Holiday Recipe Box

The BIRTHDAY Cookbook

Mary E. Bleckwehl

BLACK RABBIT BOOKS

Hi Jinx is published by Black Rabbit Books
P.O. Box 3263, Mankato, Minnesota, 56002.
www.blackrabbitbooks.com
Copyright © 2021 Black Rabbit Books

Marysa Storm, editor; Michael Sellner, designer;
Omay Ayres, photo researcher

Names: Bleckwehl, Mary Evanson, author.
Title: The birthday cookbook / Mary E. Bleckwehl.
Description: Mankato, Minnesota : Black Rabbit Books, 2021. |
Series: Hi Jinx. Holiday recipe box | Includes bibliographical references. |
Audience: Ages 8-12 | Audience: Grades 4-6 | Summary: "Teaches readers
how to make simple and delicious birthday treats through clear
directions and illustrated steps"– Provided by publisher.
Identifiers: LCCN 2019026515 (print) | LCCN 2019026516 (ebook) |
ISBN 9781623103088 (hardcover) | ISBN 9781644664049 (paperback) |
ISBN 9781623104023 (ebook)
Subjects: LCSH: Cooking. | Entertaining. | Birthdays.
Classification: LCC TX731 .B659 2021 (print) | LCC TX731 (ebook) |
DDC 641.5–dc23
LC record available at https://lccn.loc.gov/2019026515
LC ebook record available at https://lccn.loc.gov/2019026516

Printed in the United States. 1/20

Image Credits

CONTENTS

Chapter 1

Time to CELEBRATE

No birthday party is complete without delicious treats. Just follow these recipes to whip up the perfect party foods. The birthday kid will love them. These recipes are so tasty, you might even want to make them for your own birthday!

Don't forget to have a trusty adult by your side. Have them help with any cutting or tricky steps. They can also watch out for foods your guests might be allergic to.

Supplies

5 brown paper lunch bags

5 tablespoons

10-ounce (300-milliliter) plastic cups (You'll need one for each guest.)

permanent markers

stickers

Ingredients

3 cups (700 ml) raisins

3 cups (700 ml) mini pretzels

3 cups (700 ml) candy pieces

3 cups (700 ml) dried fruit

3 cups (700 ml) nuts

(You can **substitute** any of these ingredients for other treats. Try using the birthday kid's favorites!)

Chapter 2

The RECIPES

Trail Mix Station

This trail mix station makes the perfect **appetizer**. The fun starts when guests decorate their cups!

This recipe makes 15 1-cup [240-ml] servings.

Steps

1. Roll down the tops of each bag. Each bag should be about 5.5 inches (14 centimeters) tall.

2. Fill each bag with a different ingredient.

3. Put one tablespoon in each bag.

4. Set the cups, markers, and stickers near the bags.

5. Have your guests decorate their cups. Then let them use the tablespoons to fill the cups with treats. Each person can take about 16 scoops total. Happy munching!

In the United States, August 31st is National Trail Mix Day.

Critters on a Stick

Who doesn't love to eat food from a stick? Making these treats is nearly as fun as eating them!

Supplies

For Critters

4 large bowls

6 8-inch (20-cm) wooden skewers

toothpick

serving platter

plastic wrap

For Fruit Dip

large bowl

mixing spoon

plastic wrap

This makes six critters.

Ingredients

For Critters

2 pounds (900 grams) grapes

2 pounds (900 g) strawberries, stems removed

1 cantaloupe, cut into bite-sized pieces

1 pineapple, cut into bite-sized pieces

small amount of fruit dip (See page 11 for directions to make this.)

12 small candy eyes

For Fruit Dip

8 ounces (230 g) cream cheese, softened

7 ounces (200 g) marshmallow cream

2 tablespoons (30 ml) frozen orange juice **concentrate**

1 tablespoon (15 ml) orange **zest**

Turn the page for steps.

Critter Steps

1. Place each fruit in its own bowl.

2. Slide fruit pieces onto a skewer. You'll want two of each kind alternating on the stick.

3. Use a toothpick to **dab** two spots of fruit dip on the last piece of fruit. Stick a candy eye on each dab.

4. Repeat Steps 1 through 3 with the rest of the fruit and skewers. Have fun! Some critters can be one-eyed monsters.

5. Place all the critters on a platter. Cover them with plastic wrap. Store them in the fridge until you're ready to serve them.

Fruit Dip Steps

1. To make the dip, put the cream cheese in a bowl. Beat it with the spoon until smooth.

2. Add the marshmallow cream, orange concentrate, and zest to the cream cheese.

3. Mix until smooth.

4. Cover the bowl with plastic wrap.

5. Chill dip in the fridge for at least an hour before serving.

Tip

The skewers are pointy. Be careful!

11

Personal Pizzas

Getting everyone to agree on pizza toppings is hard. With personal pizzas, you don't have to!

This makes eight mini pizzas. Unless you're feeding hungry bears, plan one for each guest.

 Tip

Make sure to let your pizza cool before you eat it!

Supplies

cutting board

5-inch (13-cm) microwave-safe snack plates (You'll need one for each guest.)

pizza cutter

tablespoons

¼ measuring cup

pot holders

Ingredients

4 prebaked 10-inch (25-cm) thin pizza crusts

14-ounce (410-ml) jar pizza sauce

toppings
(Try sliced pepperoni, cooked sausage, sliced olives, and bacon bits.)

2 cups (475 ml) shredded mozzarella cheese

½ cup (45 g) grated Parmesan

Steps

1. Place one crust on the cutting board.

2. Place a plate upside down on the crust near the edge. Use the pizza cutter to cut around the plate. Cut another circle out of the same crust.

3. Repeat Step 2 to cut two circles out of each crust.

4. Place each crust on a plate.

5. For each pizza, spread about 2 tablespoons (30 ml) of sauce on the crust.

6. Add a layer of toppings.

7. Sprinkle ¼ cup (60 ml) of mozzarella cheese on top.

8. Microwave the pizza on high until the cheese is melted. This will take about 40 seconds.

9. The plate will be hot! Use pot holders to take it from the microwave.

10. Sprinkle about 1 tablespoon (15 ml) of Parmesan cheese on your creation. Ta-da! Your masterpiece is complete.

Cut Out Sandwiches

Cookie cutters aren't just for cookies! Your friends will have a blast eating sandwich shapes. They'll have even more fun answering trivia questions on top.

Supplies

cutting board

spreading knives

cookie cutters at least 1 inch (2.5 cm) deep

trivia flags (See page 24 for directions to make these.)

This recipe makes six sandwiches.

Ingredients

12 slices of bread

sandwich fixings
(such as sliced deli meat,
mayo, sliced cheese, or
peanut butter and jelly)

Steps

1. Place two slices of bread on a cutting board.

2. Put the birthday kid's favorite fixings between the slices.

3. Choose a cookie cutter. Slice through the entire sandwich. Remove the extra sandwich bits. (You can snack on these while you wait for the party to start.)

4. Repeat Steps 1 through 3 for the rest of the bread slices.

5. Poke a trivia flag into each sandwich. Ask guests to take turns reading the questions. See who can get the most right.

Birthday Ice Cream Pie

Everyone will expect cake. Surprise them with this icy delight instead! Balloon decorations make this dessert extra fun.

Supplies

ice cream scoop

spatulas

plastic wrap

about 25 inches (64 cm) of 22-gauge craft wire, washed and dried

Ingredients

1 quart (950 ml) ice cream (Use the birthday kid's favorite flavor!)

9-inch (23-cm) chocolate pie crust

1 cup (240 ml) whipped topping, thawed

small gumballs

¼ cup (60 ml) chocolate syrup

This delicious dessert serves about eight guests.

Turn the page for steps.

Steps

1. Take the ice cream from the freezer. Place it in the kitchen sink. Let it soften for about 10 to 15 minutes.

2. Use the scoop and spatula to spread the ice cream into the pie crust.

3. Use another spatula to spread the whipped topping over the ice cream.

4. Cover your pie with plastic wrap.

5. Put the pie in the freezer. Let it freeze at least five hours.

6. Now it's time for the candy balloons! Cut your wire into five to seven pieces of different lengths.

Tip Don't want balloons? Try putting other goodies on your wire! Gummy butterflies or other themed candy work well.

7. Poke a gumball onto one end of each wire.

8. Shortly before serving, take your pie from the freezer. Remove the plastic wrap.

9. Drizzle your pie with chocolate syrup.

10. Push the wires into the pie.

11. Enjoy!

Chapter 3
Get in on the HIJINX

Planning a birthday party is a lot like being an event planner. Event planners are people who professionally plan parties and celebrations. They decide on locations, decorations, and food. Maybe someday you'll have a job planning birthday parties! For now, you can do it just for fun.

Take It One Step More

1. Some people eat real critters, such as chocolate-covered ants. Would you ever try one?

2. Could any of these recipes work for other holidays? Which ones?

3. Some parties have themes. What themes would work for you? How could you change these recipes to fit them?

GLOSSARY

allergic (uh-LUR-jik)—having a medical condition that causes someone to become sick after eating, touching, or breathing something that is harmless to most people

appetizer (AP-i-tahy-zer)—a food or drink served before a meal

concentrate (KON-suhn-treyt)—a substance that is made stronger by removing water

dab (DAB)—to touch lightly

substitute (SUHB-sti-toot)—to put in the place of another

zest (ZEST)—a piece of the peel of a citrus fruit used to flavor foods

LEARN MORE

BOOKS

Heinecke, Liz. *Kitchen Science Lab for Kids: 52 Mouth-Watering Recipes and the Everyday Science that Makes Them Taste Amazing.* Beverly, MA: Quarry Books, 2019.

Kids Bake! 100+ Sweet and Savory Recipes. New York: Hearst Books, 2018.

Varozza, Georgia. *The Sugar Smart Cookbook for Kids.* Eugene, OR: Harvest House Publishers, 2019.

WEBSITES

70 Birthday Food Ideas for Your Child's Next Celebration
www.tasteofhome.com/collection/kids-birthday-party-food-ideas/view-all/

Recipes Kids Can Make
www.foodnetwork.com/recipes/packages/recipes-for-kids/cooking-with-kids/recipes-kids-can-make

Mind the rules of the kitchen.
Wash your hands. Be careful with
hot food and sharp tools.

Want to make trivia flags?
Grab construction paper,
a pen, scissors, tape, and
toothpicks. Cut out small
rectangles from the paper.
Write a trivia question on
each flag. They can be about
whatever the birthday person is into!
Then tape each flag to a toothpick.

What's Jamal's favorite soccer team?

Always clean up after yourself.
Cooking for others is great. It's not
great if you leave them with chores.

AN
INVALUABLE
COMPILATION
OF

GUIDES

**HISTORICAL
OVERVIEWS**

**GENEALOGICAL
OVERVIEWS**

MAPS

CHARTS

DRAWINGS

COMMANDMENTS

**CHARACTER
TRAITS**

**ARCHAEOLOGICAL
SITES**

BIBLICAL NAMES

HOLIDAYS

**AND MUCH
MORE...**

**PLUS THREE WEEKLY
BIBLE READINGS:**

BERESHIT

NOAH

LECH LECHA

**COMMANDMENTS
AND CHARACTER
TRAITS
HIGHLIGHTED
WITHIN
THE TEXT**

FULLY ILLUSTRATED
& USER-FRIENDLY
BIBLE
BASICS

AN INTRODUCTION
& REFERENCE GUIDE
TO THE FIVE BOOKS OF MOSES

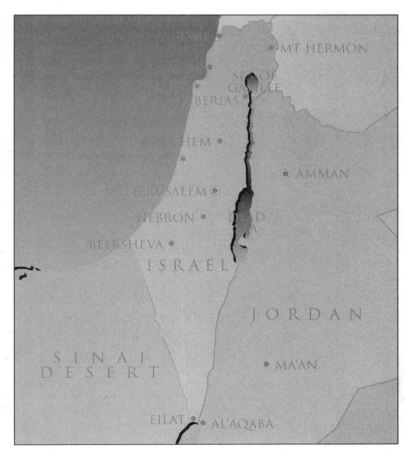

BY JEROME S. HAHN

GENEALOGICAL OVERVIEW 1 / *Adam to Moses* 0–2386/3761–1393 BCE

Birth dates

Numbered names refer to the Seventy Nations.

Bold italicized names refer to the Twelve Tribes of Israel.

Birth dates			
0/3761 BCE	Adam	Cain	Abel
130/3631 BCE	Seth		
235/3526 BCE	Enosh		
325/3426 BCE	Kenan		
395/3366 BCE	Mehalalel		
460/3301 BCE	Yered		
622/3139 BCE	Enoch		
687/3074 BCE	Methuselah		
874/2887 BCE	Lemech		
1056/2705 BCE	Noah		
1558/2203 BCE	Shem	45. Elam	
1658/2103 BCE	47. Arpachshad	46. Ashur	
1693/2068 BCE	54. Shelach	48. Lud	
		49. Aram	50. Utz
			51. Chul
			52. Geter
			53. Mash
1723/2038 BCE	55. Eber	57. Yoktan	
1757/2004 BCE	56. Peleg	58. Almodad	
1787/1974 BCE	Reu	59. Shelef	
1819/1942 BCE	Serug	60. Chatzarmavet	
1849/1912 BCE	Nachor	61. Yerach	
1878/1883 BCE	Terach	62. Hadoram	

Yefet

1. Gomer	8. Ashkenaz
	9. Rifat
	10. Togermat
2. Magog	*Russia*
3. Madai	*Persia*
4. Yavan	11. Elisha
	12. Tarshish
	13. Kittim
	14. Dodanim
5. Tuval	*Spain*

Ham

15. Cush	19. Saba
	20. Chavilah
	21. Sabta
	22. Raamah	24. Sheba
	23. Sabteka	25. Dedan
16. Mitzraim	26. Ludim
	27. Anamim
	28. Lehavim
	29. Naptuchim
	30. Patrusim
	32. Phillistines

Chacolithic Age

Early Bronze Age (3100-1850 BCE)

THE HAHN FAMILY EDITION

Dedicated to the memory

of

my parents

Irving Elias Hahn, ז״ל

Yitzchak Elchanan ben Zion

and

Viola Ruth Hahn, ז״ל

Rachel Leah bat Shmuel

לעלוי נשמת

יצחק אלחנן בן ציון ז״ל

רחל לאה בת שמואל ז״ל

TABLE OF CONTENTS

T A B L E   O F   C O N T E N T S

The Bible Summaries

T A B L E   O F   C O N T E N T S

Overviews, Maps, Charts, and Figures

Acknowledgments

A project of this type creates the need to acknowledge many people...

My introduction to using the **Bible Basics** for living my own life is only a few years new.

It all started with a Discovery Seminar held at Aish Hatorah in Jerusalem. There were many people in the classes of all ages and from all walks of life and even from many countries. The instructors were rabbis as well as lay people but their approach was indeed unique. **Everything in the Bible is relevant to your life today.**

Questions were encouraged. In fact, we were told to accept nothing at face value, and question everything we did not understand. Many of these people who taught me were involved somehow with this book.

It would be quite impossible to list all those people who have, in one way or another, made this book possible, but I'll try to list some from the beginning: Rabbi Yehuda Appel who first introduced me to the Bible, Rabbi Gedalia Gurfein, my first teacher at Aish Hatorah, Rabbi Zelig Pliskin, world famous author of many books on character traits and a principle source of inspiration for this book, and on and on.

My debt to Rabbi Noach Weinberg, the founder and leader of Aish Hatorah, is immeasurable. Others at Aish Hatorah, and its related organization, Aleynu, include Rabbis Y. Berkowitz, Moshe Pamensky, Sam Veffer, Shmuel Silinsky, Motti Berger, Avraham Goldhar, and Daniel Schloss. Others from the Old City of Jerusalem include Rabbi Mordechai Sheinberger and Rabbi Y. Ariel of the Temple Institute. It would be impossible to list all my inspirations and companions on this project.

But, for some there must be special mention. I would like to thank my friend and confidant, Martin Judovits of Boca Raton, Florida for his help on the middot and his encouragement and support at all times.

For the illustrations, I must express my thanks to Miriam Leibowitz, who was obliged to keep up with my changing interpretations of the essence of each of the *parashiyot* (sections).

I am deeply indebted to Rabbi Pinchas Winston. His responsiveness to the zigs and zags of this project were really appreciated. This book is here because of his tireless efforts.

I am also most appreciative of the help of Melanie Zeldman and her husband Moshe for editing and helping to complete many details of this book.

Marsi Tabak, Editor-in-Chief of Feldheim Publications,

Jerusalem, Israel, was exceptionally helpful in very many aspects of this book.

Of course, the beautiful design, graphics, and layouts of this book are essential to the claim of "User-Friendly" and for this I must thank Yakov Wisniewski.

Above all, I am exceptionally grateful to Rabbi Nachman Kahana, not only for being the halachic advisor for this project, but especially for his exceptional encouragement and advice in all aspects of life.

Of course there are the unsung heroes: my sons, their wives, and our 16 grandchildren. **"Teach your children so that *you* shall learn."** They have all been instrumental in the formation of this book and some of them have even contributed to its writing!

And of course, my wife, Lynn, whose patience, understanding, love, and dedication make all things possible. But mostly, I have to thank Hashem.

J. S. H.

Introduction to Bible Basics

Every one of us would like to "Win Friends and Influence People." Most of us would like to "Make a Million Dollars." All of us want to live a life of fulfillment, contentment, and peace. All of these goals are attainable if we make the right decisions in life. The problem is that most of us do not always make the right decisions. More importantly, we are not always knowledgeable enough to do so. But it is possible. We just have to find the right path to knowledge, the path to self-development. After it's found, success in these areas is almost inevitable. Millions of people have found it. It is tested, tried and true.

Why this book was written

There is a book that has been around for about 3,000 years. Its existence has no parallel in all of recorded history. There has to be a very compelling reason for its ageless existence. It has been learned and is used as a plan for living by some of the most brilliant minds that have ever existed. It is not particularly user-friendly, however, and can be most complex; it does not have visual aids to understanding, and is not written in the modern vernacular.

What this book contains

It is hoped **Bible Basics** will make it more accessible and user-friendly so that these hindrances are alleviated for "the greatest book ever written." This collection of summaries, illustrations, maps, genealogical and historical overviews, and various guides makes the Bible easier to read, to understand, and to recognize the validity of the text. Most importantly, the highlighting of commandments and the character traits within the text helps to pinpoint tools that can be used towards active self-fulfillment, as outlined in the Torah.

What this book does not contain

This book was written primarily as a beginner's book and therefore does not delve into the deep inner meanings of the Torah and other writings. As we all know, any translation from one language to another affects the reader's understanding. In this case, there is a major emphasis on simplifying the task, but in doing so, many deeper and ancillary meanings are lost. Only the essence of the message, hopefully, remains. Many additional and underlying meanings are brought out only through a study of the original Hebrew text, accompanied by the early Rabbinical commentaries.

What is the main point we are trying to make?

The essence of the Bible is to teach us how to live. This idea

After experiencing the joy and fulfillment of helping another, it becomes a "natural reaction."

is well known to anyone who has used the Bible as a guide for living. The road to success is found within your own character traits, the way you think and behave. There are literally thousands of traits throughout the Bible. Once they are pointed out to you, you may instantly agree with their worth, with regard to both positive and negative traits. We have pointed out and explained several of them... after a while, you may be be able to find your own.

What is the relationship of a commandment to a character trait?

The commandments were given by God and are all in the Bible to teach mankind to achieve the ultimate satisfaction in life, through acquiring the character traits that are essential to living a fulfilling life. A commandment is observed continuously; finally, its action and the understanding behind the action become an integral part of one's being. At this point, the action is almost done without any great intellectual effort. For example, it is a commandment to help another person with his burden. At first, one sees the person with a burden and helps him because it is a commandment to do so. Soon, after experiencing the joy and fulfillment of helping another, it becomes a "natural reaction" for many other situations. The pleasure, for you, each time the deed is done, returns again and again. The same result has been found, without exception, for everyone. Initially, your own reward at the moment of doing a commandment is very personal, but after a while, as you take on more and more of these traits, you will recognize the righteousness and the goodness that you can spread. Recognition and appreciation for your efforts is a great motivator for continuing to work on the road to self-fulfillment. You will then find yourself on the way to a complete and fulfilled life of peace and contentment. Simple, isn't it?

Who should use this book?

YOU, your family, and your friends.

Getting started

The preface and the guides are very helpful in understanding the Bible. Don't pass them by.

Preface

The Bible

The *Five Books of Moses*, the *Torah*, the *Pentateuch*—it has many names, but whatever the name, it refers to the best-selling, longest running book in the history of mankind.

Whatever one's belief, the Bible, it is agreed, is surely the single greatest source of morality that the world has ever known, and it is the foundation of many societies to this very day. These concepts which many societies take for granted, but which form the basis of our cherished civilization, such as the belief in a single God, the brotherhood of man, a just legal system, and the vision of eternal peace, are all rooted in the Bible.

"Scientific" theories continue to challenge the validity of the Torah's claim to be of Divine origin. However, as science advances, the latest discoveries only help to substantiate the claims of the Bible and to validate its authenticity in the mind of the skeptic.

All of this is secondary to the main importance of the Torah itself.

One of the Torah's main goals is human fulfillment. No matter which page a person opens to, the message is the same: humans have great potential to make themselves and the world in which they live a remarkable place. Given the history of the world with all its wars and corruption, and the lack of fulfillment of so many individuals, even of entire populations, this message seems to be all but lost.

A question comes to mind: What about the unequal distribution of wealth, which seems to leave individuals who are born into poverty little room to change their situation, and nations powerless to feed their starving? The Torah addresses all of these issues, and provides the only practical long-term solutions that benefit all of mankind. It was the Torah that taught the concept, *"Love your neighbor as yourself"* (*Leviticus 19:18*), the basis of many laws dealing with social responsibility.

Commandments in the Torah present their message directly, and often the narrative does as well. The stories themselves exemplify morality, and may offer even deeper clues to human fulfillment below the surface. No one who has ever approached the Torah intellectually, with a sincere desire to learn and better oneself, has ever walked away disappointed.

Part of the secret to the Torah's timelessness, aside from its Divine source of wisdom, is that mankind conversely seems to live within a cycle of time. We march forward in time, always changing our living conditions, and become more knowledgeable in the process, but not always wiser. We change our externals, *but the essential nature of mankind never changes*, and it is *that* which the Torah addresses.

The Purpose of Creation

The Torah teaches that man was created in the "image of God." When we are told we resemble someone else, we first need to find out what that "someone else" is like. This knowledge can provide insight into our own character. The Torah not only tells us that we were made in God's image, but it also provides information about God to help us better understand ourselves, and our potential as human beings.

The Torah then goes on to discuss various types of people: those who grapple with the purpose of creation in an effort to fulfill it, and those who don't know or ignore the reason for living, and avoid it. In each case, the consequences of the attitudes are revealed, as a lesson for future generations:

> *Remember the days of old; understand the many generations that have passed... (Deuteronomy 32:7).*

The commentators advise us to study the events of the early generations, and to think about how they brought destruction upon themselves. And, as the Torah makes clear, destruction is not always the result of a *direct* display of Divine wrath; it can also be the result of an *indirect* manifestation of Divine Providence, such as a natural disaster or a war.

Therefore, who needs the Torah? Anyone who wants to live in a moral and secure society; anyone who wants to maximize his or her potential, and his or her pleasure in life. *The Torah is not "A mission statement for mankind"; it is "THE mission statement of mankind, given to the Jewish nation, to serve as a light unto the nations."*

Personal Greatness

The newspapers often report stories about people in times of crisis rising to heights of human greatness not commonly found. Acts of heroism, acts of human kindness, and risks taken on behalf of others are only some of the things which "simple" folk achieve at times of crisis.

Everyone at some point in time, perhaps during a personal crisis when their "back is to the wall," senses something powerful within themselves. When the

We change our externals, but the essential nature of mankind never changes.

The Torah is a step-by-step plan for tapping human potential, and surging out of the world of the mundane into one of personal greatness.

demand is made, we often make supreme efforts to succeed at the task at hand, and can't believe what we can actually achieve. For many, it is just such experiences that transform them from living a life of underachieving to maximizing life's opportunities on a regular basis.

If you don't know what you have, or how to use it, then your potential can be wasted. Western society's focus, for the most part, has not been philosophical. As a technologically-based society, its major drive has always been towards making life more "comfortable."

"Personal greatness" is therefore a term usually applied to only a few, and primarily in the realm of physical accomplishment or material successes, such as sports or business. The average person, the majority of the world's population, has little understanding of just what potential he or she really has. Unaware of this crucial information, uninformed people almost always underachieve. The mundane has become the accepted norm.

Should life be exciting, even when nothing "significant" happens to make it that way? The Torah says yes, and adds that there is nothing more exciting than personal growth, which starts with realizing your own potential.

The Torah understands, however, that personal potential is something very few people learn much about without some sort of guidance and instruction. This, then, is its starting point. The Torah then continues with examples of character traits, the stories of the forefathers and their descendants, the story of the Jewish Exodus from Egypt and receiving of the Torah, many commandments, and narrations. The Torah is a step-by-step plan for tapping human potential, and surging out of the world of the mundane into one of personal greatness.

A Light Unto the Nations

One theme that has been interwoven into Jewish history is the mission to be a "light unto the nations." In essence, this mission entails being the carrier of the Divine message about personal and national fulfillment.

This mission has never translated to proselytizing the nations of the world. Unlike others, the Jewish people have believed that teaching by example is the best way to transmit the message of Divine morality. Quite simply, a consensus amongst the Jewish people about the validity of the Torah and its message, expressed by the perfected society created, would thereby beam the message worldwide.

During the "golden era" of King Solomon, during the

International brotherhood, and the distant dreams of world peace, depend upon the Torah's authentic message reaching the farthest corners of the earth.

period of the first Jewish Temple (*833–423 BCE*), this communication to the world had been the case. The Book of Kings relates how kings and queens from nations beyond the Land of Israel came to Israel to meet with Solomon, and to see for themselves the society he had built upon Torah principles. These leaders were sure to take back some of that wisdom, so that they too could improve the moral integrity of their own countries, and advance civilization.

International brotherhood, and the distant dreams of world peace, depend upon the Torah's *authentic* message reaching the farthest corners of the earth. But every light must have a source, without which there can only be darkness and confusion. And the source itself requires something to project its light, so that the illumination can be complete and all-encompassing. The Torah is that source of light; the Jewish nation is the "chosen" vehicle to project that light throughout the entire world. This description is the real message and meaning of "The Chosen People."

The Consistency and Centrality of Transmission

Every society relies upon a transmission process to convey ideas from generation to generation. This process is the basis of the continuum of society. But no society has relied upon the transmission process as much as the Jewish nation has, and still does.

At Mt. Sinai over three millennia ago, the Jewish people received the Torah in two parts. One part is the Written Law (Five Books of Moses), and the second part is the Oral Law. The Oral Law elucidates the Written Law, making it possible to put its commandments into practice *correctly*. Transmission processes have inherent dangers. Human experience has proven that transmission of a single idea from one individual to another can result in a distortion of that idea. Accuracy relies upon the ability of the transmitter to communicate the information, also in a way that the receiver of the information can receive it as sent.

Human experience has also proven that the accurate transmission of ideas is possible when necessary, but only when all the required precautions to assure accuracy have been implemented. Some of those precautions include choosing "transmitters" known for their moral integrity and fear of distorting the message, advanced methods of education and memorization, a system of information verification, and so on.

Perhaps one of the most important factors for guaranteeing the safe and accurate transmission of a body of mate-

[1] The term "Talmud" literally means "teaching." Its common usage, however, is in reference to volumes of legalistic and non-legalistic teachings that clarify points of the Oral Law. The Talmud has been, and is, the central work studied in yeshivot (traditional Jewish houses of study) around the world. See the Guide to the Bible, "The Oral Law," for more information.

rial, especially one as vast as the "sea" of *Talmud*,[1] is to make learning and transmitting the material the number one priority of that society.

All of this, and more, has been implemented by Jewish society ever since Moses came down from Mt. Sinai with the Written and Oral Torah. This system of communication and transmission is the same one in effect to this very day, over 3,300 years later. To fully understand the Torah, and its role within Jewish and world society, one must, by necessity, understand this Jewish transmission process and its consistency and centrality within Jewish thought.

Holiness

One concept that has been shared by many religious societies throughout the ages is that of *holiness*. The Hebrew word for holy is *kadosh*, which comes from the word that means "separate," as if to say, that which is holy is *separate* from that which is not.

An element that separates something from something else is purpose. If something is to be used for a *holy* purpose, that is, used in the service of God, then that object becomes imbued *spiritually* with holiness, even though the object itself does not go through any physical metamorphosis. Holiness, therefore, is a matter of perception. But by no means is the perception that leads to holiness an illusion, for it is not mankind's perception that creates holiness, but God's. Thus even if a person is unaware of the holiness of something, this does not mean the place or object is not intrinsically holy.

Through the Torah and the Oral Tradition, mankind has been told what God "thinks" about different aspects of creation, and while everything in God's world is "holy," some things are holier than others. For example, the clothing the priest wore to officiate in the Temple was holier than the clothing he might have worn for everyday purposes. As such, the priestly clothing, the Torah teaches, must be treated in a unique manner.

What determines holiness? Basically, the more something alludes to the intrinsic reality of God's presence in the physical world, the holier it is. The more direct the allusion, the holier and more "special" the place, item, or person will be to God.

Thus, just as one treats the king's guards with honor because of their relationship with the king, one must also treat things of holiness with special respect because of their affiliation with God. The Torah, being the word of God, is

Whereas most languages

are large collections of

words composed as mere

conventions to designate

places, people, and objects,

the Hebrew language is

conceptual.

deserving of the utmost respect, as was the Temple in which the Divine presence actually dwelled.

Because mankind's perception of holiness is dependent upon God's perception of what is holy, unless one has a thorough and traditional understanding of the Five Books of Moses, one will become confused and treat that which is profane as holy, and vice versa. ***The inherent and tragic result of this will be, at the very least, corrosion of the moral values of a society, and at the worst, the destruction of the society as a whole.***

Though many view holiness as a concept that applies only to those who ascribe to religious societies, the truth is, it applies to everyone. The values that *all* of mankind holds dear, such as brotherhood, freedom, and the "pursuit of happiness," all depend upon having a firm and clear understanding of the concept of holiness.

The Holy Tongue

Another element of the Torah that is often overlooked and misunderstood is the original language in which it was written: the *Holy Tongue.*

The language of Hebrew is unlike any other language. Whereas most languages are large collections of words composed as mere conventions to designate places, people, and objects, ***the Hebrew language is conceptual.***

For example, consider the Hebrew word *adam* (pronounced *a-dam*), which means "man." The word is actually a composite of the first letter of the Hebrew alphabet, *alef,* and the word *dam,* which means "blood."

Blood traditionally symbolizes physical life, being so central to physical survival. The letter *alef* (א) when written as it is pronounced (i.e., אלף), is similar to the word *aluf* (which means "chief"). Thus the name of man indicates his essence: a flesh-and-blood being (i.e. a body), made in the image of God (hinted by the allusion to "chief").

Another insight into the physical nature of man is gained when considering that the word *adam* is derived from the Hebrew word, *adamah,* which means "ground." As the verse teaches (*Genesis 2:7*), God formed man from "dust of the earth," and this is alluded to by the fact that *adam* was derived from *adamah.*

Thus, within a single Hebrew word (let alone an entire verse), there can exist many layers of meaning. And for every one of those layers revealed, there are many others that still remain a mystery, waiting for discovery by the right person at the right time, perhaps when the need is greatest.

This explanation of only a few words of the "Holy Tongue" barely touches the essence of what is surely one of the most profound aspects of all of our learning. Most of Jewish study is spent trying to uncover the many layers of meaning in the text of the original Torah. What may seem to be merely an intellectual exercise to some, is in fact a search for philosophical truths, each one crucial for deepening one's appreciation of creation, its potential, and the pleasure and fulfillment that result from such an understanding.

HISTORICAL OVERVIEW 1 / *The Five Books of Moses* 0–2488/3761–1273 BCE

Year from creation/ *Common Era year*	Five Books of Moses time periods	Landmark events		Secular historical eras
0/*3761 BCE*	Genesis 0–2309			**Chalcolithic Period** *3716–3100 BCE*
250/*3511 BCE*				
500/*3261 BCE*				
750/*3011 BCE*				**Early Bronze Age** *3100–1850 BCE*
1000/*2761 BCE*				
1250/*2511 BCE*				
1500/*2261 BCE*				
1750/*2011 BCE*		**The Flood 1656**		
2000/*1761 BCE*		**Forefathers 1948–2255**	**Tower of Babel 1996**	**Middle Bronze Age** *1850–1550 BCE*
2250/*1511 BCE*	**Exodus 2332–2448**	**Exodus 2448**	**Torah at Mt. Sinai 2448**	**Late Bronze Age** *1550–1200 BCE*
2500/*1261 BCE*	**Leviticus 2449 Numbers 2449–2488 Deuteronomy 2488**			**Iron Age** *1200–930 BCE*
2750/*1011 BCE*		**Prophets and Writings 2488–3220**		**Late Iron Age** *930–586 BCE*
3000/*761 BCE*				
3250/*511 BCE*				**Persian Empire** *586–330 BCE*
3500/*261 BCE*				**Hellenist Empire** *330–63 BCE*
3750/*11 BCE*				**Roman Empire** *63 BCE–395 CE*
4000/*239 CE*		**Mishnah 3948**		**Byzantine Empire** *395–1453 CE*
4250/*489 CE*		**Babylonian Talmud 4260**		**Western Roman Empire** *395–800 CE*
4500/*739 CE*				**Moslem Empire** *632–1300 CE*
4750/*989 CE*				**Holy Roman Empire** *800–1806 CE*
5000/*1239 CE*				
5250/*1489 CE*				**Ottoman Empire** *1300–1918 CE*
5500/*1739 CE*		**Shulchan Aruch 5316**		*Europe*
5750/*1989 CE*	**3,272 years from the end of Deuteronomy until 2000 CE**			*Middle East*

Guide to The Bible

Historical Background

In Greek, it is called the "Bible," meaning "book." The first Greek translation of the Bible (ordered by Ptolemy II, circa 285-246 BCE) was actually called the "Septuagint," which means "seventy."[1]

Traditionally, the Bible is referred to by the Jewish people as the *Torah*,[2] which means "instructions" because that is exactly its purpose: to instruct. It is also referred to as the "Five Books of Moses" (the *Chumash*, which means "five"). It is comprised of five major sections: Genesis, Exodus, Leviticus, Numbers, and Deuteronomy. Consequently, from this point onward, when the term "Torah" is used in this book, it refers to the *Five Books of Moses* only.

The Torah is over three thousand years old (see *Historical Overview 1: Five Books of Moses*). Given at Mt. Sinai in the year 2448 of the Jewish calendar (numbered from the creation of Adam), or 1313 BCE (the corresponding Western date; BCE being an acronym for the words "before common era"), the Torah has survived over three millennium and has remained intact. Traditional belief states that the Torah was dictated by God to Moses letter by letter, word by word, while Moses wrote it all down in the form of a scroll. The entire Torah, therefore, is in fact entirely the word of God.

As Moses finished a section of Torah, he would immediately add it to the additional twelve scrolls he had previously written, one for each tribe. When the Torah was complete, the procedure of writing a Torah scroll was repeated countless times throughout the ages by qualified scribes. Each adhered to the extensive rules for writing a Torah, and complied with the sacred traditions for doing so. The many strict disciplines followed by Torah scribes throughout the generations have thus protected and ensured the integrity of the Torah, for over 3,300 years.

The Jewish people arrived at the Sinai desert on the first day of the Jewish month, *Sivan*, in the year 1313 BCE, and at Mt. Sinai on the second day of *Sivan*. According to one opinion in the tradition,[3] on the sixth day of *Sivan*, the Jewish people heard the Ten Commandments (*Exodus 20:1*), and on the seventh of *Sivan*, Moses ascended the mountain to receive the tablets that were to contain the Ten Commandments (*Exodus 24:12*).

Also, according to tradition,[3] all of the 613 commandments were given to Moses later at Mt. Sinai (*Leviticus 25:1; Rashi*), even though some are not recorded until the Book of Deuteronomy. The stories and events that occurred after leaving Mt. Sinai were recorded along the way, as dictated to Moses by God. There is a disagreement in the Talmud as to whether or not Moses recorded his own death, written in the final paragraph of the Torah, or whether the words were written by his disciple, Joshua, as commanded by God.

Technical Aspects of the Five Books of Moses

Even with modern printing techniques, a *Sefer Torah* (Torah Scroll),[4] if it is to be legally certifiable according to Jewish law, must always be written according to the laws received by Moses from God at Mt. Sinai. This usually amounts to about two thousand hours of concentrated effort, and the use of over one hundred writing quills. In total, there are 304,805 letters (composing 79,976 words) in the entire Torah, written on sixty sheets of parchment.

Structure

The five books of the Torah are comprised of narratives, events, and commandments. The Torah is the original source of all Jewish law and philosophy because all of these are accepted as the word of God. For specific reasons, the names of the books either mean or allude to the following:

Hebrew	English/Latin	Translation of English/Latin
Bereshit	Genesis	origin
Shemot	Exodus	departure
VaYikra	Leviticus	Levite
BaMidbar	Numbers	census
Devarim	Deuteronomy	repetition

The Hebrew names of the five books are taken from a significant word found in the first verse of that particular book. The non-Hebrew name is based upon one of the themes found in that book.

The name "Genesis" is appropriate because the book deals with the origin of the world, the history of the world prior to the forefathers of the Jewish people, and the spiritual development of the ancestors of the Jewish people up until the Egyptian bondage begins.

Exodus is so called because it portrays the miraculous and awesome exodus of the Jewish people from Egyptian bondage. This book includes the accounts of the enslavement of the Jewish people, Moses' rise to the role of leader, the Ten Plagues that paved the way for the exodus from Egypt, the first Passover Seder, and the splitting of the Red Sea. The climax

[4] This term refers to the traditional format in which the Torah is written. Parchment made from a particular animal skin is treated and then sewn together into one continuous piece. On it are written all five books of the Torah. The first piece of parchment and the last are attached to specially designed wooden spindles, which allow for the Torah to be rolled from section to section each week in synagogues around the world according to the designated reading.

of the book involves the receiving of the Ten Commandments and the Torah at Mt. Sinai.

Leviticus, the third book, is named for the Levites, the tribe from whom the Jewish priesthood (*kohanim*) emerged. The Levites were responsible for the maintenance of the Tabernacle, and assisted with the service in the Tabernacle, which is a central topic in this book. The major emphasis, however, is on the *kohanim*, descendants of the tribe of Levi. Jewish tradition often refers to this book as *Torat Kohanim*, the laws of the priests.

The book of Numbers begins with a census of the Jewish population in the desert, and has therefore been called "Numbers." This book goes on to narrate the departure of the Jewish people from Mt. Sinai, on their way to the "Promised Land," the land of Canaan. It is in this book that the Jewish people made the grave mistake of refusing the land of Canaan, and were condemned to wander for an additional thirty-eight years in the desert.

Deuteronomy, the fifth and last book of the Torah, is a repetition of many concepts taught in earlier books. Hence the name, which means "repetition." The book ends with an account of Moses' own death, and with the next generation of Jews poised to enter the land of Canaan, forty years after leaving Egyptian slavery.

The five books have been divided into fifty-four sections (*parashiyot;* singular, *parashah*), and one section is read every Sabbath in synagogues (occasionally two portions are read together). Each weekly section, in turn, is subdivided into seven subsections called *aliyot* (plural for *aliyah*). An *aliyah* means "going up." Each section is read to the entire congregation, but one individual is called up to the *bimah* (a special podium upon which the Torah scroll is laid out for reading) for each subsection reading. The name of each section is derived from one or two main words in the first verse of the weekly portion.[5] Chapter headings and verse numbering, universally found in non-scroll versions of the Torah, were introduced in the Middle Ages by a non-Jewish source, to facilitate easy referencing.

Every Jew has an obligation to study the Torah and its explanations every moment that he or she is capable of doing so. Moses, however, established that a section of the Torah should be read on the Sabbath, and a portion of the upcoming weekly section on Monday and Thursday mornings, to make sure that the congregation does not miss such learning for even one week. Ezra the Scribe (*circa 356 BCE*) decreed that the upcoming portion be read on Sabbath afternoon as well.

[5] For example, the name of the first parashah in the Book of Genesis is *Bereshit,* because the opening verse is, **Bereshit** *bara Elokim...* ("In the beginning, God created...").

HISTORICAL OVERVIEW 2 / *Written and Oral Law* 2448-present/*1313 BCE-present*

Year from creation/ Common Era year	Historical eras	Temple dates	The Written and Oral Law	Persecuting empires
2500/*1261 BCE*			**The Written Law** *Received by Moses, the 613 commandments and narratives*	
2750/*1011 BCE*			*contained in the Five Books of Moses.*	
3000/*761 BCE*		**Construction of First Temple** **2928**/*833 BCE*	**The Oral Law** *Also received at Mt. Sinai, is a "companion" to the Written Law by providing the details*	*Babylonia*
3250/*511 BCE*		**Destruction of First Temple** **3338**/*423 BCE*	*necessary for carrying out the commandments.*	
3500/*261 BCE*	**Era of Prophecy 2448–3448/** *1313–331 BCE Prophecy was prevalent among*	**Construction of Second Temple** **3408**/*353 BCE*	*It also contains ethical teachings.*	*Greece* *Rome*
3750/*11 BCE*	*the Jewish people in this period*	**Destruction of Second Temple** **3838**/*70 CE*		*Rome*
4000/*239 CE*	*Beit Shammai/ Beit Hillel*			
4250/*489 CE*	**Era of Sanhedrin 2448–4120/** *1313–359 BCE The Sanhedrin was composed of*		**The Mishnah** **3948**/*188 CE Intense Roman persecution forced the*	
4500/*739 CE*	*seventy-one men who were the most learned in Torah and the most*		*Rabbis to commit the Oral Law to a written form. The result was the "Mishnah," which*	
4750/*989 CE*	*spiritually developed in their generation. The Sanhedrin decided disputes*		*means "teaching"— terse statements of law designed to prompt investigation so as to*	
5000/*1239 CE*	*based upon a majority vote, enabling the Oral Law to "speak" with a single voice.*		*rebuild the discussions that accompany the oral teaching.*	
5250/*1489 CE*			**Babylonian Talmud** **4260**/*499 CE A collection of the*	
5500/*1739 CE*			*Mishnah, elaborations on the Mishnah, and the Midrash. It is the principal source of study in yeshivot today.*	
5750/*1989 CE*				

All five books will be discussed in more detail in the introductions that precede each book.

The Oral Law

The term "Torah" also refers to more than the Five Books of Moses. Even a quick read through the Written Torah will cause the reader to inquire about missing details. For example, in the Torah, God commands the Jewish nation to eat only "kosher"[6] food, but does not explain how to slaughter an animal properly so that it would be *kosher*. The Torah speaks about *tefillin*, to be worn by Jewish males on their arms and on their heads, but does not give us any idea as to what they look like or to what they are.

There are many such examples of the Written Torah not providing sufficient information to execute its directives. The Written Law, by necessity demands a supplement. This critical supplement is traditionally known as the Oral Law.

The Oral Law has all the background information necessary to properly implement the instructions of the Written Law. Just as the Written Torah was dictated to Moses by God, so too was the Oral Law a direct transmission from God to Moses. It was Moses' responsibility to transmit both to the Jewish nation, and it has been the ongoing responsibility of Jews since then to maintain its integrity.

For 1,500 years, the Oral Law was taught, learned and lived and was transmitted from generation to generation in its oral form. Because dispersion, assimilation, and horrible persecution threatened the accuracy of the Oral Law, in the year 3948/186 CE (Common Era), the Oral Law was officially put into a written form called the *Mishnah*, which means "teaching" (see Historical Overview 2: *Written and Oral Law*). The less technical aspects of the Oral Law, specifically the moral teachings, were recorded into what later became the *Midrash*, which means "investigation," because they reveal deeper and usually more esoteric meanings of the verses of the Written Law.

Traditional Jewish schools around the world learn the *Mishnah* and *Talmud*,[7] together with the Written Law, to this very day.

English Translations

Every translation of the Torah is in fact another interpretation. This assertion is correct and results from the nature of the Hebrew language, and the perspective of the translator.

As explained in the *Preface* ("The Holy Tongue"), the Hebrew language is very different from all others. For

[6] "Kosher" is the technical Hebrew term used to indicate that food adheres to the Jewish dietary laws. In a broader sense, it is used to indicate that a thing or situation adheres to the laws of Torah.

[7] See the *Preface* and the footnote that defines the Talmud.

example, in the English language, most words and names are borrowed terms or were randomly chosen to represent something, with little meaning other than the fact that they can be used to identify an object, or a person. The word "chair," for instance, does not inherently mean anything, except that it is the designated name of something used to sit on.

Hebrew words function differently, in that they may act both as the name of a concept, while at the same time embody that concept. For example, the Hebrew word for "man" is *adam*. The name itself is derived from the word *adamah* meaning "ground," from which the first man was created. It is also a composite of the word *dam*, which means blood, and the first letter of the Hebrew alphabet, *alef*, which always alludes to God.

As the Talmud teaches, there are "seventy faces to Torah."

Also, one Hebrew word can require *several* English words in order to express its proper meaning. For this reason, as well as others, the translator is constantly weighing words to determine the most accurate representation of the original text, an exercise which is not an easy task. Two translations will inevitably employ different words and phraseology when rendering the same Hebrew text into English. For this reason, there is no substitute for learning the original Hebrew text.

Another point to remember is that some passages in the Torah are obscure in meaning, and require elucidation. Throughout the ages many commentators have written running commentaries to help fill the intellectual gaps for the reader of the Book. As the Talmud teaches, there are "seventy faces to Torah." The message is simple: be prepared to delve into even the simplest verse of the Torah.

Names of God

One of the most troubling aspects of the Torah for Torah critics has been the many different names of God used throughout the text. This has been the basis for the "more than one author" theory emphasized by some critics of the Torah.

The most astounding thing about this theory is that it is stated more out of ignorance of Jewish tradition than out of a scholarly investigation of the text. Long before Torah critics even came onto the scene, traditional Jewry had known the reason for the different names of God. Quite simply, because "God" is indefinable by the human language, He must be referred to only by the many different attributes He manifests in this world. His essential nature can never be "named" by the human mind; no such intellectual vocabulary exists to

[8] According to the commentator, Sforno, in Genesis (1:26). Other traditional definitions include "Omnipotent".

accurately do so. In fact, the Hebrew term for infinity, *ein sof,* is often used as a name of God.

Each name of God has always denoted a different aspect of God's nature. For example, the name *Elokim* refers to the aspect of God that is discerning and judging,[8] and for that reason, it is a term used for judges and angels as well. Man, who was made "in the image of *Elokim*" (*b'tzelem Elokim*), possesses the intellectual capacity to discern and judge.

There are many other names for God, according to Jewish tradition, some being even up to seventy-two letters long. These names are the basis of *kabbalistic* study, the more esoteric section of Jewish learning that deals with the most profound understanding of the nature of creation.

In many English translations of the Torah, the translator acknowledges the different names of God as they appear in the text by varying the English translation as well. The English may read "God," or "Lord," etc. Because the term "Lord" and others like it are less commonly used, many English translations translate all names of God as "God."

As the student becomes better versed in the Torah, and can comprehend the Hebrew text, it is obviously worthwhile knowing which name of God is being used in the context of study. Knowing this information can be the basis of a much more profound understanding of the text.

Breaks in the Text

In the Torah, there are designated breaks in the text that, according to Jewish tradition, trace back to the original Torah dictated by God to Moses. In the Hebrew text of the Bible, they are noted with either the letter *peh* (פ) or the letter *samech* (ס). They are called *petuchot* and *setumot*, "openings" and "closings" respectively. These letters do not appear in the actual Torah scrolls.

According to tradition, the purpose of these breaks was to allow Moses to integrate the information he had received, and some have been used to mark the end of the weekly *parashah* and the beginning of a new one. Most of the time, a *petucha* or a *setumah* designates the end of a particular matter thus far being discussed, and consequently, they have often been the source of subject headings in translations.

Commandments

As mentioned earlier, the Torah is comprised of specific events (e.g., the account of Creation), and commandments (e.g., "Do not steal"). The commandments, for the most part, are incumbent upon every Jewish female from the age of twelve years, and upon every Jewish male from the age of thirteen. In total, there are 613 commandments, referred to as the *Taryag Mitzvot*, because the Hebrew word *taryag* (תרי"ג) has the numerical value of 613, and *mitzvot* means commandments.

Not all commandments apply to every Jew, or at all times. Many of the commandments, which applied to the priests while the Temple stood, cannot be practiced today. In total, there are only 297 of the 613 commandments that can be applied today: 77 positive commandments, 194 negative, and 26 which apply only to Jews who live in the Land of Israel.[9]

Character Refinement

All aspects of the stories, narratives, and commandments seek to accomplish one goal: to teach the world the standards of morality as defined by man's Creator. Commandments are not merely laws. They are profound expressions of Divine truth; they are a packaged philosophy.

The stories and narration also have been recorded primarily for the sake of teaching human beings the depth of their spiritual potential. This is why the Torah is often called *Torat Chaim*, "instructions for living."

The Hebrew word for character trait is *middah*, (plural, *middot*) which also means "measure." Behavior "measures" a person, or more accurately, *weighs* the person. It is one thing to know how to behave morally; it is a whole other reality to live by that knowledge, and a whole other reality again to live by it because you *believe in being moral*. Such a person is deserving of *kavod*, the Hebrew word which means "honor" and "heavy" (a term of measuring).

A student is expected, when learning Torah, to extract *middot* from the Torah, whether learning narration, a story, or a commandment. Though this may not always be simple to do at first glance, it becomes increasingly easier to accomplish as the student penetrates the surface meaning of the text, a process of analysis commonly used by the Talmud.

The Torah has always been, and will continue to be, a vast reservoir for character refinement. "Drinking" from the waters of Torah[10] means establishing a course towards the fulfillment of one's own life.

The Many-Faceted Torah

When it comes to the Torah, what you see is not necessarily what you get, at least not entirely. The meaning of each verse is multi-layered, and though a simple meaning of the words can be derived, deeper and more profound meanings usually

[9] As listed in the *Sefer HaMitzvot HaKatzar*, compiled by the Chafetz Chaim.

[10] Torah is compared to water, in that both are life-sustaining.

lie below the surface, encoded within the text.

The Hebrew word *pardes* (פרדס), which means "garden" or "orchard," is an acronym for the words, *p'shat, remez, d'rash,* and *sod. P'shat* means "simple" and alludes to the literal meaning of the words. The word *remez* means "hint" and refers to the level of understanding alluded to by the words, though not apparent on a literal level. *D'rash* means "investigation" and refers to the level of understanding that comes from applying specific rules for deciphering the information within the text. *Sod* means "secret" and refers to the totally esoteric message hidden within the text, the basis of the Kabbalah.

Furthermore, the Talmud states, just as a hammer hits an anvil and causes sparks to fly off into many directions, so too does a verse splinter in many directions. There are "seventy faces to the Torah." Each verse has countless interpretations, all of which may be true, if derived from using the rules for doing so.[11]

᙮

When one considers all aspects of the Torah as one, an awesome picture begins to emerge that reveals a unique work, unparalleled throughout the entire history of humankind. In fact, it is absolutely remarkable that more people do not take the Torah seriously.

Despite every point in its favor and its promise of fulfillment, it is not an unnatural phenomenon that the Torah is neglected and overlooked. In life, people are often attracted to the "flowers" and ignore the "roots." The "flowers" are easy to access, enjoyable to see and smell; the roots are hidden and provide little instant pleasure.

But it is the roots that makes the flower possible, as does a foundation for a house. To overlook the roots, or a foundation, is to cause the death of the flower or the destruction of a house. Likewise, to overlook the meaning of Torah and not delve into it for its profound wisdom and insight, and therefore use it in one's own life, is to cripple one's roots and foundation, and to leave one's life, as well as the future of mankind, on shaky ground.

[11] There are thirteen specific principles for deriving meanings from the verses that are not obviously apparent, and most meanings must already be part of the Oral Tradition. Some of these rules can be found in the beginning of the daily prayer book. They begin, "Rabbi Ishmael says, there are thirteen exegetical principles...".

Guide to the Commandments

Commandments in General

Mitzvot, or commandments, are directives from God as recorded in the Five Books of Moses. When many people think of commandments, they think of the Ten Commandments, which Moses brought down from Mt. Sinai on two stone tablets. Some might even be familiar with the Seven Noahide laws (which were given to Noah and his descendants); these are binding (and generally accepted as being so) upon all individuals of all civilizations. They are:

1. Establish a system of civil justice
2. Do not curse God
3. Do not practice idolatry
4. Do not engage in one of the forbidden carnal relations
5. Do not murder
6. Do not steal
7. Do not eat a limb that was severed from a live animal

Many people, however, including a large number of Jews, are unaware that the total number of commandments incumbent upon the Jewish people, as listed in the Torah, is 613: There are 248 positive commandments (i.e., commandments to do something), and 365 negative commandments (i.e., to refrain from doing). The Ten Commandments are included in the total of 613, as are the Seven Noahide laws.

As mentioned earlier, the 613 commandments are referred to by the Hebrew word: *taryag* תרי״ג (i.e., ת = 400, ר = 200, י = 10, ג = 3 ... = 613).

Of course, not all commandments apply simultaneously. Furthermore, some only apply to specific people, such as priests, while others can only be performed in the Land of Israel. Many can only be fulfilled if a Jewish Temple stands, and for this reason, only 297 commandments today can be considered generally "applicable" (77 positive commandments, 194 negative commandments, and 26 commandments which can only be fulfilled while living in the Land of Israel).

Not Applicable does not mean that there is nothing to gain from learning about a non-functioning commandment. On the contrary, every commandment is an expression of a philosophical thought and of the Divine wisdom. The commandment may not be able to be performed today, but the concept behind its action can certainly be applied.

For instance, one commandment requiring the Temple's existence was the commandment to make an offering of an animal after transgressing certain Torah prohibitions. This practice may be difficult for the modern person to understand, but the actual act of sacrifice was considered holy, and emphasized a very great message about life: life is serious, and errors are costly. A person who had to witness an animal being slaughtered because of his actions was spiritually changed for a very long time thereafter.

Commandments are often viewed as ritual, perfunctory acts performed only by the faithful, at least by the unknowledgeable. On the contrary, for those who understand their meanings, and appreciate the goal of Torah, the commandments become opportunities — guidelines for channeling the awesome energies of human beings into worthwhile projects and endeavors.

An important point to keep in mind when doing *mitzvot* is that the action being performed is for the sake of fulfilling a Torah commandment.

Three Categories of Commandments

Aside from the fact that commandments are referred to as being either "positive" or "negative," there exists another method of categorization. The Rabbis teach that commandments are usually one of three possible types: judgments, statutes, or testimonials.

Judgments are usually considered to be commandments whose reasoning is within human grasp, such as the commandment not to steal. Most human beings can appreciate the need to have a law not to steal, so that society can function and that people can live with security, a fundamental right of a civilized society.

Statutes, by definition, are usually just the opposite of judgments, that is, beyond human reasoning. For example, why *shouldn't* a Jew cook milk and meat together, or wear clothing woven from a mixture of wool and linen? The answers to such questions are not usually available to the human mind, though certainly Divine logic was the cause of such commandments.[2]

Testimonials, such as remembering the exodus from Egypt twice a day,[3] are commandments that prevent the Jewish people from forgetting what God has done for them; they are meant to invoke a constant sense of gratitude for God's kindness.

Commandments as Structure

The very first man and woman created while inside the Garden of Eden, were given only one negative command-

[2] It is noteworthy to mention that even judgments are not *completely* fathomable by the human mind, nor are statutes entirely beyond human understanding. For example, King Solomon, the wisest of all men, was able to comprehend the reasoning behind commandments such as not cooking meat and milk together.

[3] This is done when reciting the prayer called the *Shema*, the Jewish credo recited twice a day, once in the morning and once in the evening.

[4] This, of course, is not one of the 613 commandments incumbent upon the Jewish people. It was a unique commandment given to the first man and woman before they ate from the forbidden tree.

ment[4] to observe: *Do not eat from the Tree of Knowledge of Good and Evil (Genesis 2:16).* The test proved to be too great for them, and they violated this commandment. In doing so, they caused death to enter the world, and mankind to be exiled from the garden.

Jewish mysticism teaches that the story of the Tree of Knowledge has many aspects to it, all very deep and profound with many lessons to teach mankind, and many warnings to heed. The single most important lesson to learn is that man needs structure. It is structure that "harnesses" the power of mankind, and directs it in a positive direction, very much the same way a yoke harnesses the power of an ox. Interestingly enough, the responsibility of living by the Torah is referred to as the "yoke of Heaven."

The difference between a "yoke" and a "burden" is that the latter *inhibits* while the former *channels* energy towards an ultimate positive goal. The yoke helps the ox pull the plow, while the yoke of Heaven helps mankind to fulfill its potential, and to achieve long sought after goals such as peace on earth and universal brotherhood.

To fashion a life outside the framework of commandments is to create a society that will eventually lead to anarchy, as history has proven time and time again. Commandments are expressions of Divine will, manifestations of God's intent in his creation of mankind. They are eternal, unlike the philosophies of man which are, at best, the current "opinion" of individuals who quite often lack the depth of understanding of human nature necessary for making laws that can survive epochs of history.

The goal of a law is to protect what is precious. God's commandments are no different, and behind them is the Divine philosophy of life. This philosophy points to what a human being is capable of aspiring to, and also offers a system to use to accomplish it. When one understands and appreciates this about commandments, they are no more a burden to perform than any act of love one can perform for a loved one.

Applicable Commandments

In this work, the focus is on the commandments that can be applied today. By highlighting them within the actual text, the reader has a chance to both learn the applicable commandments, and to see their original sources in the Torah. Each commandment appears in ***bold type*** in the text, and is explained briefly in a footnote indicated by the symbol, "📖".

The paragraph that describes the commandment is by no

means a complete explanation. In order to properly understand and fulfill the commandment, one has to pursue further research into traditional sources, many of which already exist, and whenever possible, consult a competent rabbi. A comprehensive listing of all 613 commandments is found on the following pages.

The 613 Commandments

T he following is a brief listing of the 613 commandments as recorded and classified by *Rambam,* Rabbi Moses ben (the son of) Maimon (*1135-1204 CE*). This listing is taken from his classic compendium of Jewish law, the *"Mishneh Torah."* The book names, such as the *"Book of Knowledge,"* refer to the names of the chapters in the *Mishneh Torah* in which the subsequent series of commandments can be found.

The following legend indicates if the commandment is currently applicable, where and for whom it is applicable.

Time Period of Applicability
A   =   all times
T   =   only during Temple times

The Place where the Commandment is Applicable
A   =   anywhere in the world a Jew may live
I   =   only in the land of Israel

To Whom the Commandment Applies
M   =   to men above the age of thirteen years
W   =   to women above the age of twelve years
A   =   to all Jewish men and women above the age of thirteen and twelve, respectively

* Please note: This list should not be used as a source for any practical Halachic ruling. There are differences of opinion over the applicability today of some commandments in this list. Similarly, distinctions must often be made between Rabbinically-decreed commandments and those that still have binding force as Torah-law today. For example, the law of resting the land every seventh year (Shemittah, see Commandment #279-283) is in practice today in Israel, but only as a Rabbinic decree. The Torah obligation to rest the land is in force only when the majority of the Jewish people reside in Israel. In all cases of doubt, a competent Rabbinical authority should be consulted.

Commandment	Source	Time	Place	Whom
Book One: The Book of Knowledge				
1 To know there is a God	Ex. 20:2	A	A	A
2 Not to entertain thoughts of other gods besides Him	Ex. 20:3	A	A	A
3 To know that He is one	Deut. 6:4	A	A	A
4 To love Him	Deut. 6:5	A	A	A
5 To fear Him	Deut. 10:20	A	A	A
6 To sanctify His Name	Lev. 22:32	A	A	A
7 Not to profane His Name	Lev. 22:32	A	A	A
8 Not to destroy objects associated with His Name	Deut. 12:4	A	A	A
9 To listen to the prophet speaking in His Name	Deut. 18:15	T	A	A
10 Not to test the prophet unduly	Deut. 6:16	T	A	A
11 To emulate His ways	Deut. 28:9	A	A	A
12 To cleave to those who know Him	Deut. 10:20	A	A	A
13 To love Jews	Lev. 19:18	A	A	A
14 To love converts	Deut. 10:19	A	A	A
15 Not to hate fellow Jews	Lev. 19:17	A	A	A
16 To reprove	Lev. 19:17	A	A	A
17 Not to embarrass others	Lev. 19:17	A	A	A
18 Not to oppress the weak	Ex. 22:21	A	A	A
19 Not to speak derogatorily of others	Lev. 19:16	A	A	A
20 Not to take revenge	Lev. 19:18	A	A	A
21 Not to bear a grudge	Lev. 19:18	A	A	A
22 To learn Torah	Deut. 6:7	A	A	A
23 To honor those who teach and know Torah	Lev. 19:32	A	A	A
24 Not to inquire into idolatry	Lev. 19:4	A	A	A
25 Not to follow the whims of your heart or what your eyes see	Num. 15:39	A	A	A
26 Not to blaspheme	Ex. 22:27	A	A	A
27 Not to worship idols in the manner they are worshiped	Ex. 20:5	A	A	A
28 Not to worship idols in the four ways we worship God	Ex. 20:5	A	A	A
29 Not to make an idol for yourself	Ex. 20:4	A	A	A
30 Not to make an idol for others	Lev. 19:4	A	A	A
31 Not to make human forms even for decorative purposes	Ex. 20:20	A	A	A
32 Not to turn a city to idolatry	Ex. 23:13	A	A	A
33 To burn a city that has turned to idol worship	Deut. 13:17	T	I	M
34 Not to rebuild it as a city	Deut. 13:17	T	I	A
35 Not to derive benefit from it	Deut. 13:18	T	I	A
36 Not to missionize an individual to idol worship	Deut. 13:12	A	A	A
37 Not to love the missionary	Deut. 13:9	A	A	A
38 Not to cease hating him	Deut. 13:9	A	A	A
39 Not to save him	Deut. 13:9	A	A	A

Commandment	Source	Time	Place	Whom
40 Not to say anything in his defense	*Deut. 13:9*	A	A	A
41 Not to refrain from incriminating him	*Deut. 13:9*	A	A	A
42 Not to prophesize in the name of idolatry	*Deut. 13:14*	A	A	A
43 Not to listen to a false prophet	*Deut. 13:4*	A	A	A
44 Not to prophesize falsely in the name of God	*Deut. 18:20*	A	A	A
45 Not to be afraid of killing the false prophet	*Deut. 18:22*	T	A	A
46 Not to swear in the name of an idol	*Ex. 23:13*	A	A	A
47 Not to perform *ov* (medium)	*Lev. 19:31*	A	A	A
48 Not to perform *yidoni* (magical seer)	*Lev. 19:31*	A	A	A
49 Not to pass your children through the fire to *Molech*	*Lev. 18:21*	A	A	A
50 Not to erect a column in a public place of worship	*Deut. 16:22*	A	A	A
51 Not to bow down on smooth stone	*Lev. 26:1*	A	A	A
52 Not to plant a tree in the Temple courtyard	*Deut. 16:21*	A	I	A
53 To destroy idols and their accessories	*Deut. 12:2*	A	A	A
54 Not to derive benefit from idols and their accessories	*Deut. 7:26*	A	A	A
55 Not to derive benefit from ornaments of idols	*Deut. 7:25*	A	A	A
56 Not to make a covenant with idolaters	*Deut. 7:2*	A	A	A
57 Not to show favor to them	*Deut. 7:2*	A	A	A
58 Not to let them dwell in our land	*Ex. 23:33*	A	I	A
59 Not to imitate them in customs and clothing	*Lev. 20:23*	A	A	A
60 Not to be superstitious	*Lev. 19:26*	A	A	A
61 Not to go into a trance to foresee events, etc.	*Deut. 18:10*	A	A	A
62 Not to engage in astrology	*Lev. 19:26*	A	A	A
63 Not to mutter incantations	*Deut. 18:11*	A	A	A
64 Not to attempt to contact the dead	*Deut. 18:11*	A	A	A
65 Not to consult the *ov*	*Deut. 18:11*	A	A	A
66 Not to consult the *yidoni*	*Deut. 18:11*	A	A	A
67 Not to perform acts of magic	*Deut. 18:10*	A	A	A
68 Men must not shave the hair off the sides of their head	*Lev. 19:27*	A	A	M
69 Men must not shave their beards with a razor	*Lev. 19:27*	A	A	M
70 Men must not wear women's clothing	*Deut. 22:5*	A	A	M
71 Women must not wear men's clothing	*Deut. 22:5*	A	A	W
72 Not to tattoo the skin	*Lev. 19:28*	A	A	A
73 Not to tear the skin in mourning	*Deut. 14:1*	A	A	A
74 Not to make a bald spot in mourning	*Deut. 14:1*	A	A	A
75 To repent and confess wrongdoings	*Num. 5:7*	A	A	A

Book Two: The Book of Adoration

76 To say the *Shema* twice daily	*Deut. 6:7*	A	A	M
77 To serve the Almighty with prayer daily	*Ex. 23:25*	A	A	A
78 The *kohanim* must bless the Jewish nation daily	*Num. 6:23*	A	A	M

Commandment	Source	Time	Place	Whom
79 To wear *tefillin* on the head	*Deut. 6:8*	A	A	M
80 To bind *tefillin* on the arm	*Deut. 6:8*	A	A	M
81 To put a *mezuzah* on each doorpost	*Deut. 6:9*	A	A	A
82 Each male must write a *Sefer Torah*	*Deut. 31:19*	A	A	M
83 The king must have a separate *Sefer Torah* for himself	*Deut. 17:18*	T	I	M
84 To have *tzitzit* on four-cornered garments	*Num. 15:38*	A	A	M
85 To bless the Almighty after eating	*Deut. 8:10*	A	A	A
86 To circumcise all males on the eighth day after their birth	*Lev. 12:3*	A	A	M

Book Three: The Book of Seasons

Commandment	Source	Time	Place	Whom
87 To rest on the seventh day	*Ex. 23:12*	A	A	A
88 Not to do prohibited labor on the seventh day	*Ex. 20:10*	A	A	A
89 The court must not inflict punishment on *Shabbat*	*Ex. 35:3*	T	A	M
90 Not to walk outside the city boundary on *Shabbat*	*Ex. 16:29*	A	A	A
91 To sanctify the day with *Kiddush* and *Havdalah*	*Ex. 20:8*	A	A	A
92 To rest from prohibited labor	*Lev. 23:32*	A	A	A
93 Not to do prohibited labor on *Yom Kippur*	*Lev. 23:32*	A	A	A
94 To afflict yourself on *Yom Kippur*	*Lev. 16:29*	A	A	A
95 Not to eat or drink on *Yom Kippur*	*Lev. 23:29*	A	A	A
96 To rest on the first day of Passover	*Lev. 23:7*	A	A	A
97 Not to do prohibited labor on the first day of Passover	*Lev. 23:8*	A	A	A
98 To rest on the seventh day of Passover	*Lev. 23:8*	A	A	A
99 Not to do prohibited labor on the seventh day of Passover	*Lev. 23:8*	A	A	A
100 To rest on *Shavuot*	*Lev. 23:21*	A	A	A
101 Not to do prohibited labor on *Shavuot*	*Lev. 23:21*	A	A	A
102 To rest on *Rosh Hashanah*	*Lev. 23:24*	A	A	A
103 Not to do prohibited labor on *Rosh Hashanah*	*Lev. 23:25*	A	A	A
104 To rest on *Sukkot*	*Lev. 23:35*	A	A	A
105 Not to do prohibited labor on *Sukkot*	*Lev. 23:35*	A	A	A
106 To rest on *Shemini Atzeret*	*Lev. 23:36*	A	A	A
107 Not to do prohibited labor on *Shemini Atzeret*	*Lev. 23:36*	A	A	A
108 Not to eat *chametz* on the afternoon of the fourteenth day of *Nisan*	*Deut. 16:3*	A	A	A
109 To destroy all *chametz* on 14th day of *Nisan*	*Ex. 12:15*	A	A	A
110 Not to eat *chametz* all seven days of Passover	*Ex. 13:3*	A	A	A
111 Not to eat mixtures containing *chametz* all seven days of Passover	*Ex. 12:20*	A	A	A
112 Not to see *chametz* in your domain seven days	*Ex. 13:7*	A	A	A
113 Not to find *chametz* in your domain seven days	*Ex. 12:19*	A	A	A

Commandment	Source	Time	Place	Whom
114 To eat *matzah* on the first night of Passover	*Ex. 12:18*	A	A	A
115 To relate the exodus from Egypt on that night	*Ex. 13:8*	A	A	A
116 To hear the *shofar* on the first day of *Tishrei* (Rosh Hashanah)	*Num. 29:1*	A	A	M
117 To dwell in a *sukkah* for the seven days of *Sukkot*	*Lev. 23:42*	A	A	M
118 To take up a *lulav* and *etrog* all seven days	*Lev. 23:40*	A	A	M
119 Each man must give a half *shekel* annually	*Ex. 30:13*	T	A	M
120 Courts must calculate to determine when a new month begins	*Ex. 12:2*	T	A	M
121 To afflict and cry out before God in times of catastrophe	*Num. 10:9*	T	I	M

Book Four: The Book of Women

Commandment	Source	Time	Place	Whom
122 To acquire a wife by means of *ketubah* and *kiddushin*	*Deut. 22:13*	A	A	M
123 Not to have relations with women not thus acquired	*Deut. 23:18*	A	A	M
124 Not to withhold food, clothing, and relations from your wife	*Ex. 21:10*	A	A	M
125 To have children with one's wife	*Gen. 1:28*	A	A	M
126 To issue a divorce by means of a *get*	*Deut. 24:1*	A	A	M
127 A man must not remarry his wife after she has married someone else	*Deut. 24:4*	A	A	M
128 To do *yibum* (marry childless brother's widow)	*Deut. 25:5*	A	A	M
129 To do *chalitzah* (freeing a widow from *yibum*)	*Deut. 25:9*	A	A	M
130 The widow must not remarry until the ties with her brother-in-law are removed	*Deut. 25:5*	A	A	W
131 The court must fine one who seduces a maiden	*Ex. 22:15-16*	T	A	M
132 The rapist must marry the maiden	*Deut. 22:29*	A	A	M
133 He must not divorce her	*Deut. 22:29*	A	A	M
134 The slanderer must remain married to his wife	*Deut. 22:19*	A	A	M
135 He must not divorce her	*Deut. 22:19*	A	A	M
136 To fulfill the laws of the *sotah*	*Num. 5:30*	T	A	M
137 Not to put oil on her meal offering	*Num. 5:15*	T	A	M
138 Not to put frankincense on her meal offering	*Num. 5:15*	T	A	M

Book Five: The Book of Holiness

Commandment	Source	Time	Place	Whom
139 Not to have relations with your mother	*Lev. 18:7*	A	A	M
140 Not to have relations with your father's wife	*Lev. 18:8*	A	A	M
141 Not to have relations with your sister	*Lev. 18:9*	A	A	M
142 Not to have relations with your father's wife's daughter	*Lev. 18:11*	A	A	M
143 Not to have relations with your son's daughter	*Lev. 18:10*	A	A	M
144 Not to have relations with your daughter	*Lev. 18:10*	A	A	M

Commandment	Source	Time	Place	Whom
145 Not to have relations with your daughter's daughter	Lev. 18:10	A	A	M
146 Not to have relations with a woman and her daughter	Lev. 18:17	A	A	M
147 Not to have relations with a woman and her son's daughter	Lev. 18:17	A	A	M
148 Not to have relations with a woman and her daughter's daughter	Lev. 18:17	A	A	M
149 Not to have relations with your father's sister	Lev. 18:12	A	A	M
150 Not to have relations with your mother's sister	Lev. 18:13	A	A	M
151 Not to have relations with your father's brother's wife	Lev. 18:14	A	A	M
152 Not to have relations with your son's wife	Lev. 18:15	A	A	M
153 Not to have relations with your brother's wife	Lev. 18:16	A	A	M
154 Not to have relations with your wife's sister	Lev. 18:18	A	A	M
155 A man must not have relations with a beast	Lev. 18:23	A	A	M
156 A woman must not have relations with a beast	Lev. 18:23	A	A	W
157 Not to have homosexual relations	Lev. 18:22	A	A	M
158 Not to have homosexual relations with your father	Lev. 18:7	A	A	M
159 Not to have homosexual relations with your father's brother	Lev. 18:14	A	A	M
160 Not to have relations with a married woman	Lev. 18:20	A	A	M
161 Not to have relations with a menstrually impure woman	Lev. 18:19	A	A	M
162 Not to marry non-Jews	Deut. 7:3	A	A	A
163 Not to let Moabite and Ammonite males marry into the Jewish people	Deut. 23:4	T	A	W
164 Don't keep a third generation Egyptian convert from marrying into the Jewish people	Deut. 23:8-9	T	A	A
165 Not to refrain from marrying a third generation Edomite convert	Deut. 23:8-9	T	A	A
166 Not to let a *mamzer* marry into the Jewish people	Deut. 23:3	A	A	A
167 Not to let a eunuch marry into the Jewish people	Deut. 23:2	A	A	A
168 Not to castrate any male (including animals)	Lev. 22:24	A	A	M
169 The High Priest must not marry a widow	Lev. 21:14	T	T	M
170 The High Priest must not have relations with a widow even outside of marriage	Lev. 21:15	T	I	M
171 The High Priest must marry a virgin maiden	Lev. 21:13	T	I	M
172 A priest must not marry a divorcee	Lev. 21:7	A	A	M
173 A priest must not marry a *zonah* (a woman who had any forbidden relations)	Lev. 21:7	A	A	M
174 A priest must not marry a *chalalah* (party to or product of 169-172)	Lev. 21:7	A	A	M
175 Not to make pleasurable contact with any forbidden woman	Lev. 18:6	A	A	M

Commandment	Source	Time	Place	Whom
176 To examine the signs of animals to distinguish between kosher and non-kosher	*Lev. 11:2*	A	A	A
177 To examine the signs of fowl to distinguish between kosher and non-kosher	*Deut. 14:11*	A	A	A
178 To examine the signs of fish to distinguish between kosher and non-kosher	*Lev. 11:9*	A	A	A
179 To examine the signs of locusts to distinguish between kosher and non-kosher	*Lev. 11:21*	A	A	A
180 Not to eat non-kosher animals	*Lev. 11:4*	A	A	A
181 Not to eat non-kosher fowl	*Lev. 11:13*	A	A	A
182 Not to eat non-kosher fish	*Lev. 11:11*	A	A	A
183 Not to eat non-kosher flying insects	*Deut. 14:19*	A	A	A
184 Not to eat non-kosher creatures that crawl on land	*Lev. 11:41*	A	A	A
185 Not to eat non-kosher maggots	*Lev. 11:44*	A	A	A
186 Not to eat worms found in fruit on the ground	*Lev. 11:42*	A	A	A
187 Not to eat creatures that live in water other than fish	*Lev. 11:43*	A	A	A
188 Not to eat the meat of an animal that died without ritual slaughter	*Deut. 14:21*	A	A	A
189 Not to benefit from an ox condemned to be stoned	*Ex. 21:28*	T		A
190 Not to eat meat of an animal that was mortally wounded	*Ex. 22:30*	A	A	A
191 Not to eat a limb torn off a living creature	*Deut. 12:23*	A	A	A
192 Not to eat blood	*Lev. 3:17*	A	A	A
193 Not to eat certain fats of clean animals	*Lev. 3:17*	A	A	A
194 Not to eat the sinew of the thigh	*Gen. 32:33*	A	A	A
195 Not to eat milk and meat cooked together	*Ex. 23:19*	A	A	A
196 Not to cook milk and meat together	*Ex. 34:26*	A	A	A
197 Not to eat bread from the new grain produce before the *Omer*	*Lev. 23:14*	A	A	A
198 Not to eat parched grains from the new grain produce before the *Omer*	*Lev. 23:14*	A	A	A
199 Not to eat ripened grains from the new grain produce before the *Omer*	*Lev. 23:14*	A	A	A
200 Not to eat fruit of a tree during its first three years	*Lev. 19:23*	A	A	A
201 Not to eat diverse seeds planted in a vineyard	*Deut. 22:9*	A	A	A
202 Not to eat untithed fruits	*Lev. 22:15*	A	I	A
203 Not to drink wine poured in service to idols	*Deut. 32:38*	A	A	A
204 To ritually slaughter an animal before eating it	*Deut. 12:21*	A	A	A
205 Not to slaughter an animal and its offspring on the same day	*Lev. 22:28*	A	A	A
206 To cover the blood of a slaughtered beast or fowl with earth	*Lev. 17:13*	A	A	A

Commandment	Source	Time	Place	Whom
207 Not to take the mother bird from her children	*Deut. 22:6*	A	A	A
208 To release the mother bird if she was taken from the nest	*Deut. 22:7*	A	A	A

Book Six: The Book of Oaths

209 Not to swear falsely in God's Name	*Lev. 19:12*	A	A	A
210 Not to take God's Name in vain	*Ex. 20:7*	A	A	A
211 Not to deny possession of something entrusted to you	*Lev. 19:11*	A	A	A
212 Not to swear in denial of a monetary claim	*Lev. 19:11*	A	A	A
213 To swear in God's Name to confirm the truth when deemed necessary by court	*Deut. 10:20*	A	A	A
214 To fulfill what was uttered and to do what was avowed	*Deut. 23:24*	A	A	A
215 Not to break oaths or vows	*Num. 30:3*	A	A	A
216 For oaths and vows annulled, there are the laws of annulling vows explicit in the Torah	*Num. 30:3*	A	A	A
217 The *nazir* must let his hair grow	*Num. 6:5*	A	A	A
218 The *nazir* must not cut his hair	*Num. 6:5*	A	A	A
219 The *nazir* must not drink wine, wine mixtures, or wine vinegar	*Num. 6:3*	A	A	A
220 The *nazir* must not eat fresh grapes	*Num. 6:3*	A	A	A
221 The *nazir* must not eat raisins	*Num. 6:3*	A	A	A
222 The *nazir* must not eat grape seeds	*Num. 6:4*	A	A	A
223 The *nazir* must not eat grape skins	*Num. 6:4*	A	A	A
224 He must not be under the same roof as a corpse	*Num. 6:6*	A	A	A
225 He must not come into contact with the dead	*Num. 6:7*	A	A	A
226 He must shave after bringing sacrifices upon completion of his period of being a *nazir*	*Num. 6:9*	T	I	A
227 To estimate the value of people as determined by the Torah	*Lev. 27:2*	A	A	A
228 To estimate the value of consecrated animals	*Lev. 27:12-13*	T	I	A
229 To estimate the value of consecrated houses	*Lev. 27:14*	T	I	A
230 To estimate the value of consecrated fields	*Lev. 27:16*	T	I	A
231 Carry out the laws of interdicting possessions (*cherem*)	*Lev. 27:28*	T	I	A
232 Not to sell the *cherem*	*Lev. 27:28*	T	I	A
233 Not to redeem the *cherem*	*Lev. 27:28*	T	I	A

Book Seven: The Book of Seeds

234 Not to plant diverse seeds together	*Lev. 19:19*	A	A	A
235 Not to plant grains or greens in a vineyard	*Deut. 22:9*	A	I	A
236 Not to crossbreed animals	*Lev. 19:19*	A	A	A
237 Not to work different animals together	*Deut. 22:10*	A	A	A

Commandment	Source	Time	Place	Whom
238 Not to wear *sha'atnez*, a cloth woven of wool and linen	*Deut. 22:11*	A	A	A
239 To leave a corner of the field uncut for the poor	*Lev. 19:10*	A	I	A
240 Not to reap that corner	*Lev. 19:9*	A	I	A
241 To leave gleanings	*Lev. 19:9*	A	I	A
242 Not to gather the gleanings	*Lev. 19:9*	A	I	A
243 To leave the gleanings of a vineyard	*Lev. 19:10*	A	I	A
244 Not to gather the gleanings of a vineyard	*Lev. 19:10*	A	I	A
245 To leave the unformed clusters of grapes	*Lev. 19:10*	A	I	A
246 Not to pick the unformed clusters of grapes	*Lev. 19:10*	A	I	A
247 To leave the forgotten sheaves in the field	*Deut. 24:19*	A	I	A
248 Not to retrieve them	*Deut. 24:19*	A	I	A
249 To separate the tithe for the poor	*Deut. 14:28*	A	I	A
250 To give charity	*Deut. 15:8*	A	A	A
251 Not to withhold charity from the poor	*Deut. 15:7*	A	A	A
252 To set aside *terumah gedolah*, tithe for the *kohen*	*Deut. 18:4*	T	I	A
253 The Levite must set aside a tenth of his tithe	*Num. 18:26*	T	I	A
254 Not to preface one tithe to the next, but separate them in their proper order	*Ex. 22:28*	T	I	A
255 A non-*kohen* must not eat *terumah*	*Lev. 22:10*	T	I	A
256 A hired worker or a Jewish bondsman of a *kohen* must not eat *terumah*	*Lev. 22:10*	T	I	A
257 An uncircumcised *kohen* must not eat *terumah*	*Ex. 12:48*	T	I	M
258 An impure *kohen* must not eat *terumah*	*Lev. 22:4*	T	I	A
259 A *chalalah* must not eat *terumah*	*Lev. 22:12*	T	I	W
260 To set aside *ma'aser* each planting year and give it to a Levite	*Num. 18:24*	T	I	A
261 To set aside the second tithe, *ma'aser sheni*	*Deut. 14:22*	T	I	A
262 Not to spend its redemption money on anything but food, drink, or ointment	*Deut. 26:14*	T	I	A
263 Not to eat *ma'aser sheni* while impure	*Deut. 26:14*	T	I	A
264 A mourner on the first day after death must not eat *ma'aser sheni*	*Deut. 26:14*	T	I	A
265 Not to eat *ma'aser sheni* grains outside Jerusalem	*Deut. 12:17*	T	I	A
266 Not to eat *ma'aser sheni* wine products outside Jerusalem	*Deut. 12:17*	T	I	A
267 Not to eat *ma'aser sheni* oil outside Jerusalem	*Deut. 12:17*	T	I	A
268 The fourth year crops must be totally for holy purposes like *ma'aser sheni*	*Lev. 19:24*	T	I	A
269 To read the confession of tithes every fourth and seventh year	*Deut. 26:13*	T	I	A
270 To set aside the first fruits and bring them to the Temple	*Ex. 23:19*	T	I	M

Commandment	Source	Time	Place	Whom
271 The *kohanim* must not eat the first fruits outside Jerusalem	*Deut. 12:17*	T	I	M
272 To read the Torah portion pertaining to their presentation	*Deut. 26:5*	T	I	M
273 To set aside a portion of dough for a *kohen*	*Num. 15:20*	T	I	A
274 To give the shoulder, two cheeks, and stomach of slaughtered animals to a *kohen*	*Deut. 18:3*	T	I	A
275 To give the first sheering of sheep to a *kohen*	*Deut. 18:4*	A	I	A
276 To redeem the firstborn sons and give the money to a *kohen*	*Num. 18:15*	A	A	M
277 To redeem the firstborn donkey by giving a lamb to a *kohen*	*Ex. 13:13*	A	A	A
278 To break the neck of the donkey if the owner does not intend to redeem it	*Ex. 13:13*	A	A	A
279 To rest the land during the seventh year by not doing any work which enhances growth	*Ex. 34:21*	T	I	A
280 Not to work the land during the seventh year	*Lev. 25:4*	T	I	A
281 Not to work with trees to produce fruit during that year	*Lev. 25:4*	T	I	A
282 Not to reap crops that grow wild that year in the normal manner	*Lev. 25:5*	T	I	A
283 Not to gather grapes which grow wild that year in the normal way	*Lev. 25:5*	T	I	A
284 To leave free all produce which grew in that year	*Ex. 23:11*	T	I	A
285 To release all loans during the seventh year	*Deut. 15:2*	T	A	A
286 Not to pressure or claim from the borrower	*Deut. 15:2*	T	A	A
287 Not to refrain from lending immediately before the release of the loans for fear of monetary loss	*Deut. 15:9*	T	A	A
288 The *Sanhedrin* must count seven groups of seven years	*Lev. 25:8*	T	I	M
289 The *Sanhedrin* must sanctify the fiftieth year	*Lev. 25:10*	T	I	M
290 To blow the *shofar* on the tenth of *Tishrei* to free the slaves	*Lev. 25:9*	T	I	M
291 Not to work the soil during the fiftieth year	*Lev. 25:11*	T	I	A
292 Not to reap in the normal manner that which grows wild in the fiftieth year	*Lev. 25:11*	T	I	A
293 Not to pick grapes which grew wild in the normal manner in the fiftieth year	*Lev. 25:11*	T	I	A
294 Carry out the laws of sold family properties	*Lev. 25:24*	T	I	A
295 Not to sell the land in Israel indefinitely	*Lev. 25:23*	T	I	A
296 Carry out the laws of houses in walled cities	*Lev. 25:29*	T	I	A
297 The Tribe of Levi must not be given a portion of the land in Israel, rather they are given cities to dwell in	*Deut. 18:1*	T	I	A

Commandment	Source	Time	Place	Whom
298 The Levites must not take a share in the spoils of war	*Deut. 18:1*	T	I	A
299 To give the Levites cities to inhabit and their surrounding fields	*Num. 35:2*	T	I	A
300 Not to sell the fields but they shall remain the Levites' before and after the Jubilee year	*Lev. 25:34*	T	I	A

Book Eight: The Book of Service
301 To build a Sanctuary	*Ex. 25:8*	T	I	A
302 Not to build the altar with stones hewn by metal	*Ex. 20:22*	T	I	A
303 Not to climb steps to the altar	*Ex. 20:23*	T	I	A
304 To show reverence to the Temple	*Lev. 19:30*	A	A	A
305 To guard the Temple area	*Num. 18:2*	T	I	M
306 Not to leave it unguarded	*Num. 18:5*	T	I	M
307 To prepare the anointing oil	*Ex. 30:31*	T	A	A
308 Not to reproduce the incense formula	*Ex. 30:32*	A	A	A
309 Not to anoint with it	*Ex. 30:32*	A	A	A
310 Not to reproduce the incense formula	*Ex. 30:37*	A	A	A
311 Not to burn anything on the Golden Altar besides incense	*Ex. 30:9*	T	I	M
312 The Levites must transport the ark on their shoulders	*Num. 7:9*	T	I	M
313 Not to remove the staves from the ark	*Ex. 25:15*	T	I	M
314 The Levites must work in the Temple	*Num. 18:23*	T	I	M
315 No Levite must do another's work of either a *kohen* or a Levite	*Num. 18:3*	T	I	M
316 To dedicate the *kohen* for service	*Lev. 21:8*	A	A	A
317 The kohanic work shifts must be equal during holidays	*Deut. 18:6-8*	T	I	M
318 The *kohanim* must wear their priestly garments during service	*Ex. 28:2*	T	I	M
319 Not to tear them	*Ex. 28:32*	T	I	A
320 The breastplate must not be loosened from the *efod*	*Ex. 28:28*	T	I	A
321 A *kohen* must not enter the Temple intoxicated	*Lev. 10:9*	T	I	M
322 A *kohen* must not enter the Temple with long hair	*Lev. 10:6*	T	I	M
323 A *kohen* must not enter the Temple with torn clothes	*Lev. 10:6*	T	I	M
324 A *kohen* must not enter the Temple indiscriminately	*Lev. 16:2*	T	I	M
325 A *kohen* must not leave the Temple during service	*Lev. 10:7*	T	I	M
326 To send the impure from the Temple	*Num. 5:2*	A	I	A

Commandment	Source	Time	Place	Whom
327 Impure people must not enter the Temple	*Num. 5:3*	A	I	A
328 Impure people must not enter the Temple Mount area	*Deut. 23:11*	A	I	A
329 Impure *kohanim* must not do service in the Temple	*Lev. 22:2*	T	I	M
330 An impure *kohen,* following immersion, must wait until after sundown before returning to service	*Lev. 22:7*	T	I	M
331 A *kohen* must wash his hands and feet before doing the service	*Ex. 30:19*	T	I	M
332 A *kohen* with a physical blemish must not enter the sanctuary or approach the altar	*Lev. 21:23*	T	I	M
333 A *kohen* with a physical blemish must not serve	*Lev. 21:17*	T	I	M
334 A *kohen* with a temporary blemish must not serve	*Lev. 21:17*	T	I	M
335 One who is not a *kohen* must not serve	*Num. 18:4*	A	I	A
336 To offer only unblemished animals	*Lev. 22:21*	T	I	M
337 Not to dedicate a blemished animal for the altar	*Lev. 22:20*	A	A	A
338 Not to slaughter it	*Lev. 22:22*	T	I	M
339 Not to sprinkle its blood	*Lev. 22:24*	T	I	M
340 Not to burn its fat	*Lev. 22:22*	T	I	M
341 Not to offer a temporarily blemished animal	*Deut. 17:1*	T	I	M
342 Not to sacrifice blemished animals even if offered by non-Jews	*Lev. 22:25*	T	I	M
343 Not to inflict wounds upon dedicated animals	*Lev. 22:21*	A	A	A
344 To redeem dedicated animals which have become disqualified	*Deut. 12:15*	T	I	A
345 To offer only animals which are at least eight days old, for younger animals are unfit for service	*Lev. 22:27*	T	I	M
346 Not to offer animals bought with the wages of a harlot or the animal exchanged for a dog	*Deut. 23:19*	T	I	A
347 Not to burn honey or yeast on the altar	*Lev. 2:11*	T	I	M
348 To salt all sacrifices	*Lev. 2:13*	T	I	M
349 Not to omit the salt from sacrifices	*Lev. 2:13*	T	I	M
350 Carry out the procedure of the burnt offering as prescribed in the Torah	*Lev. 1:3*	A	A	A
351 Not to eat its meat	*Deut. 12:17*	T	I	M
352 Carry out the procedure of the sin offering	*Lev. 6:18*	T	I	M
353 Not to eat the meat of the inner sin offering	*Lev. 6:23*	T	I	A
354 Not to decapitate a fowl brought as a sin offering	*Lev. 5:8*	T	I	A
355 Carry out the procedure of the guilt offering	*Lev. 7:1*	T	I	M
356 The *kohanim* must eat the sacrificial meat in the Temple	*Ex. 29:33*	T	I	A
357 The *kohanim* must not eat the meat outside the Temple courtyard	*Deut. 12:17*	A	A	A

Commandment	Source	Time	Place	Whom
358 A non-*kohen* must not eat sacrificial meat	*Ex. 29:33*	T	I	A
359 To follow the procedure of the peace offering	*Lev. 7:11*	T	I	M
360 Not to eat the meat of minor sacrifices before sprinkling the blood	*Deut. 12:17*	A	A	A
361 To bring meal offerings as prescribed in the Torah	*Lev. 2:1*	T	I	M
362 Not to put oil on the meal offerings of wrongdoers	*Lev. 5:11*	T	I	M
363 Not to put frankincense on the meal offerings of wrongdoers	*Lev. 5:11*	T	I	M
364 Not to eat the meal offering of the High Priest	*Lev. 6:16*	T	I	A
365 Not to bake a meal offering as leavened bread	*Lev. 6:10*	T	I	A
366 The *kohanim* must eat the remains of the meal offerings	*Lev. 6:9*	T	I	M
367 To bring all avowed and freewill offerings to the Temple on the first subsequent festival	*Deut. 12:5-6*	T	I	M
368 Not to withhold payment incurred by any vow	*Deut. 23:22*	A	A	A
369 To offer all sacrifices in the Temple	*Deut. 12:11*	A	A	A
370 To bring all sacrifices from outside Israel to the Temple	*Deut. 12:26*	T	A	A
371 Not to slaughter sacrifices outside the courtyard	*Lev. 17:4*	A	A	A
372 Not to offer any sacrifices outside the courtyard	*Deut. 12:13*	A	A	A
373 To offer two lambs every day	*Num. 28:3*	T	I	M
374 To light a fire on the altar every day	*Lev. 6:6*	T	I	M
375 Not to extinguish this fire	*Lev. 6:6*	T	I	A
376 To remove the ashes from the altar every day	*Lev. 6:3*	T	I	M
377 To burn incense every day	*Ex. 30:7*	T	I	M
378 To light the Menorah every day	*Ex. 27:21*	T	I	M
379 The *Kohen Gadol* must bring a meal offering every day	*Lev. 6:13*	T	I	M
380 To bring two additional lambs as burnt offerings on *Shabbat*	*Num. 28:9*	T	I	M
381 To make the show bread	*Ex. 25:30*	T	I	M
382 To bring additional offerings on the New Month	*Num. 28:11*	T	I	M
383 To bring additional offerings on Passover	*Num. 28:19*	T	I	M
384 To offer the wave offering from the meal of the new wheat	*Lev. 23:10*	T	I	M
385 Each man must count seven weeks from the day the new wheat offering was brought	*Lev. 23:15*	A	A	M
386 To bring additional offerings on *Shavuot*	*Num. 28:26*	T	I	M
387 To bring two loaves to accompany the above sacrifice	*Lev. 23:17*	T	I	M
388 To bring additional offerings on *Rosh HaShanah*	*Num. 29:2*	T	I	M
389 To bring additional offerings on *Yom Kippur*	*Num. 29:8*	T	I	M
390 To bring additional offerings on *Sukkot*	*Num. 29:13*	T	I	M

Commandment	Source	Time	Place	Whom
391 To bring additional offerings on *Shemini Atzeret*	*Num. 29:35*	T	I	M
392 Not to eat sacrifices which have become unfit or blemished	*Deut. 14:3*	A	A	A
393 Not to eat from sacrifices offered with improper intentions	*Lev. 7:18*	T	I	A
394 Not to leave sacrifices past the time allowed for eating them	*Lev. 22:30*	T	I	A
395 Not to eat from that which was left over	*Lev. 19:8*	T	I	A
396 Not to eat from sacrifices which became impure	*Lev. 7:19*	T	I	A
397 An impure person must not eat from sacrifices	*Lev. 7:20*	T	I	A
398 To burn the leftover sacrifices	*Lev. 7:17*	T	I	M
399 To burn all impure sacrifices	*Lev. 7:19*	T	I	M
400 To follow the procedure of *Yom Kippur* in the sequence prescribed in *parashat Acharei Mot*	*Lev. 16:3*	T	I	M
401 One who profaned property must repay what he profaned plus a fifth and bring a sacrifice	*Lev. 5:16*	T	I	A
402 Not to work consecrated animals	*Deut. 15:19*	A	A	A
403 Not to shear the fleece of consecrated animals	*Deut. 15:19*	A	A	A

Book Nine: The Book of Sacrifices

Commandment	Source	Time	Place	Whom
404 To slaughter the paschal sacrifice at the specified time	*Ex. 12:6*	T	I	A
405 Not to slaughter it while in possession of leaven	*Ex. 23:18*	T	I	A
406 Not to leave the fat overnight	*Ex. 23:18*	T	I	M
407 To slaughter the second paschal lamb	*Num. 9:11*	T	I	A
408 To eat the paschal lamb with *matzah* and *maror* on the night of the 15th of *Nisan*	*Ex. 12:8*	T	I	A
409 To eat the second paschal lamb on the night of the 15th of *Iyar*	*Num. 9:11*	T	I	A
410 Not to eat the paschal meat raw or boiled	*Ex. 12:9*	T	I	A
411 Not to take the paschal meat from the confines of the group	*Ex. 12:46*	T	I	A
412 An apostate must not eat from it	*Ex. 12:43*	T	I	A
413 A permanent or temporary hired worker must not eat from it	*Ex. 12:45*	T	I	A
414 An uncircumcised male must not eat from it	*Ex. 12:48*	T	I	M
415 Not to break any of its bones	*Ex. 12:46*	T	I	A
416 Not to break any bones from the second paschal offering	*Num. 9:12*	T	I	A
417 Not to leave its meat over until morning	*Ex. 12:10*	T	I	A
418 Not to leave the second paschal meat over until morning	*Num. 9:12*	T	I	A
419 Not to leave the meat of the holiday offering of the 14th until the 16th	*Deut. 16:4*	T	I	A

Commandment	Source	Time	Place	Whom
420 To be seen at the Temple on *Pesach* (Passover), *Shavuot,* and *Sukkot*	*Deut. 16:16*	T	I	M
421 To celebrate on these three Festivals (bring a peace offering)	*Ex. 23:14*	T	I	M
422 To rejoice on these three Festivals (bring a peace offering)	*Deut. 16:14*	A	A	A
423 Not to appear at the Temple without offerings	*Deut. 16:16*	T	I	M
424 Not to refrain from rejoicing with, and giving gifts to, the Levites	*Deut. 12:19*	T	I	M
425 To assemble all the people on the *Sukkot* following the seventh year	*Deut. 31:12*	T	I	A
426 To set aside the firstborn animals	*Ex. 13:12*	A	A	A
427 The *kohanim* must not eat unblemished firstborn animals outside Jerusalem	*Deut. 12:17*	A	I	M
428 Not to redeem the firstborn	*Num. 18:17*	A	I	A
429 Separate the tithe from animals	*Lev. 27:32*	A	A	A
430 Not to redeem the tithe	*Lev. 27:33*	A	A	A
431 Every person must bring a sin offering for his transgression	*Lev. 4:27*	T	I	A
432 Bring an *asham talui* when uncertain of guilt	*Lev. 5:17-18*	T	I	A
433 Bring an *asham vadai* when guilt is ascertained	*Lev. 5:25*	T	I	A
434 Bring an *oleh v'yored* offering. If the person is wealthy, an animal; if poor, a bird or meal offering for prescribed sins	*Lev. 5:7-11*	T	I	A
435 The *Sanhedrin* must bring an offering when it rules in error	*Lev. 4:13*	T	I	M
436 A woman who had a running issue must bring an offering after she goes to the *mikveh*	*Lev. 15:28-29*	T	I	W
437 A woman who gave birth must bring an offering after she goes to the *mikveh*	*Lev. 12:6*	T	I	W
438 A man who had a running issue must bring an offering after he goes to the *mikveh*	*Lev. 15:13-14*	T	I	M
439 A *metzora* must bring an offering after going to the *mikveh*	*Lev. 14:10*	T	I	A
440 Not to substitute another beast for one set apart for sacrifice	*Lev. 27:10*	A	A	A
441 The new animal, in addition to the substituted one, retains consecration	*Lev. 27:10*	A	A	A
442 Not to change consecrated animals from one type of offering to another	*Lev. 27:26*	A	A	A

Book Ten: The Book of Purity

443 Carry out the laws of impurity of the dead	*Num. 19:14*	T	I	A
444 Carry out the procedure of the Red Heifer	*Num. 19:2*	T	I	A

Commandment	Source	Time	Place	Whom
445 Carry out the laws of the sprinkling water	Num. 19:21	T	I	A
446 Rule the laws of human *tzara'at* as prescribed in the Torah	Lev. 13:12	A	A	A
447 The *metzora* must not remove his signs of impurity	Deut. 24:8	A	A	A
448 The *metzora* must not shave signs of impurity in his hair	Lev. 13:33	A	A	A
449 The *metzora* must publicize his condition by tearing his garments, allowing his hair to grow and covering his lips	Lev. 13:45	A	A	A
450 Carry out the prescribed rules for purifying the *metzora*	Lev. 14:2	A	A	A
451 The *metzora* must shave off all his hair prior to purification	Lev. 14:9	A	A	A
452 Carry out the laws of *tzara'at* of clothing	Lev. 13:47	A	A	A
453 Carry out the laws of *tzara'at* of houses	Lev. 13:34	A	I	A
454 Observe the laws of menstrual impurity	Lev. 15:19	A	A	W
455 Observe the laws of impurity caused by childbirth	Lev. 12:2	A	A	W
456 Observe the laws of impurity caused by a woman's running issue	Lev. 15:25	T	A	W
457 Observe the laws of impurity caused by a man's running issue	Lev. 15:3	A	A	M
458 Observe the laws of impurity caused by a dead beast	Lev. 11:39	A	A	A
459 Observe the laws of impurity caused by the eight *sheratzim*	Lev. 11:29	A	A	A
460 Observe the laws of impurity of a seminal emission	Lev. 15:16	A	A	M
461 Observe the laws of impurity concerning liquid and solid foods	Lev. 11:34	A	A	A
462 Every impure person must immerse himself in a *mikveh* to become pure	Lev. 15:16	A	A	A

Book Eleven: The Book of Damages

Commandment	Source	Time	Place	Whom
463 The court must judge the damages incurred by a goring ox	Ex. 21:28	T	A	M
464 The court must judge the damages incurred by an animal eating	Ex. 22:4	A	A	M
465 The court must judge the damages incurred by a pit	Ex. 21:33	A	A	M
466 The court must judge the damages incurred by fire	Ex. 22:5	A	A	M
467 Not to steal money stealthily	Lev. 19:11	A	A	A
468 The court must implement punitive measures against the thief	Ex. 21:37	A	A	M

Commandment	Source	Time	Place	Whom
469 Each individual must ensure that his scales and weights are accurate	*Lev. 19:36*	A	A	A
470 Not to commit injustice with scales and weights	*Lev. 19:35*	A	A	A
471 Not to possess inaccurate scales and weights even if they are not for use	*Deut. 25:13*	A	A	A
472 Not to move a boundary marker to steal someone's property	*Deut. 19:14*	A	A	A
473 Not to kidnap	*Ex. 20:13*	A	A	A
474 Not to rob openly	*Lev. 19:13*	A	A	A
475 Not to withhold wages or fail to repay a debt	*Lev. 19:13*	A	A	A
476 Not to covet and scheme to acquire another's possession	*Ex. 20:14*	A	A	A
477 Not to desire another's possession	*Deut. 5:18*	A	A	A
478 Return the robbed object or its value	*Lev. 5:23*	A	A	A
479 Not to ignore a lost object	*Deut. 22:3*	A	A	A
480 Return the lost object	*Deut. 22:1*	A	A	A
481 The court must implement laws against the one who assaults another or damages another's property	*Ex. 21:18*	A	A	M
482 Not to murder	*Ex. 20:13*	A	A	A
483 Not to accept monetary restitution to atone for the murderer	*Num. 35:31*	T	I	A
484 The court must send the accidental murderer to a city of refuge	*Num. 35:25*	T	I	M
485 Not to accept monetary restitution instead of being sent to a city of refuge	*Num. 35:32*	T	I	A
486 Not to kill the murderer before he stands trial	*Num. 35:12*	A	A	A
487 Save someone being pursued even by taking the life of the pursuer	*Deut. 25:12*	A	A	A
488 Not to pity the pursuer	*Num. 35:12*	A	A	A
489 Not to stand idly by if someone's life is in danger	*Lev. 19:16*	A	A	A
490 Designate cities of refuge and prepare routes of access	*Deut. 19:3*	T	I	M
491 Break the neck of a calf by the river valley following an unsolved murder	*Deut. 21:4*	T	I	M
492 Not to work nor plant that river valley	*Deut. 21:4*	A	I	A
493 Not to allow pitfalls and obstacles to remain on your property	*Deut. 22:8*	A	A	A
494 Make a guard rail around flat roofs (parapet)	*Deut. 22:8*	A	A	A
495 Not to put a stumbling block before a blind man nor give harmful advice, lead someone to sin, or trip somebody	*Lev. 19:14*	A	A	A
496 Help another remove the load from a beast which can no longer carry it	*Ex. 23:5*	A	A	A

Commandment	Source	Time	Place	Whom
497 Help others load their beast	*Deut. 22:4*	A	A	A
494 Not to leave them distraught with their burdens but help to either load or unload	*Deut. 22:4*	A	A	A

Book Twelve: The Book of Acquisition

Commandment	Source	Time	Place	Whom
499 Buy and sell according to Torah law	*Lev. 25:14*	A	A	A
500 Not to overcharge or underpay for an article	*Lev. 25:14*	A	A	A
501 Not to insult or harm anybody with words	*Lev. 25:17*	A	A	A
502 Not to cheat a sincere convert monetarily	*Ex. 22:20*	A	A	A
503 Not to insult or harm a sincere convert with words	*Ex. 22:20*	A	A	A
504 Purchase a Hebrew slave in accordance with the prescribed laws	*Ex. 21:2*	T	I	M
505 Not to sell him as a slave is sold	*Lev. 25:42*	T	I	A
506 Not to work him oppressively	*Lev. 25:43*	T	I	A
507 Not to allow a non-Jew to work him oppressively	*Lev. 25:53*	T	I	A
508 Not to have him do menial slave labor	*Lev. 25:39*	T	I	A
509 Give him gifts when he goes free	*Deut. 15:14*	T	I	A
510 Not to send him away empty-handed	*Deut. 15:13*	T	I	A
511 Redeem Jewish maidservants	*Ex. 21:8*	T	I	M
512 Betroth the Jewish maidservant	*Ex. 21:8*	T	I	M
513 The master must not sell his maidservant	*Ex. 21:8*	T	I	M
514 Canaanite slaves must work forever unless injured in one of their limbs	*Lev. 25:46*	A	A	A
515 Not to extradite a slave who fled to Israel	*Deut. 23:16*	A	I	A
516 Not to wrong a slave who who has come to Israel for refuge	*Deut. 23:17*	A	I	A

Book Thirteen: The Book of Judgments

Commandment	Source	Time	Place	Whom
517 The courts must carry out the laws of a hired worker and hired guard	*Ex. 22:9*	A	A	M
518 Pay wages on the day they were earned	*Deut. 24:15*	A	A	A
519 Not to delay payment of wages past the agreed time	*Lev. 19:13*	A	A	A
520 The hired worker may eat from the unharvested crops where he works	*Deut. 23:25*	A	A	A
521 The worker must not eat while on hired time	*Deut. 23:26*	A	A	A
522 The worker must not take more than he can eat	*Deut. 23:25*	A	A	A
523 Not to muzzle an ox while plowing	*Deut. 25:4*	A	A	A
524 The courts must carry out the laws of a borrower	*Ex. 22:13*	T	A	M
525 The courts must carry out the laws of an unpaid guard	*Ex. 22:6*	A	A	M
526 Lend to the poor and destitute	*Ex. 22:24*	A	A	A
527 Not to press them for payment if you know they don't have it	*Ex. 22:24*	A	A	A

Commandment	Source	Time	Place	Whom
528 Press the idolater for payment	*Deut. 15:3*	A	A	A
529 The creditor must not forcibly take collateral	*Deut. 24:10*	A	A	A
530 Return the collateral to the debtor when needed (i.e., blanket at night)	*Deut. 24:13*	A	A	A
531 Not to delay its return when needed	*Deut. 24:12*	A	A	A
532 Not to demand collateral from a widow	*Deut. 24:17*	A	A	A
533 Not to demand as collateral utensils needed for preparing food	*Deut. 24:6*	A	A	A
534 Not to lend with interest	*Lev. 25:37*	A	A	A
535 Not to borrow with interest	*Deut. 23:20*	A	A	A
536 Not to intermediate in an interest loan, guarantee, witness, or write the promissory note	*Ex. 22:24*	A	A	A
537 Lend to and borrow from idolaters with interest	*Deut. 23:21*	A	A	A
538 The courts must carry out the laws of the plaintiff, admitter, or denier	*Ex. 22:8*	A	A	M
539 Carry out the laws of the order of inheritance	*Num. 27:8*	A	A	A

Book Fourteen: The Book of Judges

Commandment	Source	Time	Place	Whom
540 Appoint judges	*Deut. 16:18*	A	I	M
541 Not to appoint judges who are not familiar with judicial procedure	*Deut. 1:17*	A	A	M
542 Decide by majority in case of disagreement	*Ex. 23:2*	A	A	A
543 The court must not execute through a majority of one; at least a majority of two is required	*Ex. 23:2*	T	I	M
544 A judge who presented an acquittal plea must not present an argument for conviction in capital cases	*Deut. 23:2*	T	I	M
545 The courts must carry out the death penalty of stoning	*Deut. 22:24*	T	I	M
546 The courts must carry out the death penalty of burning	*Lev. 20:14*	T	I	M
547 The courts must carry out the death penalty of the sword	*Ex. 21:20*	T	I	M
548 The courts must carry out the death penalty of strangulation	*Lev. 20:10*	T	I	M
549 The courts must hang those stoned for blasphemy or idolatry	*Deut. 21:22*	T	I	M
550 Bury the executed on the day they are killed	*Deut. 21:23*	T	I	M
551 Not to delay burial overnight	*Deut. 21:23*	T	I	M
552 The court must not let the sorcerer live	*Ex. 22:17*	T	I	M
553 The court must flog the wrongdoer	*Ex. 25:2*	T	I	M
554 The court must not exceed the prescribed number of lashes	*Deut. 25:3*	T	I	A
555 The court must not kill anybody on circumstantial evidence	*Ex. 23:7*	T	I	M

Commandment	Source	Time	Place	Whom
556 The court must not punish anybody who was forced to do a crime	*Deut. 22:26*	A	A	M
557 The judge must not pity the murderer or assaulter at the trial	*Deut. 19:13*	A	A	A
558 The judge must not have mercy on the poor man at the trial	*Lev. 19:15*	A	A	A
559 The judge must not respect the great man at the trial	*Lev. 19:15*	A	A	M
560 The judge must not decide unjustly the case of the habitual transgressor	*Ex. 23:6*	A	A	M
561 The judge must not pervert justice	*Lev. 19:15*	A	A	M
562 The judge must not pervert the case involving a convert or orphan	*Deut. 24:17*	A	A	M
563 Judge righteously	*Lev. 19:15*	A	A	M
564 The judge must not fear the violent man in judgment	*Deut. 1:17*	A	A	M
565 Judges must not accept bribes	*Ex. 23:8*	A	A	M
566 Judges must not accept testimony unless both parties are present	*Ex. 23:1*	A	A	M
567 Not to curse judges	*Ex. 22:27*	A	A	A
568 Not to curse the head of state or leader of the *Sanhedrin*	*Ex. 22:27*	A	A	A
569 Not to curse any upstanding Jew	*Lev. 19:14*	A	A	A
570 Anybody who knows evidence must testify in court	*Lev. 5:1*	A	A	M
571 Carefully interrogate the witness	*Deut. 13:15*	A	A	M
572 A witness must not serve as a judge in capital crimes	*Deut. 19:17*	T	I	M
573 Not to accept testimony from a lone witness	*Deut. 19:15*	A	A	A
574 Transgressors must not testify	*Ex. 23:1*	A	A	M
575 Relatives of the litigants must not testify	*Deut. 24:16*	A	A	M
576 Not to testify falsely	*Ex. 20:13*	A	A	M
577 Do to the false witnesses what they tried to do to the defendant	*Deut. 19:19*	T	I	M
578 Act according to the ruling of the *Sanhendrin*	*Deut. 17:11*	T	A	A
579 Not to deviate from their word (the *Sanhendrin*)	*Deut. 17:11*	A	A	A
580 Not to add to the Torah commandments or their oral explanations	*Deut. 13:1*	A	A	A
581 Not to diminish from the Torah any commandments, in whole or in part	*Deut. 13:1*	A	A	A
582 Not to curse your father and mother	*Ex. 21:17*	A	A	A
583 Not to strike your father and mother	*Ex. 21:15*	A	A	A
584 Respect your father or mother	*Ex. 20:12*	A	A	A
585 Fear your father or mother	*Lev. 19:3*	A	A	A

Commandment	Source	Time	Place	Whom
586 Not to be a rebellious son, not heeding your father's and mother's voice	*Deut. 21:18*	T	I	M
587 Mourn for relatives	*Lev. 10:19*	A	A	A
588 The High Priest must not defile himself for any relative	*Lev. 21:11*	T	I	M
589 The High Priest must not enter under the same roof as a corpse	*Lev. 21:11*	T	A	M
590 A *kohen* must not defile himself for anyone except relatives	*Lev. 21:1*	T	A	M
591 Appoint a king from Israel	*Deut. 17:15*	T	I	A
592 Not to appoint a convert	*Deut. 17:15*	A	A	A
593 The king must not have too many wives	*Deut. 17:17*	T	I	M
594 The king must not have too many horses	*Deut. 17:16*	T	I	M
595 The king must not have too much silver and gold	*Deut. 17:17*	T	I	M
596 Destroy the seven Canaanite nations	*Deut. 20:17*	A	A	A
597 Not to let any of them remain alive	*Deut. 20:16*	A	A	A
598 Wipe out the descendants of Amalek	*Deut. 25:19*	A	A	M
599 Remember what they did to the Jewish people	*Deut. 25:17*	A	A	A
600 Not to forget their atrocities and ambush on our journey from Egypt in the desert	*Deut. 25:19*	A	A	A
601 Not to dwell permanently in Egypt	*Deut. 17:16*	A	A	A
602 Offer peace terms to the inhabitants of a city while holding siege, and treat them according to the Torah if they accept the terms	*Deut. 20:10*	T	A	M
603 Not to offer peace to Ammon and Moab while besieging them	*Deut. 23:7*	T	A	M
604 Not to destroy fruit trees even during the siege	*Deut. 20:19*	A	A	A
605 Prepare latrines outside the camps	*Deut. 23:13*	T	A	M
606 Prepare a shovel for each soldier to dig with	*Deut. 23:14*	T	A	M
607 Appoint a priest to speak to the soldiers during the war	*Deut. 20:2*	T	I	M
608 He who has taken a wife, built a new home, or planted a vineyard is given a year to rejoice with his possessions	*Deut. 24:5*	A	A	M
609 Not to demand from the above any involvement, communal or military	*Deut. 24:5*	T	I	M
610 Not to panic and retreat during battle	*Deut. 20:3*	T	I	M
611 Keep the laws of the captive woman	*Deut. 21:11*	T	I	M
612 Not to sell her into slavery	*Deut. 21:14*	T	I	M
613 Not to retain her for servitude after having relations with her	*Deut. 21:14*	T	I	M

Guide to the Character Traits

The Nature of Character Traits

I t is inherent in the human condition to constantly go through self-evaluation. Even Western society, which has tended to move away from absolute values and towards relativism, can't escape the inborn need to quantify and qualify human behavior. In fact, the only aspect of humanity that changes from society to society, and from generation to generation, is the standard by which people measure themselves.

As mentioned in the Preface, the Hebrew word for "character trait" is *middah,* which means "measure." According to Jewish philosophy, the true measure of human success is in the area of refinement of character traits. From the Torah, it is clear that refinement means moving closer towards the "Divine image" in which we were created.

The Talmud tells about a potential convert to Judaism. The non-Jew approached the great scholar, Hillel (*circa 260 BCE*), and asked him to teach him the entire Torah while standing on one foot. Hillel's response was, "Do not do to others what you would not like done to you. The rest is commentary, now go and learn!"

This statement, of course, was a highly unusual response to give to a potential convert, considering that the Torah is composed of many commandments; those that deal with human relationships form only a portion. Hillel's message was, however, that as technical as the Torah may become, whether dealing with the laws of torts, or the laws of ritual slaughtering, the underlying theme behind all commandments, stories, and narratives is righteousness.

The Thirteen Attributes of God

When God described Himself to Moses, He did so in terms of character traits:[1]

> "God, God, Omnipotent, merciful and gracious, slow to anger, abundant in kindness and truth. Preserver of kindness for thousands of generations, forgiving transgression, rebellious sins and error. He does not clear [the unrepentant], but keeps in mind the transgressions of the fathers to their children and grandchildren, to the third and fourth generation..."

The above statement isolates thirteen main attributes:

1. *God...*   He has mercy on the person before he transgresses.

[1] Exodus 34:6

According to Jewish philosophy, the true measure of human success is in the area of character traits.

2. *God...*   He has mercy on the person after he transgresses.

3. *Omnipotent...*   He is all-powerful.

4. *compassionate...* He is a sympathetic God.

5. *gracious...*   He is merciful to all.

6. *slow to anger...*   He does not hasten to punish, so the person might repent.

7. *abundant in kindness...*   He never reneges on his word and he does kindness even to those who don't deserve it.

8. *and truth...*   He will faithfully reward those who do his will.

9. *Preserver of kindness*   He stores up the mercy done before Him for thousands of generations.

10. *forgiver of iniquity...*   He forgives intentional wickedness upon repenting.

11. *willful sin...*   He forgives transgressions performed in rebellion upon repenting.

12. *and error...*   He forgives accidental transgressions upon repenting.

13. *He does not clear [the unrepentant], but keeps in mind the transgressions of the fathers to their children and grandchildren, to the third and fourth generation...*

Ethics of our Fathers (Pirkei Avot)

Ethics of our Fathers shows us an interesting point. It is a series of teachings that focuses entirely on character development,[2] yet it was placed amidst the most technical aspect of Jewish law, in *Nezikin,* the Book of Damages, which deals with the laws of torts and damages.

The Rabbis' message: All damages, whether to property or to people, result from negligence, and all negligence results from bad character traits. When a person refines his personality, he automatically becomes more aware and sensitive to the important issues in life, and is thus motivated to act morally.

In *Ethics of our Fathers* (*5:13*), the measure of a person

[2] Ethics of our Fathers was compiled by the Rabbis of the Second Temple and post-Second Temple eras (circa 70 CE).

Self-growth can be the source of one's sense of fulfillment and joy, and the Torah of all time to achieve both.

is described by the way a person relates to his or her own possessions, and the possessions of others. The pious person is the one who believes, "What's mine is yours, and what's yours is yours," whereas the wicked person is the one who thinks, "What's yours is mine, and what's mine is mine." In between these two extremes is the "average" person, and the ignoramus, the one who does not understand.

Likewise, the charitable person is described as one "who gives and wishes others to give"; the best type of student is one "who is quick to learn, and slow to forget."

This is just the beginning. There are countless character traits to learn and to implement, and though the list is daunting, the mission is exciting. The never ending list of *middot* (plural for traits) shows us that self-growth is also never ending. A comprehensive list of character traits has been indexed in alphabetical order and is presented at the end of this chapter.

Fulfillment through Self-Growth

It is up to the individual to learn how to extract the message of personal fulfillment from every aspect of Torah. Self-growth can be the source of one's sense of fulfillment and joy, and the Torah is the guidebook for all time to achieve both. To this end, this work has used the weekly Torah portions as opportunities to focus on a sampling of traits that can be learned from the verses.

In each weekly Torah portion, verses will be printed in **bold italics**, followed by the symbol, " ⚖ ". This symbol will refer the reader to the footnotes, which will provide a brief note on the trait being learned from the verse. For example:

> ⚖ 1:4 **Orderly**
> ***"And God separated between the light and the dark"*** (Good and Evil?—Life and Death?) Arranging things in a clear and orderly manner in every aspect of one's life is the way to begin any undertaking and is the key to success.

This discussion about character refinement is probably the most important one in this work. Because it is, there is one last point to consider. Anyone who has ever attended the eulogy for a deceased person knows that the most fitting description of the person who has passed away is one of his or her character traits. Sometimes, our own obsessions with material success may cause us to admire him or her for being adept in business, sports or the like.

Business success, however, matters little to us at

funerals. What concerns us is what the person was like. What did he or she do with his or her opportunity in life? How did he or she behave with other people, especially the needy? These are the issues that are usually addressed on such sobering occasions.

Jewish consciousness states that if you want to know how to live your life, and not get distracted from the true purpose, ask yourself the question, "What would I want others to say about me after I die? That I made a lot of money? That I knew how to make a good business deal? That I was a great athlete? Or, that I was a good spouse and a good parent... that I showed concern for the well-being of others?"

Questions such as these make it clear why your character refinement should be a major concern for every conscious moment of your life. As the Torah teaches in the weekly Torah portion, *Noah*, what you become and the good name you create is essentially the inheritance you leave to your family, friends, and the world.[3]

Try it. You'll see that it works!

[3] The portion begins with the words, *"These are the generations of Noah. Noah was a righteous man..."* (Genesis 6:9). The question is asked, if the Torah intended to discuss the "generations" of Noah, why did it mention Noah's righteousness? The answer given is that the Torah wishes to teach that a person's *true* legacy is the good reputation he leaves behind after living a life filled with the performance of good deeds.

The Character Traits

Listed here are two sets of character traits (adapted from the book *Begin Again Now by Zelig Pliskin*), one of positive traits and the other of negative traits. Positive traits are to be integrated into one's personality; negative ones are to be uprooted. Knowing these traits and thinking about them is already a change in the right direction—an important first step towards becoming a success in the eyes of Torah, one's fellow man, and, of course, in your own eyes as well.

Positive Character Traits

1. Accepting
2. Accessible
3. Accomplished
4. Accurate
5. Acknowledging
6. Adaptable
7. Adventurous
8. Agreeable
9. Alacritous
10. Altruistic
11. Ambitious
12. Analytic
13. Appreciative
14. Articulate
15. Attentive to details
16. Authentic
17. Aware
18. Awed by wonders
19. Balanced
20. Beloved
21. Benevolent
22. Blissful
23. Brave
24. Buoyant
25. Calm
26. Careful
27. Caring
28. Cautious
29. Charismatic
30. Charitable
31. Cheerful
32. Compassionate
33. Composed
34. Concerned about others
35. Concentrating well
36. Confident
37. Conscientious
38. Considerate
39. Consistent
40. Cooperative
41. Courageous
42. Creative
43. Decisive
44. Deliberative
45. Dependable
46. Devoted
47. Devout
48. Dexterous
49. Dignified
50. Diligent
51. Diplomatic
52. Discreet
53. Driven
54. Dutiful
55. Dynamic
56. Easygoing
57. Ecstatic
58. Effective
59. Efficient
60. Eloquent
61. Emotionally honest
62. Emotionally strong
63. Empathic
64. Encouraging
65. Energetic
66. Enthusiastic
67. Ethical
68. Evenhanded
69. Expert
70. Expressive
71. Fair
72. Faithful
73. Family devoted
74. Family oriented
75. Fearless
76. Filial
77. Flexible
78. Fluent
79. Forgiving
80. Forward looking
81. Friendly
82. Generous
83. Gentle
84. Genuine
85. Giving
86. Goal-oriented
87. Good natured
88. Graceful
89. Grateful
90. Handy

91. Happy
92. Hardworking
93. Healthy
94. Helpful
95. Honest
96. Honors others
97. Hopeful
98. Hospitable
99. Humble
100. Idealistic
101. Imaginative
102. Imperturbable
103. Industrious
104. Inner-directed
105. Innovative
106. Insightful
107. Intuitive
108. Joyful
109. Just
110. Keeping secrets
111. Keeping his/her word
112. Kind
113. Knowledgeable
114. Leadership qualities
115. Levelheaded
116. Likeable
117. Lively
118. Logical
119. Loving
120. Loyal
121. Magnanimous
122. Mature
123. Meeting obligations
124. Merciful
125. Methodical
126. Meticulous
127. Mild
128. Modest
129. Moral
130. Natural
131. Neat
132. Noble
133. Objective
134. Open

135. Optimistic
136. Orderly
137. Organized
138. Original
139. Patient
140. Peace loving
141. Peaceful of mind
142. Peaceful
143. Peace pursuing
144. Perceptive
145. Persevering
146. Persistent
147. Persuasive
148. Philanthropic
149. Planning goals
150. Poised
151. Polite
152. Positive in thinking
153. Practical
154. Productive
155. Proficient
156. Prompt
157. Punctual
158. Rapport with people
159. Rational
160. Real
161. Realistic
162. Reasonable
163. Reassuring
164. Relaxed
165. Reliable
166. Resilient
167. Resourceful
168. Respectful
169. Responsible
170. Righteous
171. Scholarly
172. Scrupulous
173. Selective
174. Self-assuring
175. Self-actualized
176. Self-composed
177. Self-controlled
178. Sincere

179. Skillful
180. Sociable
181. Soft
182. Speedy
183. Spirited
184. Spiritual
185. Spontaneous
186. Stable
187. Steadfast
188. Straightforward
189. Studious
190. Sunny
191. Supportive
192. Sweet
193. Swift
194. Sympathetic
195. Systematic
196. Tactful
197. Talented
198. Tenacious
199. Testing
200. Thankful
201. Thorough
202. Thoughtful
203. Thrifty
204. Tidy
205. Time efficient
206. Tolerant
207. Tranquil
208. Trusting
209. Trustworthy
210. Truthful
211. Unafraid
212. Unconditionally loving
213. Understanding
214. Unselfish
215. Versatile
216. Vigorous
217. Visionary
218. Warm
219. Will-power
220. Wise
221. Zestful

Negative Character Traits

1. Abrasive
2. Abrupt
3. Absent-minded
4. Abusive
5. Afraid of people
6. Aggressive
7. Aimless
8. Alarming
9. Alcoholic
10. Aloof
11. Angry
12. Antagonistic
13. Argumentative
14. Attention-seeking
15. Avoiding
16. Awkward
17. Babyish
18. Barbaric
19. Base
20. Beating around the bush
21. Belligerent
22. Bigoted
23. Bitter
24. Blame passer
25. Blaming
26. Blocked
27. Blunt
28. Boastful
29. Boisterous
30. Boorish
31. Boring
32. Brazen
33. Brooding
34. Brutal
35. Bullying
36. Calculating
37. Callous
38. Careless
39. Caustic
40. Characterless
41. Charlatan
42. Chatter-box
43. Cheater
44. Cheerless
45. Childish
46. Closed
47. Clumsy
48. Coarse
49. Coercive
50. Cold
51. Cold-hearted
52. Colorless
53. Competitive
54. Complacent
55. Complaining
56. Compulsive
57. Concealing
58. Conceited
59. Confrontational
60. Confused
61. Contemptuous of others
62. Contradictory
63. Controlling
64. Covetous
65. Cranky
66. Critical
67. Crooked
68. Cross
69. Crude
70. Cruel
71. Cunning
72. Cynical
73. Dawdling
74. Decadent
75. Deceitful
76. Deceptive
77. Defensive
78. Deficient in attention
79. Defiant
80. Dejected
81. Demanding
82. Dependent
83. Depressed
84. Derisive
85. Deserting
86. Despairing
87. Destructive
88. Detached
89. Devious
90. Dishonest

91. Disloyal
92. Disobedient
93. Disorderly
94. Disrespectful
95. Distracted
96. Distrustful
97. Divisive
98. Domineering
99. Downcast
100. Dreamy
101. Drowsy
102. Dull
103. Egoistic
104. Egotistic
105. Elusive
106. Envious
107. Evasive
108. Evilly inclined
109. Excessive
110. Excitable
111. Exhibitionist
112. Exploitative
113. Extravagant
114. Faint-hearted
115. Faraway
116. Fearful
117. Ferocious
118. Fickle
119. Fierce
120. Finicky
121. Flaky
122. Flattering
123. Flighty
124. Flippant
125. Flustered
126. Foggy
127. Foolish
128. Forgetful
129. Frantic
130. Fraudulent
131. Frivolous
132. Frustrated
133. Garrulous
134. Glib
135. Gloomy
136. Gluttonous

137. Gossiping
138. Graceless
139. Grandiose
140. Greedy
141. Gross
142. Gruff
143. Grumpy
144. Guilt-ridden
145. Gullible
146. Hardhearted
147. Harsh
148. Hasty
149. Histrionic
150. Headstrong
151. Hostile
152. Hyper
153. Hypercritical
154. Hypersensitive
155. Hypochondriac
156. Hypocritical
157. Hysterical
158. Idle
159. Ignorant
160. Illogical
161. Ill-tempered
162. Illusive
163. Immature
164. Immoderate
165. Immoral
166. Impatient
167. Impetuous
168. Impractical
169. Impudent
170. Impulsive
171. Inaccessible
172. Inactive
173. Incompetent
174. Inconsiderate
175. Inconsistent
176. Indecisive
177. Indifferent
178. Indiscreet
179. Ineffective
180. Inefficient
181. Infantile
182. Inferiority complex

183. Inflexible
184. Insecure
185. Intimidated
186. Intimidating
187. Intolerant
188. Intrusive
189. Irrational
190. Irresponsible
191. Irritable
192. Irritating
193. Isolated
194. Jealous
195. Judgmental
196. Jumping to conclusions
197. Juvenile
198. Loafing
199. Lonely
200. Loner
201. Loud
202. Lowly
203. Lustful
204. Malicious
205. Manipulative
206. Mean
207. Mediocre
208. Meddlesome
209. Mercenary
210. Merciless
211. Mischievous
212. Miserable
213. Misleading
214. Monotonous
215. Moody
216. Myopic
217. Nagging
218. Naive
219. Narcissistic
220. Negative-thinking
221. Neglectful
222. Negligent
223. Nervous
224. Neurotic
225. Nosy
226. Obnoxious
227. Obstinate

228. Odd
229. Offensive
230. Oppressive
231. Opportunistic
232. Ostentatious
233. Overbearing
234. Overeater
235. Paranoid
236. Passive
237. Passive-aggressive
238. Patronizing
239. Pessimistic
240. Petty
241. Phobic
242. Phony
243. Pitiless
244. Pompous
245. Possessive
246. Prejudiced
247. Procrastinating
248. Punitive
249. Pushy
250. Quarrelsome
251. Quixotic
252. Quitter
253. Rebellious
254. Reckless
255. Reclusive
256. Regretful
257. Remorseful
258. Repulsive
259. Resentful
260. Restless
261. Revengeful
262. Rigid

263. Rough
264. Rude
265. Ruthless
266. Sad
267. Sadistic
268. Sarcastic
269. Scolding
270. Secretive
271. Self-blaming
272. Self-centered
273. Self-conscious
274. Self-tempting
275. Self-contemptuous
276. Self-deceptive
277. Self-destructive
278. Self-hating
279. Self-important
280. Selfish
281. Self-pitying
282. Self-righteous
283. Self-serving
284. Sensation-seeking
285. Servile
286. Shabby
287. Shallow
288. Shortsighted
289. Showing off
290. Shy
291. Sloppy
292. Slow
293. Smug
294. Snobbish
295. Spiteful
296. Squeamish
297. Stiff

298. Stingy
299. Stubborn
300. Submissive
301. Sulky
302. Superficial
303. Suspicious
304. Sycophant
305. Tactless
306. Tasteless
307. Tense
308. Thoughtless
309. Timid
310. Tyrannical
311. Uncertain of oneself
312. Uncompromising
313. Underhanded
314. Unethical
315. Unfair
316. Unforgiving
317. Unfriendly
318. Unhappy
319. Unproductive
320. Unrealistic
321. Unreliable
322. Unsociable
323. Unstable
324. Vain
325. Vengeful
326. Vindictive
327. Violent
328. Weak
329. Withdrawn
330. Worrying

Guide to the Overviews

One picture is worth a thousand words. A picture helps a person to gain an instant perspective of what may amount to at least hundreds, if not thousands of words of data.

The overviews in this book have been provided to help the reader put the information of the Torah into historical perspective, something the narration of the Torah doesn't always readily facilitate. Two different types of overviews are presented: Historical and Genealogical. Each type clarifies details of the text and allows the reader to gain a broader perspective of the Torah.

The historical overviews juxtapose historical information (see diagram below), in order to allow a person to understand the order in which events occurred in the Torah (the Torah does not always record events in chronological order). Genealogic overviews focus on the lineage of Biblical personalities, information that is not always available from the reading of the text.

Using the Historical Overview

The first number of the left dateline, which begins with the number "1940," refers to the Jewish year. The Jewish people have always dated events according to a dateline that begins with the formation of man on the sixth day after creation. Adam's creation, therefore, began the first year in this calendar. Hence the date of the Western year 1997 CE is 5757, according to the Jewish dating system.

HISTORICAL OVERVIEW 3 / *The Life of Abraham* 1948—2123/*1813—1638 BCE*

Year from creation *Common Era year*	Portion of the week	Landmark events * Involving Abraham	Abraham's location	Abraham's age	Others' ages
1940/*1821 BCE*	**Noah** *Genesis 6:9—12:1*			**birth**	
1950/*1811 BCE*				**10**	
1960/*1801 BCE*			***Ur Kasdim*** *(Iraq)*	**20**	
1970/*1791 BCE*					
			Haran (Iraq)	**30**	
1980/*1781 BCE*				**40**	
1990/*1771 BCE*					**Noah** *950 years (892 years old at*
		Tower of Babel		**50**	

Date Conversion

Common year to Jewish year
  BCE   Subtract from 3761
  CE   Add to 3761

Jewish year to Common year
  Subtract 3761; negative
  number means BCE

The second number refers to the currently used Western, or Gregorian calendar introduced in 1582, as a corrected form of the Julian calendar. Unlike the Jewish calendar, the Gregorian calendar works in two directions from either side of a point in history designated by the Christian Church.

The terms BCE and CE are acronyms for "Before the Common Era" and "Common Era" respectively. The "Common Era" refers to the period of history from the designated point until now, while "Before the Common Era" refers to the period of history prior to the designated point in time. All dates from Creation (Jewish years) in the overviews are in bold and Gregorian dates are in regular italic.

To use the historical overview, you can look straight along a given point on the timeline and see the Jewish year, Gregorian year, and the various events that occurred in that time frame.

One more point to consider: the Jewish new year (*Rosh Hashanah*) falls approximately three to four months prior to the Western new year. Thus an event that occurs in the spring of 1996 will occur in the Jewish year 5756. However, an event that occurs in the fall of 1996 (after *Rosh Hashanah*) will occur in the year 5757.

Historical Overviews
Overview #1: *The Five Books of Moses* shows the period of history covered by the Five Books of Moses, in relation to the various historical periods established by Western historians.

Overview #2: *Written and Oral Law* shows the historical evolution of the Oral Law through the generations, since its inception with the Written Law at Mt. Sinai.

Overview #3: *The Life of Abraham* puts into perspective the events of the first forefather's life, as recorded in the Torah.

Overview #4: *Isaac to Moses* illustrates the generations that led from Isaac, the second forefather, until Moses, the leader and teacher, who redeemed the Jewish people from Egyptian slavery.

Overview #5: *Countdown to Sinai* displays the events and places of encampment on the way to receiving the Torah at Mt. Sinai.

Overview #6: *Historical Sequence of Leviticus and Numbers* chronologically arranges the weekly Torah portions of the Books of Leviticus and Numbers. As seen in the Torah, the portions seem to follow a sequential order when in fact they occur out of historical order, as the overview reveals.

Overview #7: *Forty Years in the Desert* is a collection of the historical information of the 40 years of desert travel and presents it in perspective of the major events, showing the order of encampments on the way to the Promised Land of Canaan.

Overview #8: *The Life of Moses* traces the life of Moses from his birth until his death.

Overview #9: *The Unbroken Chain* communicates the link that has ensured the safe transmission of the Written and Oral Laws throughout the generations, until today.

Using the Genealogical Overviews

The Genealogical Overviews are historically accurate, but graphically not to scale. It is not practical to determine the number of years that passed between the life of one individual and that of another by the spacing between their names. These overviews only juxtapose historical information in chronological sequence, but not according to a measured dateline.

In all cases, the overviews were designed for easy use. In some cases, their simplicity may belie the amount of information actually being presented, while in other cases, the overview may appear more complex than it actually is. When used as a supplement to the text, however, each overview should provide valuable information and perspectives.

Genealogical Overviews

Overview #1: *Adam to Moses (Seventy Nations)* is the most complex of all overviews in *Bible Basics*. After the great flood that destroyed the entire world, Noah and his family, the sole survivors, were designated to propogate the world. This overview traces Noah's descendants, the seventy nations that emanated from his sons, and the generations until Moses.

Overview #2: *The Matriarchs* shows the family ties that link the four matriarchs of the Jewish people.

Overview #3: *Abraham to Moses* shows the generations from Abraham to Moses.

Overview #4: *The Twelve Tribes* traces the descendants of the twelve sons of Jacob for six generations.

Overview #5: *Generations of Levi* shows the descendants of Levi through the generation of Moses, and Aaron his brother, the first High Priest of the Jewish people. The Tribe of Levi became the source of both the priests and those who would help serve in the Tabernacle and later in the Temple.

Overview #6: *David's Lineage* traces the line of descent from Peretz, Judah's and Tamar's son, until King David himself. The episode of Judah and Tamar seemed to be a spiritual catastrophe until the end, when the child who was born of the union became an ancestor of King David, from whom the ultimate Messiah will descend.

It is worth pointing out that the average lifespan of a human being was not always the same. After Adam was exiled from the Garden of Eden and made mortal, he still lived 930 years. In fact, it wasn't uncommon for the average person at that time to live a couple of hundred years with vitality. However, around the time of the Great Flood (**1656**/*2104 BCE*), the Torah teaches, God shortened the average lifespan, and gradually over the millennia it became what it is today.

Guide to the Maps and Charts

This book could not be complete without an appropriate series of maps and charts. Maps bring life to the events of the Torah, and charts clarify information that at first seems somewhat obscure. The following maps and charts are found in *Bible Basics*.

Maps

Map 1. *Archaeological Sites* locates some of the known archaeological sites that date back to the time of the Torah and to the period of the Prophets, many locations of which have since been excavated and opened to the public.

Map 2. *Travels of the Patriarchs* shows the routes the forefathers took as they traveled from one location to another. The lives of the forefathers (*Genesis 12:1-46:28*) were hectic ones, often causing them to travel to different locations.

Map 3. *Egypt to Mt. Sinai* shows the route the Jewish people followed when they left Egypt for Mt. Sinai, where the giving of the Torah took place (*Exodus 12:37-19:1*).

Map 4. *Biblical Borders of Israel* outlines specific borders of the Land of Israel, as stated in the Book of Numbers only (*34:1*). The actual borders of the Land have changed many times throughout the millennium.

Map 5. *Division of the Land of Israel* shows how the Land was divided up amongst the twelve tribes: ten and one-half tribes located west of the Jordan river, and the tribes of Reuben and Gad and half the tribe of Menashe, located on the east of the Jordan (*Numbers 32:1*).

Map 6. *Forty Years in the Desert* shows the various stations made during the forty-year journey of the Jewish people in the desert. They were supposed to travel from Mt. Sinai right to the land of Canaan. The incident of the spies (*Numbers 13:1*), however, brought about a decree of thirty-eight extra years of wandering in the desert.

Map 7. *The Seventy Nations* shows the original locations wherein some of Noah's seventy descendants settled. (Not all of the descendants' locations are known today.) In Genesis (*10:1-32*), the Torah lists the descendants of Noah through his sons Shem, Ham, and Yefet. According to tradition, after the Great Flood (*Genesis 6:13*), seventy of Noah's descendants (*see Genealogical Overview 1, Adam to Moses*) migrated to different parts of Europe, Asia, and Africa, and became the ancestors of all nationalities that have evolved since then.

Charts

Chart 1. *Lifespan from Adam to Moses* shows how the lifespans steadily decreased from the time of Adam until the life of Moses. Today, hoping that someone will live until 120 years of age sounds like wishful thinking. The Torah, however, illustrates a time when dying at the age of 120 years meant dying early, as revealed in this chart.

Chart 2. *Exile to Exodus* recounts the events from the time that Jacob came down with his small family to Egypt (*Genesis 46:28*), until the nation of three million people left Egypt and slavery (*Exodus 12:37*).

Chart 3. *The Offerings* lists the various types of sacrifices mentioned in the Torah, and the details concerning how they were offered.

Chart 4. *The Census* compares the three occasions that the Jewish people were counted, as mentioned in the Torah. For each census, they were counted either according to individual tribes, or as a whole.

Guide to the Holidays

Jewish tradition teaches us that the Jewish year is made up of holidays which can afford us certain spiritual, psychological, and material knowledge and understandings. For example, the fifteenth day of the Jewish month, *Nisan*, is a day for gaining freedom. For this reason, only on the *fifteenth* day of *Nisan* (after the first Passover seder the previous night), not the fourteenth day of *Nisan*, were the Jewish people finally able to overcome Pharaoh and leave Egypt.

Likewise, in every year and generation, the fifteenth day of *Nisan* (and the week that follows), is a propitious time to gain freedom, from either physical or spiritual enslavement. It is for this reason that the Jewish holidays are called "appointed times" (*mo'adim*), and that they are celebrated as unique spiritual opportunities.

However, not all Jewish holidays have their source in the Torah. They may have been established long after the Torah was completed. Nevertheless, because all days of the year possess special opportunities, the Tradition teaches us that even Rabbinically-ordained holidays create the potential for spiritual growth.

The following chart shows the Biblical source and date for each of the *main* holidays of the Jewish calendar. (Note: One should consult a regular Jewish calendar for the other days of significance that are observed throughout the year.)

Holiday	Hebrew name	Source	Jewish date
Passover	*Pesach*	Exodus 12:24	15 *Nisan*
Festival of weeks	*Shavuot*	Exodus 23:16	6 *Sivan*
Ninth of Av	*Tishah b'Av*	Zechariah 8:19	9 *Av*
New Year	*Rosh Hashanah*	Leviticus 23:23	1 *Tishrei*
Day of Atonement	*Yom Kippur*	Leviticus 16:29	10 *Tishrei*
Feast of Tabernacles	*Sukkot*	Exodus 23:16	15 *Tishrei*
Eighth Day of Assembly	*Shemini Atzeret*	Leviticus 23:36	22 *Tishrei*
Celebration of Torah	*Simchat Torah*	Oral tradition	23 *Tishrei* *
Chanukah (165 BCE)	*Chanukah*	Oral tradition	25 *Kislev*
Purim (351 BCE)	*Purim*	Book of Esther	14 *Adar*

* *Simchat Torah* is celebrated on the same day as *Shemini Atzeret* in the Land of Israel

Themes and Opportunities

Jewish holidays are called "appointed times" (mo'adim), and they are celebrated as unique spiritual opportunities.

The following is a brief description of the theme and opportunity of each holiday:

Passover *Pesach* celebrates the miraculous departure from Egypt and the first step towards the beginning of nationhood for the Jewish people. It is a time to work on overcoming spiritual shortcomings.

Festival of Weeks *Shavuot* celebrates the giving of the Torah at Mt. Sinai, and it is a time to reaffirm one's commitment to Torah ideals.

Tishah b'Av The Ninth day of *Av* marks the date of many Jewish misfortunes, most notably the destruction of both Temples. It is a time of great national mourning.

Rosh Hashanah is the Jewish New Year, and a day of judgment, during which time Jews reexamine their potential and make commitments to be more ethical in the upcoming year.

Yom Kippur The Day of Atonement is the day Moses achieved atonement for the Jewish people after the making of the golden calf, and has since been a day during which Jews fast and beg God for forgiveness of their transgressions.

Feast of Tabernacles *Sukkot* is the week that Jews live in outdoor temporary structures to commemorate the shelters they lived in after leaving Egypt, and to recall the "Clouds of Glory" that God used to protect them from the dangers of the desert. It is a good time to reexamine and reassess one's dependence on material possessions.

Eighth Day of Assembly *Shemini Atzeret* is a designated time for Jews to focus on their unique relationship with God.

Celebration of Torah *Simchat Torah* is the day on which we celebrate the completion of the yearly cycle of reading the Torah, and the commencement of another cycle.

Chanukah commemorates the miraculous victory of the Jewish army, an army which was few in number, over the Greco-Syrian army in the time of the Maccabees. It is a time to consider the miraculous and obvious intervention of God in the affairs of the Jewish people throughout history, including in recent history.

Purim celebrates the miraculous victory over the Persian people, specifically the destruction of the evil Haman, who tried to annihilate the Jewish people. It is a time to contemplate how God interacts with man from "behind the scenes."

Each and every holiday adds a depth of meaning and understanding, not only of the Jewish people, but of the world we live in. Each of us will take away a measure of pleasure and wisdom in direct proportion to the time and effort we put into each of the holidays. All holidays begin at sundown the day before the dates listed below.

Thirty Year Calendar

	Purim	Pesach	Shavuot	Tishah b'Av	Rosh Hashanah	Yom Kippur	Sukkot	Shemini Atzeret	Simchat Torah	Chanukah
1997	Feb 21	Apr 22	Jun 11	Aug 12	Oct 2	Oct 11	Oct 16	Oct 23	Oct 24	Dec 24
1998	Mar 12	Apr 11	May 31	Aug 2	Sep 21	Sep 30	Oct 5	Oct 12	Oct 13	Dec 14
1999	Mar 2	Apr 1	May 21	Jul 22	Sep 11	Sep 20	Sep 25	Oct 2	Oct 3	Dec 4
2000	Feb 20	Apr 20	Jun 9	Aug 10	Sep 30	Oct 9	Oct 14	Oct 21	Oct 22	Dec 22
2001	Mar 9	Apr 8	May 28	Jul 29	Sep 18	Sep 27	Oct 2	Oct 9	Oct 10	Dec 10
2002	Feb 26	Mar 28	May 17	Jul 18	Sep 7	Sep 16	Sep 21	Sep 28	Sep 29	Nov 30
2003	Feb 16	Apr 17	Jun 6	Aug 7	Sep 27	Oct 6	Oct 11	Oct 18	Oct 19	Dec 20
2004	Mar 7	Apr 6	May 26	Jul 27	Sep 16	Sep 25	Sep 30	Oct 7	Oct 8	Dec 8
2005	Feb 23	Apr 24	Jun 13	Aug 14	Oct 4	Oct 13	Oct 18	Oct 25	Oct 26	Dec 26
2006	Mar 14	Apr 13	Jun 2	Aug 3	Sep 23	Oct 2	Oct 7	Oct 14	Oct 15	Dec 16
2007	Mar 4	Apr 3	May 23	Jul 24	Sep 13	Sep 22	Sep 27	Oct 4	Oct 5	Dec 5
2008	Feb 20	Apr 20	Jun 9	Aug 10	Sep 30	Oct 9	Oct 14	Oct 21	Oct 22	Dec 22
2009	Mar 10	Apr 9	May 29	Jul 30	Sep 19	Sep 28	Oct 3	Oct 10	Oct 11	Dec 12
2010	Feb 28	Mar 30	May 19	Jul 20	Sep 9	Sep 18	Sep 23	Sep 30	Oct 1	Dec 2
2011	Feb 18	Apr 19	Jun 8	Aug 9	Sep 29	Oct 8	Oct 13	Oct 20	Oct 21	Dec 21
2012	Mar 8	Apr 7	May 27	Jul 29	Sep 17	Sep 26	Oct 1	Oct 8	Oct 9	Dec 9
2013	Feb 24	Mar 26	May 15	Jul 16	Sep 5	Sep 14	Sep 19	Sep 26	Sep 27	Nov 28
2014	Feb 14	Apr 15	Jun 4	Aug 5	Sep 25	Oct 4	Oct 9	Oct 16	Oct 17	Dec 17
2015	Mar 5	Apr 4	May 24	Jul 26	Sep 14	Sep 23	Sep 28	Oct 5	Oct 6	Dec 7
2016	Feb 23	Apr 23	Jun 12	Aug 14	Oct 3	Oct 12	Oct 17	Oct 24	Oct 25	Dec 25
2017	Mar 12	Apr 11	May 31	Aug 1	Sep 21	Sep 30	Oct 5	Oct 12	Oct 13	Dec 13
2018	Mar 1	Mar 31	May 20	Jul 22	Sep 10	Sep 19	Sep 24	Oct 1	Oct 2	Dec 3
2019	Feb 19	Apr 20	Jun 9	Aug 11	Sep 30	Oct 9	Oct 14	Oct 21	Oct 22	Dec 23
2020	Mar 10	Apr 9	May 29	Jul 30	Sep 19	Sep 28	Oct 3	Oct 10	Oct 11	Dec 11
2021	Feb 26	Mar 28	May 17	Jul 18	Sep 7	Sep 16	Sep 21	Sep 28	Sep 29	Nov 29
2022	Feb 15	Apr 16	Jun 5	Aug 7	Sep 26	Oct 5	Oct 10	Oct 17	Oct 18	Dec 19
2023	Mar 7	Apr 6	May 26	Jul 27	Sep 16	Sep 25	Sep 30	Oct 7	Oct 8	Dec 8
2024	Feb 23	Apr 23	Jun 12	Aug 13	Oct 3	Oct 12	Oct 17	Oct 24	Oct 25	Dec 26
2025	Mar 14	Apr 13	Jun 2	Aug 3	Sep 23	Oct 2	Oct 7	Oct 14	Oct 15	Dec 15
2026	Mar 3	Apr 2	May 22	Jul 23	Sep 12	Sep 21	Sep 26	Oct 3	Oct 4	Dec 5
2027	Feb 21	Apr 22	Jun 11	Aug 12	Oct 2	Oct 11	Oct 16	Oct 23	Oct 24	Dec 25

Four minor fast days not included: 10th of Tevet, Fast of Esther (13 Adar), 17th of Tammuz, Fast of Gedaliah (3 Tishrei)

MAP 1 / *Archaeological Sites* *present day with references to ancient sites*

LEBANON

• *Laish*

• *Acco*   *Hazor* •   SYRIA

Sea of Galilee

Mediterranean Sea   • Haifa

• *Megiddo*

Beth She'an •

• *Shechem*   • *Sukkos*

• Tel Aviv
• *Jaffa*   • *Shiloh*

ISRAEL
• *Bethel*
Jericho •   JORDAN

Salem •
(Jerusalem)
• *Gezer*   • *Bethlehem*
• *Ashkelon*
• *Hebron*

Dead Sea

• *Gaza*   • *Lachish*

• *Arad*
Beersheva •

EGYPT

• *Kadesh Barnea*

Guide to Archaeological Sites

Like many places in the Middle East, Israel is a gold mine of archaeological sites. However, what makes Israel unique in this respect is that many of these sites are mentioned in the Torah and the books of the Prophets, often allowing today's tourist to link, in time, the places and the events that occurred there so long ago. See *Map 1: Archaeological Sites*, on opposite page.

List of Sites *(probable sources)*

Site	Source	In Israel?
Acco	*Judges 1:31*	Y
Arad	*Numbers 21:1*	Y
Ashkelon	*Judges 1:18*	Y
Be'er Sheva	*Genesis 21:31*	Y
Bethel	*Genesis 12:8*	Y
Bethlehem	*Genesis 35:19*	Y
Beth She'an	*Joshua 17:11*	Y
Gaza	*Genesis 10:19*	Y
Gezer	*Joshua 10:33*	Y
Hazor	*Joshua 11:1*	Y
Hebron	*Genesis 13:18*	Y
Jaffa	*Joshua 19:46*	Y
Jericho	*Numbers 22:1*	Y
Kadesh Barnea	*Genesis 14:7*	N
Lachish	*Joshua 10:3*	Y
Laish	*Judges 18:7*	Y
Megiddo	*Joshua 12:21*	Y
Salem (Jerusalem)	*Genesis 14:18*	Y
Shechem	*Genesis 12:6*	Y
Shiloh	*Genesis 49:10*	Y
Sukkot	*Genesis 33:17*	N

Many of the places mentioned in the Bible may be visited by you today. There have even been some restorations at some of the sites. Visit Mamre, in modern Hebron, and see where Abraham built the altar to God (*Genesis 13:18*), or visit the Tomb of Rachel on the main road from Jerusalem to Bethlehem (*Genesis 35:19*).

Locations, History and Highlights

Acco *(current name: Acre)*
Located 4 km east of present-day Acco, on the northern sea coast. On the border of the tribe of Asher, at the valley of the tribe of Zevulun.

During the First Temple period (*833-423 BCE*), Acco was a Phoenician town, and thus outside the boundaries of Israel. In the days of the Maccabean Revolt (*135-132 BCE*), this city played a significant role in the struggle for the independence of the Jews.

It reached its most significant period in the time of the Crusaders (*1104-1291 CE*), where it was a commercial link between the Latin Kingdom and Europe. During the time of the British mandate, Acco housed the central jail, where almost all Jewish underground fighters sentenced to death, were hung. The Museum of Jewish Heroism houses the only gallows in Israel today.

Arad *(current name: Tel-Arad)*
Located 37 km east of modern-day Beersheva, in the north-eastern Negev.

Arad is first mentioned as a Canaanite town (*originating around 2700 BCE*), in the Five Books of Moses, when the King of Arad prevented the Israelites from entering Canaan through this territory. During the period of the Judges, according to the Midrash, the first Judge after Joshua, Otniel ben Kenaz of Judah, the brother of Caleb (*1245-1205 BCE*), set up a learning center in Arad.

Ancient Arad of the First Temple period (*833-423 BCE*) is found on the new Arad-Hebron road to the present-day new settlements. In the north-eastern corner of the *tel*, a First Temple period Israelite fortress has been uncovered.

Ashkelon *(current name: Ashkelon)*
Located 56 km south of Tel Aviv, on the coast.

Ashkelon was conquered and built by the Philistines around the 13th century BCE. It became one of the five major Philistine cities. The city was conquered by the Israelites after Joshua's death. Herod the Great, whose slaves and laborers built the present-day Western wall in Jerusalem, was probably born in Ashkelon.

In describing King Saul's death in a tragic clash with the Philistines, the Bible quotes David as saying (*Samuel II 1:19*): *"The beauty, O Israel, is slain upon your high places; how are the mighty fallen! Tell it not in Gat, proclaim it not in the streets of Ashkelon, lest the daughters of the Philistines rejoice..."*

Only from the Mishnah/Talmud period and onwards (*188 CE*), did Ashkelon have Jewish inhabitants, but during this time it was not included within the boundaries of Israel.

Beit-El (current name: Beit El)
Located 4 km northeast of present-day Ramallah, in the territory of the tribe of Efraim.

Bethel was an Israelite town during the era of the kings of the First Temple period. It was originally called Beit El, "House of God," after Jacob, the third Patriarch, had his dream of angels ascending and descending a ladder, whose base was in Beit El and whose top was in heaven, and heard the voice of God, on this spot.

As written in the Book of Kings, in 797 BCE, after the Kingdom of Judah was split, Yarovam ben Nevat of Ephraim, the first king of the ten separated tribes of Israel (Judah and Benjamin only remained for the house of David) wanted to prevent the population from going on pilgrimage to the Temple in Jerusalem. He therefore set up two temples conveniently located at Dan in the north and at Beit El near the border of Judah, in order for the populace to bring their sacrifices there instead of to the Temple itself.

In these temples, he deemed it necessary to have some symbol of God, so he placed an idol of a golden calf at each altar. The idols were eventually destroyed by the righteous kin of Judah, Josiah, in approximately 476 BCE. Beit El was visited by the prophets Elijah and Elisha. There are also ruins from the First Temple period located here.

Beit Lechem (current name: Bethlehem)
Located 7 km south of Jerusalem.

Beit Lechem was first inhabited by the Israelites from the 13th century BCE. The burial site of the Matriarch, Rachel, is located here, and serves as a holy site of worship for the Jewish people.

According to legend, Jacob was told by God of the future exile of his sons by Nebuchadnezzar, who would pass by the tomb of Rachel. She would then be able to beseech God for their redemption, and their prayers would be answered. Jacob's prophecy was fulfilled when the Israelites were exiled after the destruction of the First Temple, only to return to build the Second Temple in Jerusalem seventy years later.

The story of Ruth (*964 BCE*) also took place in Beit Lechem, as did the birth of David (*907 BCE*), and his subsequent anointment by the prophet Samuel.

Tel-Beit She'an (current name: Beth She'an)
Located 1 km north of modern-day Beit She'an, in the territory of the tribe of Menashe, on the ancient biblical road between Egypt and Babylon.

Spread out over 325 acres, the *tel* contains over twenty layers of civilization, including ruins from as early as the fourth millennium BCE, as well as ruins from a Hellenistic city, and a large Roman-Byzantine city whose six thousand seat amphitheater is visible today. The city was conquered from the Canaanites in King David's reign (*877-837 BCE*).

As written in the Book of Samuel, King Saul and his sons were captured and killed near Mount Gilboa (*around 877 BCE*), and their bodies were hung on the walls of Beit She'an. Climb the tel and you will see in the south, *Yavesh Gilad* (*yavesh* means dry), where King Saul was buried after they took his body from the wall.

Gezer (current name: Gezer)
Located 2 km south of Kibbutz Gezer.

Gezer was a strategic military site dating from the Chalciolithic period (*4020-3000 BCE*), and was conquered by Joshua. Four hundred years later, Pharaoh gave Gezer as a dowry for his daughter upon her marriage to King Solomon (*837-707 BCE*). An agricultural calendar explaining harvesting times for the country, written in ancient Hebrew, was found here.

Tel Hazor (current name; Hazor)
Located 9 km north of Rosh Pina, on the modern-day road to Kiryat Shemonah.

First inhabited as the most important northern Canaanite city in Israel, Hazor was conquered by Joshua between 1273-1266 BCE, and its king, Yavin, was killed. Joshua destroyed its pagan sanctuary used by the Canaanites to worship the sun and the moon; it can be seen at Jerusalem's Israel Museum. King Solomon fortified Hazor, and after his reign, an impressive water system was dug here between 740-718 BCE by King Ahab of Israel, similar to the one found in Jerusalem, dug by King Hezekiah.

Ahab was married to Jezebel, the princess of Tyre and of Sidon, and thus idolatry was introduced into Israel. As is written in Kings I, 21:25: *"There was no one like Ahab, who sold himself to do what was evil in the eyes of God, which his wife Jezebel persuaded him."*

Ruins from the First Temple period can be found there.

Hazor was destroyed by the Assyrians in 732 BCE. Near the *tel*, at the entrance to the kibbutz, are finds from the area housed in a museum.

Hebron *(current name: Hebron)*
Located 37 km south of Jerusalem.

Hebron is one of the oldest cities in the world, known as the City of the Patriarchs. The most important site is the Cave of Machpelah, where Adam, Eve, Abraham, Isaac, Jacob, Sarah, Rebecca, and Leah are all buried. Abraham purchased the Cave as a burial site for Sarah from Ephron the Hittite for a huge sum. According to the Midrash, the resurrection of the dead, during the time of the Messiah, will first occur in the Cave of Machpelah.

The structure now standing over the site of the cave was originally built by King Herod (*36 BCE - 4 CE*), although an earlier structure dating back to the Hasmonean kings (*187 BCE*) has been documented.

The road from Jerusalem to Hebron was the route that David took from Bethlehem, bringing his brothers food for battle in the area of the Valley of Elah, where he killed the giant Philistine, Goliath. Hebron was the capital of the kingdom of Judah from 877-870 BCE, where King David ruled, until he transferred his capital to the conquered Jerusalem.

Jaffa *(current name: Jaffa)*
Located south of modern day Tel Aviv, in the territory of the tribe Dan.

Jaffa was, and still is, a seaport dating back to the 17th century BCE. The book of Jonah begins at Jaffa port, where the Prophet boarded a ship bound for the Mediterranean city of Tarshish, in order to flee from God's Presence and the command to rebuke the Assyrian city of Nineveh (*between 837-707 BCE*). Although the tribe of Dan failed to conquer Jaffa, King Solomon finally conquered it in his reign, and designated it his major seaport.

About half of the ruins are Moslem, dating back to the 16th-20th centuries (*CE*) during the Ottoman period, although Roman and Byzantine ruins can be found as well.

Aside from the Museum of Jaffa and a photographic Museum of Finds, you will find a tremendous stone gate depicting three biblical scenes: the sacrifice of Isaac, Jacob's dream in Beit El of the ascending and descending Angels on a ladder, and the conquest of Jericho.

Tel Jericho *(current name: Jericho)*
Located 35 km east of Jerusalem, at the edge of modern day Jericho.

Jericho is the oldest city in the world, having a recorded history of at least five thousand years. The Israelites, under the leadership of Joshua, first entered the Land of Israel, at Jericho in 1273 BCE. The walls that came tumbling down can still be viewed today, exactly in the position that they fell, as well as the remains of a tremendous inner tower from the eighth millennium BCE. This great victory was accomplished through Divine intervention as a result of the Israelites raising their voices in prayer. Joshua destroyed the city, and it was cursed, never to be rebuilt (*Joshua 6:26*). Over five hundred years later, in the reign of King Ahab, Chiel of Beit El dared to rebuild Jericho. The curse was fulfilled: each of his sons died during its reconstruction.

Jericho is the site where the prophets Elijah and Elisha crossed the Jordan river and where tradition depicts Elijah being taken alive to Gan Eden. During the periods of the First and Second Temples, one could smell the pleasant aroma of the Temple's sacrifices and hear the Temple's musical instruments being played in Jericho, although it was over thirty kilometers away from the Holy City.

Lachish *(current name: Lachish)*
Located on the road from Jerusalem to Kiryat Gat.

The site is easily reachable from the famous grape-growing Moshav Lachish. The deepest well in the country is carved on the peak of the *tel*: it is 135 meters deep. After being conquered by Joshua, Lachish became one of Israel's major fortifications in the southwest, against Egypt.

Rechavam, King Solomon's son (*707-690 BCE*), also used Lachish during the campaign against the Assyrian king, Sancheriv. A relief depicting it was found in Nineveh, the ancient Assyrian capital located on the east bank of the Tigris River. An accurate copy of the relief can be viewed at Jerusalem's Israel Museum. Many finds of the First Temple period come from Lachish.

Laish *(current name: Tel Dan)*
Located 2 km north of Kibbutz Dan, in the territory of the tribe of Dan.

Laish was first inhabited by the Canaanites, and was conquered by the tribe of Dan in the twelfth century BCE. During the First Temple period between 797-776 BCE, Yarovam ben

Nevat of the tribe of Efraim placed idols at Tel Dan and at Beit El in order to roadblock pilgrims to Jerusalem, thus maintaining a political and spiritual division in the Jewish people. As a result, Tel Dan became a cult center and a place of idol worship during this time: an altar for an idol of a Golden Calf has been discovered.

A city has been uncovered here, as well as a gate complex (worth seeing), dating back to Yarovam's time. A brick arch, the oldest arch in the world, dating back to four thousand years ago can also be found. More archaeology of the *tel* can be viewed at the Israel Museum in Jerusalem, including a huge model of the site. While you're at the tel, you should visit the beautiful Tel Dan nature reserve, one of the Jordan River's sources.

Megiddo
Located 10 km south of Afulah, in the Jezebel Valley.

Non-Jews call Megiddo "Armageddon," a distortion of the Hebrew *Har Mageddon*, the mountain on which Megiddo is built. Excavations carried out in the 1930s revealed twenty-two layers of civilization, ranking Megiddo as one of the most significant tels in the world.

In the Israelite period, Megiddo was an administrative center. King Solomon built a monumental gate and two palaces, while King Ahab refortified Megiddo and housed his biggest supply system, running through hundreds of feet of solid rock.

Because Megiddo overlooks the opening of the narrow Wadi Ara into the Jezreel Valley, it was a strategically located city. Its location brought Megiddo benefits in times of peace, but much misfortune in times of war, when armies chose the open Jezreel plain as a battlefield. One of the most famous battles fought here occurred between Egypt and the King of Judah, Josiah, in 476 BCE, leaving Josiah dead. The demise of the kingdom of Judah occurred less than a hundred years later, resulting in the exile to Babylon.

The entrance to the archaeological site is via a small museum. A lookout above the section offers an excellent view of the Jezreel Valley. Try descending into the water shaft that leads from the summit of the mound to the foot of the slope.

Salem *(namely Jerusalem)*
Salem is the old city of Jerusalem, located in modern day Jerusalem.

Everything is holy and exciting in the city of God. Jerusalem is first mentioned in Genesis 14:18, when Abraham is met by Shalem's righteous king, Malkitzedek;

the monarch blesses Abraham in recognizing that Abraham was blessed by God and was thus victorious in war. It can be concluded that Jerusalem is over four thousand years old, and was a religious city from its start. King David conquered Jerusalem during his reign, moving the capital of his kingdom there from Hebron. King Solomon built the glorious First Temple here, where God's Divine presence hovered for four hundred and ten years.

King Solomon "overlaid the whole House with gold," *(Kings I 6:22)*, and supplied it with doors of carved olive wood *(Kings I 6:31)*. All of the stones were hewn before they arrived at the Mount, so that *"there was neither hammer nor axe nor any tool of iron heard in the House, while it was being built"* *(Kings I 6:7)*. It was a house of peace, was glorious to behold, and was world renowned.

The old city, specifically the Jewish Quarter, has extensive ruins dating from the First and Second Temple periods. These ruins include the City of David, the Ophel, the Wohl Archaeological Museum, the Western Wall (the *Kotel HaMa'aravi*) ruins of the First and Second Temples and southern excavations, the Burnt House (a basement of a Priest's home during Temple times, replete with finds), and the Tower of David Museum.

The Tower, located at Jaffa Gate, covers the Canaanite *(3000-1200 BCE)*, First Temple *(833-423 BCE)*, Second Temple *(353 BCE-70 CE)*, Late Roman *(135-324 CE)*, Byzantine *(324-638 CE)*, Early Arab Age *(638-1099 CE)*, Crusader and Ayyubid *(1099-1250 CE)*, Mameluke *(1250-1517 CE)*, Ottoman *(1517-1917 CE)*, British Mandate *(1917-1948 CE)*, and State of Israel periods and how Jews were affected during these times. Each period is presented with three-dimensional relief maps depicting the size of the city.

The Roman, Byzantine, and Moslem ruins include the Cardo, the ramparts on top of the high city outer wall, and the Dome of the Rock. The Temple Mount, where the Dome of the Rock is located, is halachically forbidden to Jews to visit, although the periphery may be visited under specific halachic conditions. The mosque is situated on top of the site where Abraham bound Isaac for sacrifice and where the First and Second Temples stood.

Also in the Quarter, a partially restored synagogue, The Hurva, dating from 1701 stands, as well as the Ramban synagogue, and the Sephardic synagogue, dating from the 16th century. At the Museum of the Yishuv, you can find photographs and artifacts from life in Jerusalem in the 18th and 19th centuries.

Shechem *(current name: Nablus)*
Located in the center of the Samaria mountains, on the borders of the territory of the tribes of Efraim and Menashe, between Mount Eval and Mount Gerizim.

The earliest settlers of Shechem were the Canaanites. During this era, first Abraham (*1813-1638 BCE*) and then his grandson, Jacob (*1653-1506 BCE*) both visited Shechem and built altars to God (*Genesis 12:6-7, ibid. 33:20*) in the area, thus sanctifying the town and region. The last ruler of Shechem was Chamor, before the city and its population were destroyed by Simeon and Levi, after their sister Dinah was violated there.

After the Israelites entered the land, Joshua led the people to Shechem. Half of the population stood on Mount Gerizim and the other half stood on Mount Eval, and the Priests and Levites stood in the valley. Joshua turned to the population on one mountain and communicated the curses they would undergo if they strayed away from God, and then he turned to the opposite mountain and enumerated the blessings the Israelites would receive from God if they would follow in the ways of the Torah. To this day, the mountain upon which the Israelites received the blessings is called *Har Berachah* ("Mountain of Blessing"); a Jewish settlement stands there today.

After the conquest of the land, Shechem was a city designated to the Levites. The tomb of Joseph, Jacob's son from Rachel, is located in ancient Shechem; the name of the ancient tel is Tel Balata. Joseph's bones were brought out of Egypt with the Exodus (*1313 BCE*). Today, a modern Yeshiva has been built here called *Od Yosef Chai* ("Joseph still lives").

After the Kingdom was split in 797 BCE, Shechem was the capital of Israel under the reign of Yarovam ben Nevat, of the tribe of Efraim. After the land of Israel was conquered until the end of the Second Temple period (*70 CE*), Shechem was one of five designated cities of refuge.

Shiloh *(current name: Shiloh)*
On the road between Ramallah and Shechem, in the territory of the tribe of Efraim. Today, a new settlement named Shiloh stands next to the ancient site.

Shiloh was established and became famous, after the exodus from Egypt. It housed the Tabernacle, the *Mishkan*, for 369 years between 1260 and 891 BCE. The Tabernacle was then moved to Nob and Giveon for fifty-seven years. The Book of Samuel begins with the Tabernacle of Shiloh. This place was the heart of the nation, for there rested the Ark of God's Covenant from the days of Joshua. It became a place of frequent pilgrimage and Torah learning. The Ark was finally taken from Shiloh in the battle with the Philistines in 891 BCE. The Tabernacle of Shiloh was not quite the same as it was in the wilderness of Sinai, for now it was a stone building, whose roof consisted of a covering of sheets.

Its semi-permanent structure symbolized its intermediary status between the wandering Tabernacle of the wilderness and the First and Second Temples, both built from stone, and the final Third Temple, still to be built and never destroyed, in the coming days of the Messiah.

Remnants of houses found on the *tel*, indicate that Shiloh was a fairly large and wealthy community in the period of the Judges. The final forty years of Shiloh (*931-891 BCE*) was a very interesting period, because the Judge of the nation, Eli the Kohen, was at the same time the *Kohen Gadol*, the High Priest. The famous story of Hannah praying to God for a son took place there. She gave birth to the famous prophet Samuel, who developed under Eli's tutelage, and who later became the prophet who both anointed and rebuked kings. The 98-year-old Eli died of a broken neck after fainting from the news of the Ark's capture by the Philistines. This battle marked the end of the period of the Judges, and was followed by the growing need for a king to unite the nation.

Guide to Biblical Names

N ames from the Bible are often unusual and difficult to pro-
nounce since they are usually a composition of words, each
having their own specific meaning. The name also becomes more
meaningful because it may embody a trait or traits either apparent in the child from birth, or desired for the child in his or her
lifetime. Many parents carry on this tradition today (though most
Jewish names are chosen to give memory to a departed relative).

Below is a partial list of names from the Five Books of Moses,
including their most likely meanings and their sources. Men's
names begin here. Women's names begin on page 99.

The names of the men in the Torah

Aaron	*mountain* or *shining;* the first High Priest, Moses' brother. (Ex. 4:14)
Abel	*breath;* son of Adam and Eve, brother of Cain. (Gen. 4:3)
Avimelech	*my father, the king;* king of Phillistine. (Gen. 20:2)
Abram	*my father is noble;* Abraham's original name. (Gen. 11:26)
Abraham	*father of many nations;* first patriarch of the Jewish people. (Gen. 17:5)
Achiezer	*my brother is my helper;* prince of the tribe of Dan. (Num. 1:12)
Achiman	*my brother is a gift;* son of Anak, a giant. (Num. 13:22)
Achira	*my brother is evil;* leader of the tribe of Naftali. (Num. 1:15)
Achiram	*my brother is noble;* son of Benjamin. (Num. 26:38)
Achisamach	*my brother is my support;* father of Oholiav, a craftsman of the Temple. (Ex. 31:6)
Achran	*disturbed* or *troubled;* member of tribe of Asher. (Num. 1:13)
Adbe'el	*God has established;* grandson of Abraham, son of Ishmael. (Gen. 25:13)
Adam	*earth;* name of the first man. (Gen. 2:7)
Alvah	*sin* or *transgression;* leader of a family of Esau. (Gen. 36:40)
Alvan	Edomite name (Gen. 36:23).
Amishadai	*my people belong to God;* member of the tribe of Dan. (Num. 1:12)
Amram	*mighty nation;* father of Moses. (Ex. 6:18)
Anah	*to sing* or *chant;* father of a wife of Esau. (Gen. 36:2)
Aner	*meaning uncertain;* ally of Abraham. (Gen. 14:13)
Aram	*high* or *heights;* grandson of Noah. (Gen. 10:22)
Aran	*sarcophagus* or *chest;* son of Seir the Chorite. (Gen. 36:28)
Ard	*bronze* or *wild ox;* son of Benjamin. (Gen. 46:21)
Arnon	*roaring scream;* stream flowing from Moab into the Dead Sea. (Num. 21:13)
Arodi	*bronze;* son of Gad, grandson of Jacob. (Gen. 46:16)
Arioch	*measurement;* king of Elasar. (Gen. 14:1)
Ashbel	*the fire of Bel;* son of Benjamin. (Gen. 46:21)

Asher	*blessed* or *fortunate;* son of Jacob and Zilpah. (Gen. 30:13)
Ashkenaz	*meaning uncertain;* son of Gomer, great-grandson of Noah. (Gen. 10:3)
Assir	*imprisoned* or *bound;* son of Korach. (Ex. 6:24)
Asriel	*prince of God;* son of Gilad, grandson of Menashe. (Num. 26:31)
Aviasaf	*father of multitude;* son of Korach. (Ex. 6:24)
Avida	*my father knows;* grandson of Abraham and Keturah. (Gen. 25:4)
Avidan	*my father judges;* a leader of the tribe of Benjamin. (Num. 1:11)
Avihu	*he is my father;* second son of Aaron. (Ex. 6:23)
Avimael	*God is my father;* descendant of Shem, who was Noah's son. (Gen. 10:28)
Aviram	*my father is mighty;* conspirator against Moses. (Num. 16:1)
Avrech	*kneel down;* a salutation for Joseph. (Gen. 41:43)
Ayah	*to fly swiftly;* descendant of Esau. (Gen. 36:24)
Bela	*swallow* or *engulf;* son of Benjamin. (Gen. 46:21)
Ben-Ami	*son of my people;* son of one of Lot's daughters. (Gen. 19:38)
Ben-Oni	*son of my sorrow;* Rachel's name for her son Benjamin. (Gen. 35:18)
Be'eri	*my well;* father of Judith (one of Esau's wives). (Gen. 26:34)
Betuel	*house of God;* father of Rebecca, nephew of Abraham. (Gen. 22:22)
Betzalel	*shadow of God;* builder of the Tabernacle. (Ex. 31:2)
Benjamin	*son of my right hand;* youngest of Jacob's twelve sons. (Gen. 35:18)
Bukki	*tested* or *investigated;* leader of the tribe of Dan. (Num. 34:22)
Buz	*contempt;* son of Nachor. (Gen. 22:21)
Cain	*to acquire;* son of Adam and Eve, he was the brother of Abel. (Gen. 4:1)
Caleb	*dog* or *heart;* one of the twelve spies. (Num. 13:6)
Carmi	*my vineyard;* son of Reuben, grandson of Jacob. (Gen. 46:9)
Chadad	*sharp;* sixth son of Ishmael, grandson of Abraham. (Gen. 25:15)
Chagai	*festive;* son of Gad, grandson of Jacob. (Gen. 46:16)
Chamul	*spared* or *saved;* son of Peretz, grandson of Judah. (Gen. 46:12)
Chavilah	*soft, damp sand* or *mud;* grandson of Noah. (Gen. 10:7)
Chazo	*breast of animal;* son of Nachor, the nephew of Abraham. (Gen. 22:22)
Chefer	*to dig;* father of Tzelofchad. (Num. 26:33)
Chelon	*fortress;* member of the tribe of Zevulun. (Num. 1:9)
Chemdan	*precious* or *desirable.* Descendant of Seir the Horite. (Gen. 36:26)
Chori	*to dig* or *make a hole;* father of a leader of tribe of Simeon. (Num. 13:5)
Chuppim	*enclosure;* son of Benjamin, grandson of Jacob. (Ex. 46:21)
Chushim	*feeling;* member of the tribe of Dan. (Gen. 46:23)
Datan	*meaning uncertain;* member of the tribe of Reuben, one of the conspirators against Moses. (Num. 16:1)
Deuel	*knowledge of God;* member of the tribe of Gad. (Num. 1:14)

Diklah	*palm tree;* descendant of Noah. (Gen. 10:27)
Divri	*orator;* father of an Israelite daughter who married an Egyptian. (Lev. 24:11)
Dumah	*silence;* son of Ishmael. (Gen. 25:14)
Eber	*other side;* descendant of Shem, grandson of Noah. (Gen. 10:21)
Edom	*red;* name applied to Esau and his descendants. (Gen. 25:30)
Efer	*mountain goat* or *deer;* son of Midian, grandson of Abraham. (Gen. 25:4)
Efod	*vest;* father of a leader of the tribe of Menashe. (Num. 34:23)
Efraim	*fruitful;* second son of Joseph, grandson of Jacob. (Gen. 41:52)
Efron	*bird;* Hittite who sold burial plot to Abraham. (Gen. 23:8)
Eilam	*eternal;* eldest of Shem's five sons. (Gen. 10:22)
Einan	*yes;* father of a leader of the tribe of Naftali. (Num. 1:15)
Elon	*oak tree;* son of Zevulun, grandson of Jacob. (Gen. 46:14)
Elda'ah	*God knows;* descendant of Abraham and Keturah. (Gen. 25:4)
Eldad	*beloved of God;* Israelite who prophesied in the desert. (Num. 11:26)
Elazar	*my God is my help;* son of Aaron the high priest. (Ex. 6:23)
Eliav	*my God is my father;* a leader of the tribe of Zevulun. (Num. 1:9)
Elidad	*my God is my friend;* a leader of the tribe of Benjamin. (Num. 34:21)
Eliezer	*my God is my help;* Abraham's servant (Gen. 15:2); also name of Moses' son. (Ex. 18:4)
Elishama	*my God hears;* a prince of the tribe of Efraim. (Num. 1:10)
Elitzur	*my God is a rock;* a prince of the tribe of Reuben. (Num. 1:5)
Eltzafan	*God has hidden;* cousin of Moses and Aaron. (Ex. 6:22)
Elyassaf	*God will increase;* a leader of the tribe of Gad. (Num 1:14)
Enoch	*dedicated;* son of Cain, also father of Methuselah. (Gen. 4:17)
Er	*guardian* or *awake;* son of Judah. (Gen. 38:3)
Eri	*my guardian;* son of Gad. (Gen. 46:16)
Esau	*hairy;* son of Isaac and Rebecca. (Gen. 25:25)
Eshban	*galley;* descendant of Seir the Horite. (Gen. 36:26)
Eshkol	*cluster of grapes;* a man who made a covenant with Abraham. (Gen. 13:24)
Evi	*desire;* one of the five kings of Midian. (Num. 31:8)
Gacham	*to kindle, burn,* or *flame;* Abraham's nephew. (Gen. 22:24)
Gad	*happy* or *fortunate;* one of Jacob's sons from Zilpah. (Gen. 30:11)
Gadiel	*God is my blessing;* of the tribe of Zevulun, one of the spies. (Num. 13:10)
Gamliel	*God is my reward;* a leader of the tribe of Menashe. (Num. 1:10)
Gemali	*my reward;* member of the tribe of Dan. (Num. 13:12)
Gera	*combat* or *dispute;* one of the sons of Benjamin. (Gen. 46:21)
Gershom	*stranger;* son of Moses. (Ex. 2:22)
Gershon	*stranger;* son of Levi. (Gen. 46:11)
Geuel	*redeemed by God;* member of tribe of Gad, one of the spies. (Num. 13:15)

Gomer	*to end;* son of Yefet. (Gen. 10:2)
Guni	*tinge of color;* son of Naftali. (Gen. 46:24)
Ham	*warm* or *dark;* Noah's second son. (Gen. 5:32)
Haran	*mountain air;* brother of Abraham. (Gen. 11:26)
Hoshea	*salvation;* original name of Joshua. (Num. 13:8)
Irad	*to escape;* grandson of Cain. (Gen. 4:18)
Iram	*to escape;* a prince in Esau's family. (Gen. 36:43)
Isaac	*he will laugh;* second of the three Patriarchs. (Gen. 17:19)
Ishmael	*God will hear;* son of Abraham and the brother of Isaac. (Gen. 16:11)
Israel	*wrestled with God;* the name given to Jacob. (Gen. 32:28)
Issachar	*there is a reward;* son of Jacob and Leah, one of the tribes. (Gen. 30:18)
Itamar	*island of palms;* Aaron's youngest son. (Ex. 6:23)
Jacob	*held by the heel;* the third Patriarch. (Gen. 25:26)
Jethro	*abundance, riches,* or *excellence;* Moses' father-in-law. (Ex. 3:1)
Joseph	*God will add, increase;* one of Jacob's twelve sons. (Gen. 30:24)
Joshua	*God is salvation;* Moses' disciple and the leader after Moses' death. (Ex. 16:9)
Judah	*God will be praised;* son of Jacob and Leah, one of the tribes. (Gen. 29:35)
Kedar	*black* or *dark;* son of Ishmael. (Gen. 25:13)
Kedem	*eastward;* son of Ishmael. (Gen. 25:15)
Kehat	*faint* or *weak;* son of Levi, grandson of Jacob. (Gen. 46:11)
Kemuel	*to stand up for God;* son of Nachor, Abraham's brother. (Gen. 22:21)
Kenan	*acquire* or *possess;* great-grandson of Adam, son of Enosh. (Gen. 5:9)
Kenaz	*reed;* grandson of Esau, the son of Elifaz. (Gen. 36:11)
Korach	*bald;* a Levite who led a rebellion against Moses and Aaron. (Num. 16:1)
Lavan	*white;* father of Leah and Rachel, brother of Rebecca. (Gen. 24:29)
Lael	*belonging to God;* a Levite, father of a leader of the Gershon family. (Num. 3:24)
Lemech	*meaning uncertain;* descendant of Cain. (Gen. 4:18)
Levi	*one who accompanies* or *attends;* son of Jacob and Leah. (Gen. 29:34)
Livni	*white;* a Levite, son of Gershom. (Ex. 6:17)
Lot	*myrhh, a precious resin;* nephew of Abraham. (Gen. 11:27)
Lotan	*to envelop;* son of Seir the Horite. (Gen. 36:20)
Lud	*meaning uncertain;* grandson of Noah. (Gen. 10:22)
Ma'achah	*to press;* nephew of Abraham, son of Nachor. (Gen. 22:24)
Machi	*to diminish;* member of the tribe of Gad, father of one of the twelve spies. (Num. 13:15)

Machir	*merchandise;* son of Menashe, grandson of Joseph. (Gen. 50:23)
Machli	*my affiliation;* grandson of Levi, the eldest son of Merari. (Ex. 6:19)
Madai	*strife* or *war;* Grandson of Noah, son of Yefet. (Gen. 10:2)
Magdiel	*goodness* or *excellence of the Lord;* descendant of Esau. (Gen. 36:43)
Mahalalel	*praise to God;* son of Kenan, grandson of Enosh. (Gen. 5:12)
Malkiel	*God is my king;* grandson of Asher. (Gen. 46:17)
Malki-tzedek	*my king is righteousness;* King of Salem. (Gen. 14:18)
Medad	*friend;* a leader and prophet in the time of Moses. (Num. 11:26)
Medan	*strife, contention,* or *war;* son of Abraham and Keturah. (Gen. 25:2)
Mehuyael	*man who asks;* descendant of Cain. (Gen. 4:18)
Mei Zahav	*golden water;* an Edomite. (Gen. 36:39)
Menashe	*causing to forget;* eldest son of Joseph, brother of Efraim. (Gen. 41:51)
Merari	*bitter;* son of Levi, grandson of Jacob. (Ex. 6:19)
Methuselah	*messenger;* the longest living man (969 years). (Gen. 5:21)
Metushael	*man who was asked;* descendant of Cain. (Gen. 4:18)
Michael	*who is like God?;* member of the tribe of Asher. (Num. 13:13)
Midian	*strife, war,* or *contention;* son of Abraham and Keturah. (Gen. 25:2)
Mishael	*borrowed;* a cousin of Moses and Aaron. (Ex. 6:22)
Mishma	*hear* or *news;* son of Ishmael, grandson of Abraham. (Gen. 25:14)
Mitzvar	*secure place;* descendant of Esau. (Gen. 36:42)
Mizza	*to empty;* grandson of Esau. (Gen. 36:17)
Moses	*drawn out (of the water);* leader of the Israelites. (Ex. 2:10)
Mushi	*touch* or *remove;* grandson of Levi, the younger son of Merari. (Ex. 6:19)
Nachbi	*to hide* or *to withdraw;* one of the twelve spies. (Num. 13:14)
Nachor	*nostril;* brother of Abraham, son of Terach. (Gen. 11:26)
Nachshon	*diviner;* brother-in-law of Aaron, became prince of Judah. (Ex. 6:23)
Nadav	*generous* or *noble;* eldest son of Aaron. (Ex. 6:23)
Nafish	*to refresh oneself;* son of Ishmael, grandson of Abraham. (Gen. 25:15)
Naftali	*to wrestle* or *to compare;* second son of Jacob and Bilhah. (Gen. 30:8)
Nefeg	*casualty* or *wounded;* a Levite, the son of Yitzhar. (Ex. 6:21)
Nemuel	*ant,* therefore, *industrious;* member of the tribe of Reuben. (Num. 26:9)
Nebayot	*behold* or *see;* elder son of Ishmael. (Gen. 25:13)
Nimrod	*rebel;* son of Kush, grandson of Ham. (Gen. 10:8)
Noah	*rest;* main character in the story of the flood. (Gen. 5:29)
Nun	*offspring* or *to grow;* father of Joshua (successor to Moses). (Ex. 33:11)

Ohad   *beloved;* the third son of Simeon, grandson of Jacob.
               (Gen. 46:10)
Oholiav   *father (God) is my tent;* assistant of Betzalel. (Ex. 31:6)
Omar   *to praise* or *to revere;* descendant of Esau. (Gen. 36:11)
On   *strength* or *wealth;* leader of the rebellious Korach group.
               (Num. 16:1)
Onam   *strength* or *wealth;* descendant of Esau. (Gen. 36:23)
Onan   *pain or iniquity;* second son of Judah. (Gen. 38:4)
Ophir   *gold;* son of Yoktan. (Gen. 10:29)
Ozni   *my ear* or *my hearing;* son of Gad, grandson of Jacob.
               (Num. 26:16)
Pagiel   *to pray* or *to entreat God;* a leader of the tribe of Asher. (Num. 1:13)
Palu   *miracle;* Reuben's second son, grandson of Jacob. (Gen. 46:9)
Pedael   *God has redeemed; a* leader of the tribe of Naftali. (Num. 34:28)
Pelet   *escape* or *deliverance;* son of Reuben, grandson of Jacob.
               (Num. 16:1)
Peretz   *burst forth;* son of Judah and Tamar. (Gen. 38:29)
Pinchas   *mouth of a snake;* grandson of Aaron, later a High Priest.
               (Ex. 6:25)
Potifar   *servant of the (sun) god;* prefect in Pharaoh's court. (Gen. 39:1)
Potifera   *servant of the (sun) god;* Joseph's father-in-law, Priest of On.
               (Gen. 46:20)
Putiel   *servant of God;* father-in-law of Eleazar. (Ex. 6:25)
Ra'amah   *mane (of an animal)* or *crest;* great-grandson of Noah, son of
               Cush. (Gen. 10:7)
Rafu   *to heal;* member of the tribe of Benjamin. (Num. 13:9)
Reu   *friend* or *companion;* son of Peleg. (Gen. 11:18)
Reuel   *friend of God;* another name for Jethro (father-in-law of Moses).
               (Ex. 2:18)
Reuben   *behold, a son!;* Jacob's firstborn son from Leah. (Gen. 29:32)
Rifat   *meaning uncertain (possibly a grain or fruit);* grandson of
               Yefet. (Gen. 10:3)
Rosh   *chief* or *bitter;* son of Benjamin, grandson of Jacob. (Gen. 46:21)
Salu   *basket;* the father of Zimri, a leader of the tribe of Simeon.
               (Num. 25:14)
Samlah   *garment* or *left-handed;* King of Edom. (Gen. 36:36)
Savtah   *old* or *grandfather;* son of Cush. (Gen. 10:7)
Seba   *imbibers of wine;* the eldest son of Cush. (Gen. 10:7)
Sered   *frightened* or *fearful;* son of Zevulun, grandson of Jacob.
               (Gen. 46:14)
Serug   *twig* or *intertwine;* descendant of Shem. (Gen. 11:20)
Seth   *appointed;* son of Adam born after the death of Abel. (Gen. 5:3)
Shechem   *shoulder;* son of Chamor, who kidnapped Dinah (the daughter
               of Jacob). (Gen. 34:2)
Shede'ur   *flame;* member of the tribe of Reuben. (Num. 1:5)
Sheshai   *ivory;* descendant of Anak, the giant. (Num. 13:22)

Shelah	*peaceful;* youngest son of Judah. (Gen. 38:5)
Shelach	*missile, weapon,* or *sprout;* father of Eber. (Gen. 10:24)
Shelef	*to draw (a sword)* or *to plunder;* son of Yoktan. (Gen. 10:26)
Shelumiel	*God is my reward;* a leader of the tribe of Simeon. (Num. 1:6)
Shem	*name, connoting reputation;* eldest of Noah's three sons. (Gen. 5:32)
Shiftan	*judge;* leader of the tribe of Efraim. (Num. 34:24)
Shilem	*peace* or *reward;* son of Naftali, grandson of Jacob. (Gen. 46:24)
Simeon	*to hear;* second son of Jacob and Leah. (Gen. 29:33)
Shimron	*guard;* son of Issachar. (Gen. 46:14)
Shlomi	*my peace;* father of the leader of the tribe of Asher. (Num. 34:27)
Shoval	*barren;* descendant of Seir the Horite. (Gen. 36:2)
Shua	*salvation* or *victory;* father-in-law of Judah. (Gen. 38:2)
Shuach	*to walk;* son of Abraham and Keturah. (Gen. 25:2)
Shuni	*harbor* or *seashore;* son of Gad, grandson of Jacob. (Gen. 46:16)
Sitri	*my secret* or *my hidden place;* a Levite of the Kehat family. (Gen. 6:22)
Sodi	*my secret;* father of Gadiel (spy from the tribe of Zevulun). (Num. 13:10)
Susi	*my horse;* father of the spy from the tribe of Menashe. (Num. 13:11)
Tachash	*wild one-horned beast;* son of Nachor, nephew of Abraham. (Gen. 22:24)
Terach	*wild goat;* father of Abraham, a descendent of Shem. (Gen. 11:24)
Tevach	*slaughter;* son of Nachor. (Gen. 22:24)
Tola	*worm* or *scarlet material;* son of Issachar, one of Israel's judges. (Gen. 46:13)
Tzelofchad	*protection from fear;* member of the tribe of Menashe. (Num. 26:33)
Tzifion	*watchtower;* son of Gad, grandson of Jacob. (Gen. 46:16)
Tzipor	*bird;* father of Balak. (Num. 22:2)
Tzochar	*tan, reddish-grey;* son of Simeon, grandson of Jacob. (Gen. 46:10)
Tzuar	*small;* leader of the tribe of Issachar. (Num. 1:8)
Tzuriel	*God is my rock;* leader of the Merari family. (Num. 3:35)
Tzuri-shaddai	*God is my rock;* father of a leader of the tribe of Simeon. (Num. 1:6)
Uri	*my flame;* member of the tribe of Judah. (Ex. 31:2)
Uz	*advice, wisdom* or *to make haste;* grandson of Shem. (Gen. 10:23)
Uzal	*to leave* or *to be exhausted;* descendant of Shem. (Gen. 10:27)
Uziel	*God is my strength;* son of Kehat, grandson of Levi. (Ex. 6:18)
Vofsi	*meaning uncertain;* member of the tribe of Naftali. (Num. 13:14)
Yachin	*(God) will establish;* son of Simeon, grandson of Jacob. (Gen. 46:10)
Yachle'el	*waiting for God* or *faith in God;* member of the tribe of Zevulun. (Gen. 46:14)

Yair	*to light up, enlighten;* son of Menashe, grandson of Joseph. (Deut. 3:14)
Yamin	*right hand;* son of Simeon, grandson of Jacob. (Gen. 46:10)
Yaval	*stream;* son of Lemech and his wife Adah. (Gen. 4:20)
Yefet	*beautiful;* youngest of Noah's three sons. (Gen. 5:32)
Yefuneh	*(God) will face;* father of Caleb. (Num. 13:6)
Yemuel	*day of the Lord;* son of Simeon, grandson of Jacob. (Gen. 46:10)
Yerach	*moon* or *month;* son of Yoktan, descendant of Shem. (Gen. 10:26)
Yered	*descend;* father of Enoch. (Gen. 5:15)
Yetur	*row;* son of Ishmael. (Gen. 25:15)
Yetzer	*desire* or *inclination;* son of Naftali, grandson of Jacob. (Gen. 46:24)
Yigal	*he will redeem;* one of the twelve spies. (Num. 13:7)
Yimnah	*good fortune* or *right side;* son of Asher, grandson of Jacob. (Gen. 46:17)
Yishbak	*to let go;* son of Abraham and Keturah. (Gen. 25:2)
Yishvah	*smooth* or *agreeable;* son of Asher; grandson of Jacob. (Gen. 46:17)
Yitzhar	*fresh oil* or *he will shine;* son of Korach, grandson of Levi. (Ex. 6:21)
Yoktan	*small;* descendant of Shem. (Gen. 10:25)
Yov	*he will return;* son of Issachar, grandson of Jacob. (Gen. 46:13)
Yovav	*to lament* or *to cry;* son of Yoktan. (Gen. 10:29)
Yuval	*stream;* son of Lemech. (Gen. 4:21)
Zaccur	*remembrance;* father of one of the spies. (Num. 13:4)
Zerach	*light* or *shine;* son of Judah and Tamar. (Gen. 38:30)
Zevulun	*to honor,* or *lofty house;* sixth son of Jacob and Leah. (Gen. 30:20)
Zichri	*my memory* or *my remembrance;* grandson of Levi. (Ex. 6:21)
Zimran	*mountain-sheep* or *goat;* son of Abraham and Keturah. (Gen. 25:2)

Names of Women in the Torah

Adah	*adorned* or *beautiful;* wife of Lemech (Gen. 4:19); and of Esau. (Gen. 36:2)
Bilhah	*weak, troubled,* or *old;* maidservant of Jacob's wife Rachel. (Gen. 30:3)
Bosmat	*perfumed, sweet odor;* wife of Esau. (Gen. 26:34)
Chaglah	*hop* or *hobble;* one of the five daughters of Tzelofchad. (Num. 26:33)
Deborah	*to speak kind words;* nurse of Rebecca. (Gen. 35:8)
Dinah	*judgment;* daughter of Jacob and Leah. (Gen. 30:21)
Elisheva	*God is my oath;* wife of Aaron (Ex. 6:23)
Eve	*life;* the first woman, wife of Adam. (Gen. 3:20)
Hagar	*wanderer;* concubine of Abraham, mother of Ishmael. (Gen. 16:1)
Judith	*praise;* wife of Esau. (Gen. 26:31)
Ketura	*burned* or *perfumed;* Abraham's wife. (Gen. 25:1)
Kozbi	*lie* or *falsehood;* a Midianite woman. (Num. 25:15)
Leah	*to be weary;* daughter of Lavan, first of Jacob's four wives. (Gen. 29:16)
Machalat	*plague;* one of Esau's wives, daughter of Ishmael. (Gen. 28:9)
Machlah	*affliction;* one of the five daughters of Tzelofchad. (Num. 26:33)
Matred	*to pursue* or *to continue uninterrupted;* mother-in-law of Hadar. (Gen. 36:39)
Milkah	*divine* or *queen;* wife of Nachor, Abraham's brother. (Gen. 11:29); also one of the five daughters of Tzelofchad. (Num. 26:33)
Miriam	*sea of bitterness* or *sorrow;* sister of Moses and Aaron. (Ex. 15:20)
Noah	*tremble* or *shake;* one of the five daughters of Tzelofchad. (Num. 26:33)
Ohalivamah	*tent of the high place;* wife of Esau. (Gen. 36:2)
Osnat	*unfortunate;* wife of Joseph, mother of Efraim and Menashe. (Gen. 41:45)
Puah	*to coo;* a Hebrew midwife. (Ex. 1:15)
Rachel	*female sheep;* wife of Jacob, sister of Leah. (Gen. 29:16)
Rebecca	*to tie* or *to bind;* wife of Isaac (Gen. 24:15)
Reumah	*antelope;* concubine of Nachor, Abraham's brother. (Gen. 22:24)
Sarah	*princess;* first of the Matriarchs, Abraham's wife. (Gen. 17:15)
Sarai	*my princess, original form of Sarah;* Abraham's wife. (Gen. 11:29)
Serach	*to be unrestrained, to be free,* or *excess;* daughter of Asher. (Gen. 46:17)
Shifrah	*good* or *beautiful;* a Hebrew midwife. (Ex. 1:15)
Shelomit	*peaceful;* daughter of Divri of the tribe of Dan. (Lev. 24:11)
Tamar	*palm tree, upright* or *righteous;* wife of Judah. (Gen. 38:6)

Tirtzah	*willing* or *pleasing;* one of the five daughters of Tzelofchad. (Num. 26:33)
Tzipporah	*bird;* wife of Moses. (Ex. 2:21)
Yiskah	*anointed;* daughter of Haran, Abraham's brother. (Gen. 11:29)
Yocheved	*God's honor;* wife of Amram, mother of Moses, Aaron and Miriam. (Ex. 6:20)
Zilpah	*to trickle* or *youthful;* maidservant of Jacob's wife, Leah. (Gen. 29:24)

The Bible Summaries

with Section Summaries and Illustrations, Maps, Drawings, and Overviews

Book One: *Genesis/Bereshit*

Book Two: *Exodus/Shemot*

Book Three: *Leviticus/VaYikra*

Book Four: *Numbers/BaMidbar*

Book Five: *Deuteronomy/Devarim*

Introduction to Genesis/Bereshit

B E R E S H I T

- Six days of creation
- The mistake of eating from the Tree of Knowledge
- Expulsion from the Garden • Cain kills Abel
- Decree of destruction

N O A H

- The Flood • Covenant
- Curse of Canaan
- The Tower of Babel
- Ten generations to Abram

L E C H   L E C H A

- Abram journeys to Canaan • Pharaoh takes Sarah • Abram battles the Kings • The Covenant with God • The birth of Ishmael
- Abram's & Sarai's names change • Circumcision

V A Y E R A

- Sodom destroyed
- Sarah and Avimelech
- Sarah gives birth to Isaac • Covenant with Avimelech • Binding of Isaac • Rebecca is born

C H A Y E I   S A R A H

- Sarah dies • The purchase of Machpelah
- Isaac and Rebecca
- Abraham dies
- Descendants of Ishmael

T O L D O T

- The birth of Jacob and Esau • Jacob buys Esau's birthright • Jacob takes the blessing due Esau

The name of the first book of the Five Books of Moses is "Genesis," a Greek word for "origin," because the book begins with an account of the origin of existence. In Hebrew, the name is *"Bereshit"* (the first Hebrew word in the opening sentence), which means "in the beginning of."

Although Genesis opens with a step-by-step account of the creation, this is just an introduction. The real purpose of Genesis is to teach mankind what our purpose in life is and how to achieve the ultimate success in living.

This goal becomes apparent from the beginning of the book, through the initial errors of mankind (i.e., eating from the forbidden tree, *Chapter 3:6,* and the generation of the Flood, *Chapter 6:3*). Eventually, the messages are clarified through the successes of Abraham and his descendants, who grapple with the purpose of life and try to achieve its goals.

The common thread that binds all of Genesis together is its beautiful, fascinating, and often heart-warming narrative, forever reminding all of us how great mankind can become. Genesis provides the foundation upon which all of history rests and must continue to be built upon.

The book is divided into twelve weekly readings (*parashiyot*). The first two weekly readings cover an amazing 1,948 years of history and twenty generations and include

V A Y E T Z E

• *Jacob's ladder* • *Jacob meets Rachel* • *Jacob marries* • *Birth of the eleven tribes* • *Jacob's journey home*

V A Y I S H L A C H

• *Confrontation with Esau* • *Rape of Dinah* • *Jacob becomes Israel* • *The birth of Benjamin* • *Isaac dies* • *Esau's and Seir's descendants* • *Kings of Edom*

V A Y E S H E V

• *Jacob settles in Canaan* • *Joseph's dreams* • *Joseph sold into slavery* • *Judah and Tamar* • *Joseph imprisoned in Egypt*

M I K E T Z

• *Joseph interprets Pharaoh's dreams* • *Joseph becomes the viceroy* • *Famine strikes* • *Joseph's brothers are accused as spies* • *Benjamin arrested*

V A Y I G A S H

• *Joseph reveals himself to his brothers* • *Jacob brings his family to Egypt* • *Israel settles in Goshen* • *Effects of the famine on Egypt*

V A Y E C H I

• *Joseph's promise to Jacob* • *Jacob's blessing of Efraim and Menashe* • *Jacob's blessing of the twelve Tribes* • *Jacob's death* • *Joseph's death and promise*

accounts of the creation of the world and mankind, mankind's expulsion from Paradise, Noah and the great Flood, and the Tower of Babel. These readings are in contrast to the third and fourth readings, which focus only on one hundred years of Abraham's life. The message is quite clear: what Abraham stood for is what Creation is all about—what Abraham represented is what concerns the Torah. The Torah therefore dwells on the lives of the forefathers.

The balance of the Book of Genesis (eight weekly readings) is devoted to following the course of Abraham's descendants (Isaac, Jacob, and the Twelve Tribes) as they further develop the philosophy and approach to life of their illustrious ancestor, Abraham. Eventually the ideology developed by Abraham becomes the basis for a unique nation. The further evolution and progress of this nation is presented in the following book, Exodus.

The Book of Genesis not only describes the origins of the Jewish people, but traces the origins of all peoples of the human family. Many, such as the Jewish people and the Arab nations, share a common ancestor, Abraham, as the *Genealogical Overviews* reveal. All of mankind, of course, can trace their ancestry all the way back to the original man and woman, Adam and Eve.

CHART 1 / *Lifespans from Adam to Moses* 0–2488/3761–1273 BCE

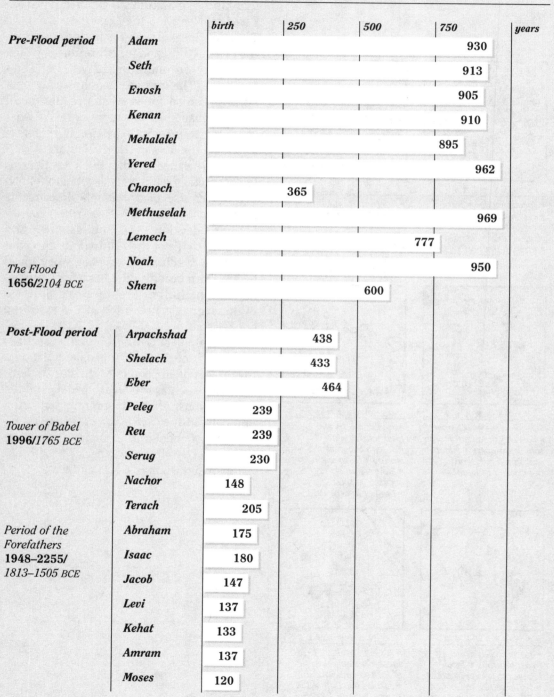

		birth	250	500	750	years
Pre-Flood period	Adam				930	
	Seth				913	
	Enosh				905	
	Kenan				910	
	Mehalalel			895		
	Yered				962	
	Chanoch	365				
	Methuselah				969	
	Lemech			777		
The Flood	Noah				950	
1656/*2104* BCE	Shem		600			
Post-Flood period	Arpachshad	438				
	Shelach	433				
	Eber	464				
	Peleg	239				
Tower of Babel	Reu	239				
1996/*1765* BCE	Serug	230				
	Nachor	148				
	Terach	205				
Period of the	Abraham	175				
Forefathers	Isaac	180				
1948–2255/	Jacob	147				
1813–1505 BCE	Levi	137				
	Kehat	133				
	Amram	137				
	Moses	120				

HISTORICAL OVERVIEW 3 / *The Life of Abraham* 1948—2123/*1813—1638 BCE*

Year from creation *Common Era year*	Portion of the week	Landmark events * Involving Abraham	Abraham's location	Abraham's age	Others' ages
1940/*1821 BCE*	**Noah** *Genesis 6:9—12:1*			birth	
1950/*1811 BCE*					
				10	
1960/*1801 BCE*			**Ur Kasdim** *(Iraq)*	20	
1970/*1791 BCE*					
			Haran (Iraq)	30	
1980/*1781 BCE*					
				40	
1990/*1771 BCE*					**Noah** *950 years (892 years old at Abraham's birth)*
				50	
2000/*1761 BCE*		**Tower of Babel** *Genesis 11:1* *1996/1765 BCE*		60	
2010/*1751 BCE*					
				70	
2020/*1741 BCE*	**Lech Lecha** *Genesis 12:1—18:1*	**Journey to Canaan*** *Genesis 12:1* *2023/1738 BCE*	**Canaan** *(Israel)*	80	
2030/*1731 BCE*			**Egypt** **Canaan** *(Israel)*		
		War with Kings *Genesis 14:1* *2023/1738 BCE*		90	
2040/*1721 BCE*				100	
2050/*1711 BCE*	**VaYera** *Genesis 18:1—23:1*	**Circumcision*** *Genesis 17:1* *2047/1714 BCE*		110	
2060/*1701 BCE*		**Sodom destroyed** *Genesis 18:1* *2047/1714 BCE*		120	**Terach** *205 years (70 years old at Abraham's birth)*
2070/*1691 BCE*				130	
2080/*1681 BCE*	**Chayei Sarah** *Genesis 23:1—25:19*	**Binding of Isaac*** *Genesis 22:1* *2085/1676 BCE*		140	**Sarah** *127 years*
2090/*1671 BCE*				150	
2100/*1661 BCE*				160	
2110/*1651 BCE*				170	
2120/*1641 BCE*				death at 175 years	**Isaac** *75 years old at Abraham's death*
2130/*1631 BCE*					

MAP 2 / *Travels of the Patriarchs* 2018–2238/1743–1523 BCE

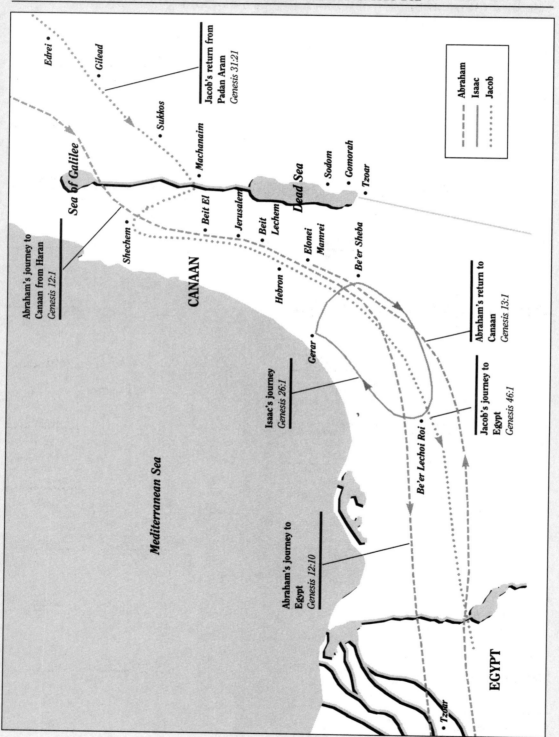

Jacob's return from Padan Aram
Genesis 31:21

Abraham
Isaac
Jacob

Edrei

Gilead

Sukkos

Machanaim

Sea of Galilee

Beit El

Jerusalem

Beit Lechem

Dead Sea

Sodom

Gomorah

Tzoar

Abraham's journey to Canaan from Haran
Genesis 12:1

Shechem

Elonei Mamrei

Be'er Sheba

Abraham's return to Canaan
Genesis 13:1

CANAAN

Hebron

Gerar

Isaac's journey
Genesis 26:1

Jacob's journey to Egypt
Genesis 46:1

Be'er Lechoi Roi

Mediterranean Sea

Abraham's journey to Egypt
Genesis 12:10

EGYPT

Tzoar

GENEALOGICAL OVERVIEW 2 / *The Matriarchs* 1958–2216/*1803–1545 BCE*

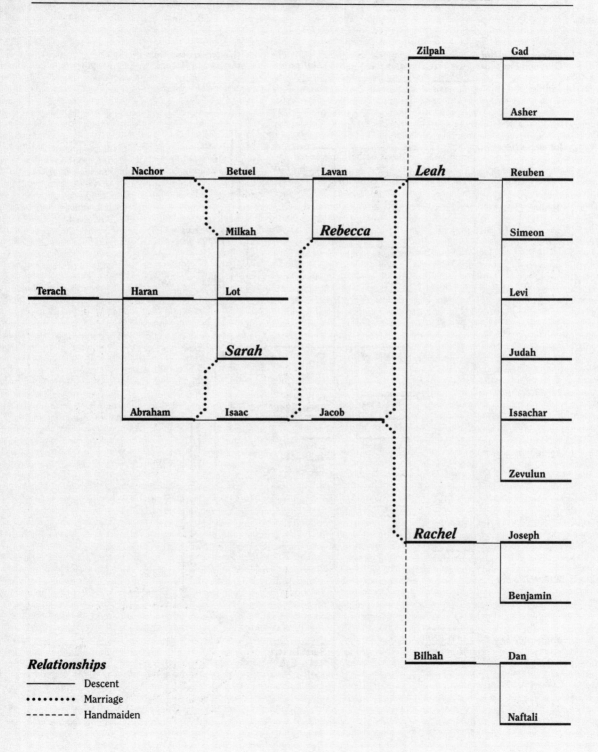

Relationships
———— Descent
•••••••• Marriage
- - - - - Handmaiden

GENEALOGICAL OVERVIEW 3 / *Abraham to Moses* 1948—2248/*1813—1273* BCE

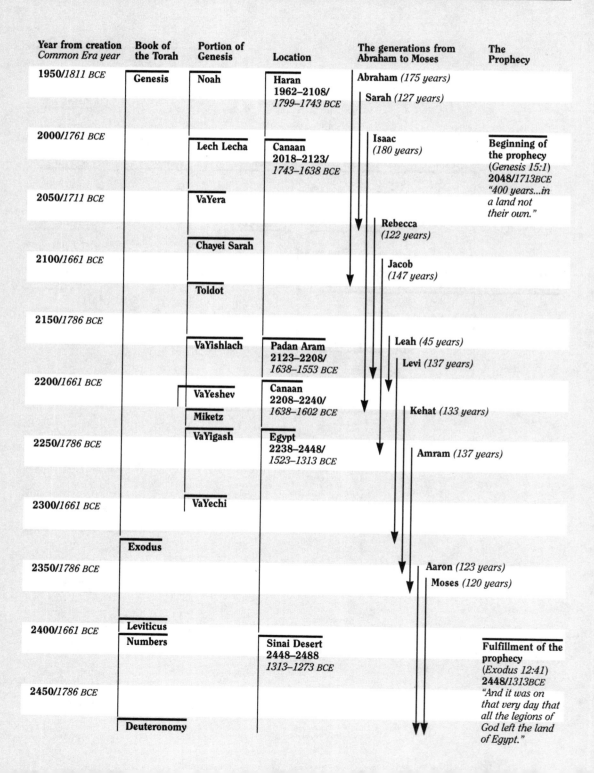

Year from creation / Common Era year	Book of the Torah	Portion of Genesis	Location	The generations from Abraham to Moses	The Prophecy
1950/*1811* BCE	Genesis	Noah	Haran 1962–2108/ *1799–1743* BCE	Abraham (175 years) / Sarah (127 years)	
2000/*1761* BCE		Lech Lecha	Canaan 2018–2123/ *1743–1638* BCE	Isaac (180 years)	Beginning of the prophecy (*Genesis 15:1*) 2048/*1713*BCE "400 years...in a land not their own."
2050/*1711* BCE		VaYera			
2100/*1661* BCE		Chayei Sarah		Rebecca (122 years)	
		Toldot		Jacob (147 years)	
2150/*1786* BCE					
		VaYishlach	Padan Aram 2123–2208/ *1638–1553* BCE	Leah (45 years) / Levi (137 years)	
2200/*1661* BCE		VaYeshev	Canaan 2208–2240/ *1638–1602* BCE		
		Miketz		Kehat (133 years)	
2250/*1786* BCE		VaYigash	Egypt 2238–2448/ *1523–1313* BCE		
				Amram (137 years)	
2300/*1661* BCE		VaYechi			
	Exodus				
2350/*1786* BCE				Aaron (123 years) / Moses (120 years)	
2400/*1661* BCE	Leviticus				
	Numbers		Sinai Desert 2448–2488 *1313–1273* BCE		Fulfillment of the prophecy (*Exodus 12:41*) 2448/*1313*BCE "And it was on that very day that all the legions of God left the land of Egypt."
2450/*1786* BCE					
	Deuteronomy				

HISTORICAL OVERVIEW 4 / *Isaac to Moses* 2048–2368/*1713–1393 BCE*

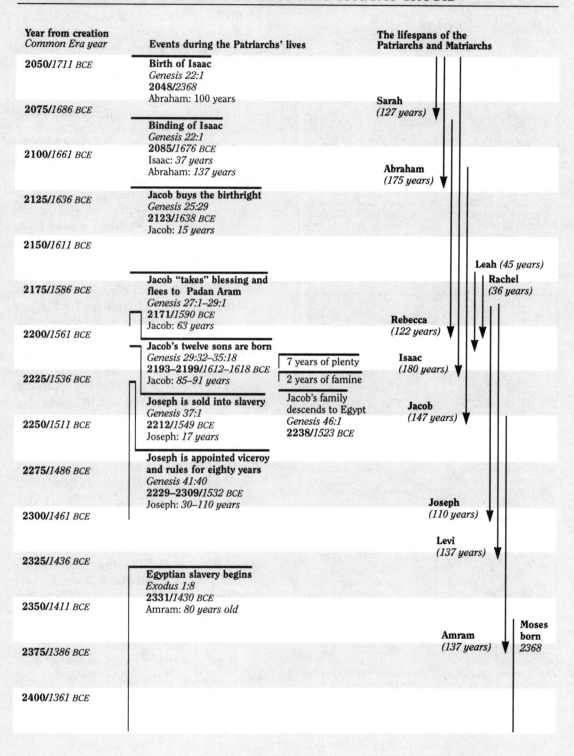

Year from creation *Common Era year*	Events during the Patriarchs' lives	The lifespans of the Patriarchs and Matriarchs
2050/*1711 BCE*	**Birth of Isaac** *Genesis 22:1* **2048/2368** Abraham: 100 years	
2075/*1686 BCE*		**Sarah** *(127 years)*
2100/*1661 BCE*	**Binding of Isaac** *Genesis 22:1* **2085/***1676 BCE* Isaac: *37 years* Abraham: *137 years*	
2125/*1636 BCE*	**Jacob buys the birthright** *Genesis 25:29* **2123/***1638 BCE* Jacob: *15 years*	**Abraham** *(175 years)*
2150/*1611 BCE*		
2175/*1586 BCE*	**Jacob "takes" blessing and flees to Padan Aram** *Genesis 27:1–29:1* **2171/***1590 BCE* Jacob: *63 years*	**Leah** *(45 years)* **Rachel** *(36 years)* **Rebecca** *(122 years)*
2200/*1561 BCE*	**Jacob's twelve sons are born** *Genesis 29:32–35:18* **2193–2199/***1612–1618 BCE* Jacob: *85–91 years*	
2225/*1536 BCE*	7 years of plenty 2 years of famine	**Isaac** *(180 years)*
2250/*1511 BCE*	**Joseph is sold into slavery** *Genesis 37:1* **2212/***1549 BCE* Joseph: *17 years*	Jacob's family descends to Egypt *Genesis 46:1* **2238/***1523 BCE* **Jacob** *(147 years)*
2275/*1486 BCE*	**Joseph is appointed viceroy and rules for eighty years** *Genesis 41:40* **2229–2309/***1532 BCE* Joseph: *30–110 years*	
2300/*1461 BCE*		**Joseph** *(110 years)*
2325/*1436 BCE*		**Levi** *(137 years)*
2350/*1411 BCE*	**Egyptian slavery begins** *Exodus 1:8* **2331/***1430 BCE* Amram: *80 years old*	
2375/*1386 BCE*		**Amram** *(137 years)* **Moses born 2368**
2400/*1361 BCE*		

Introduction to Exodus/Shemot

SHEMOT

• *Pharaoh enslaves the Jews* • *Birth of Moses* • *Moses is forced to flee* • *The burning bush* • *Moses is sent to Pharaoh* • *Pharaoh's response*

VAERA

• *Moses refuses the mission* • *Moses' genealogy* • *Moses returns to Pharaoh* • *The staff becomes a serpent* • *The Ten Plagues begin*

BO

• *Final plagues* • *The first Passover seder* • *The Exodus from Egypt* • *Sanctification of the firstborn*

BESHALACH

• *Escape from Egypt* • *Splitting of the Red Sea* • *Song at the Sea* • *Bitter waters* • *Manna from heaven* • *Sabbath laws* • *Water from a rock* • *Amalek attacks*

YITRO

• *On the advice of Yitro, Moses appoints judges* • *Preparation for receiving the Torah* • *The Jewish nation receives The Ten Commandments* • *Other laws*

MISHPATIM

• *Social laws* • *Sealing the covenant* • *Moses ascends Mount Sinai*

The name of the second book of the Five Books of Moses is "Exodus," which in Greek means "a departure," and refers to the departure of the people from the land of Egypt. In Hebrew, the name is *"Shemot"* (the second Hebrew word in the opening sentence), which means "names."

Exodus begins with an account of how the Jewish people went from the status of royal visitors in Egypt (*see Genesis 45:17*), to that of slaves (*Exodus 1:8*), to a liberated people (*ibid. 12:51*). All of this happens within the first four Torah readings. The rest of Exodus follows the journey of the Jewish people from Egypt to Mt. Sinai, via the Sinai Peninsula (*see Map 3: Egypt to Sinai*), where the entire people had a revelation of God as He spoke two of the Ten Commandments and delivered His Torah (*ibid. 20:1-40:38*).

Highlights of Exodus are the Ten Plagues that destroyed Egypt and paved the way for Jewish redemption, the first Passover Seder (observed in Egypt), the splitting of the Red Sea which provided lasting freedom from Egyptian slavery, the giving of the Torah and the Ten Commandments, and the making of the infamous golden calf.

The theme of Exodus is twofold. First, it is about the Jewish people who grappled with freedom after over one hundred years in bondage (**2332-2448/1429-1313** BCE.). It is about how they struggled within a very short period of time to grow into their role as a people "unique [to God] above all peoples... a kingdom of priests [to God], a holy nation" (*Exodus 19:5-6*)—the mission statement of the Jewish people. It is about their initial successes and failures at fulfilling this mission; lessons to all subsequent generations concerning the need to constantly monitor and maintain spiritual growth.

The second theme is about Jewish leadership, and the struggles, setbacks, and rewards inherent in trying to forge the Jewish people into a unified nation. The life of Moses, "the humblest man on earth," is

TERUMAH

• *Contributions for building the Tabernacle*
• *Instructions for building the Tabernacle*

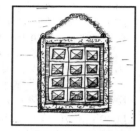

TETZAVEH

• *Oil for the Menorah*
• *The Priestly clothing*
• *Consecration of the Priests and the altar*
• *The incense altar*

KI TISA

• *The half-Shekel for census* • *The Sabbath*
• *The Golden calf* • *Moses breaks the Tablets* • *Plea for Divine mercy* • *The Thirteen Attributes*
• *The second Tablets*

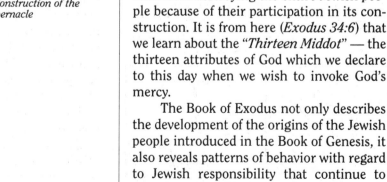

VAYAKHEL

• *The Sabbath* • *Materials for building the Tabernacle*
• *Construction of the Tabernacle*

PEKUDEI

• *An accounting*
• *Making the priests' garments* • *Placements into the Tabernacle*
• *The Cloud of Glory descends*

used as the vehicle to impart this theme until the end of Deuteronomy. Both themes dovetail towards the end of Exodus with the building of the Tabernacle, the construction of which draws out, of both leader and people, their greatest potential to relate to God and to each other.

The book is divided into eleven weekly readings *(parashiyot)*. Unlike Genesis, which covered a period of over 2,300 years, Exodus covers only 116. The first three weekly portions focus on Moses' efforts, at God's behest, to free the Jewish people from Egyptian slavery. The next three deal with Jewish preparation to receive, and the receiving of, commandments directly from God. The next two contain the instructions for the construction of the Tabernacle and all its implements, as do the final two weekly portions. The third to last portion begins with a census of the Jewish people, and contains the episode of the golden calf and the destruction of the first set of stone tablets upon which the Ten Commandments were engraved.

Perhaps one of the most moving and telling scenes in the entire Torah is in the portion containing the episode of the golden calf, when Moses pleads with God to hold back from destroying the entire Jewish people because of their participation in its construction. It is from here *(Exodus 34:6)* that we learn about the *"Thirteen Middot"* — the thirteen attributes of God which we declare to this day when we wish to invoke God's mercy.

The Book of Exodus not only describes the development of the origins of the Jewish people introduced in the Book of Genesis, it also reveals patterns of behavior with regard to Jewish responsibility that continue to resurface throughout our long history. It brings into focus the deeper meaning of what it means to be Jewish and provides the footing upon which all of Jewish history has been and will be built.

CHART 2 / *Exile to Exodus* 2238–2448/ *1523–1313 BCE (210 years)*

	Date from creation	BCE	Passage of time	Event	Source
Exile begins	**2238**	*1523*	0	Jacob descends to Egypt with "seventy souls"	*Genesis 46:1*
	2309	*1452*	71	Joseph dies	*Genesis 50:26*
	2331	*1430*	93	Levi dies (the last of Joseph's brothers to die)	*Exodus 6:16*
	2332	*1429*	94	Egyptian bondage begins	*Exodus 1:8*
	2361	*1400*	123	New pharaoh who "did not know Joseph" rises to power and institutes harsh decrees:	*Exodus 1:8*
				1. Hard labor and taxes	*Exodus 1:11*
				2. Throw all newborn Jewish males into the river	*Exodus 1:16*
				Miriam (Moses' sister) is born	
	2365	*1396*	127	Aaron (Moses' brother) is born	
	2368	*1393*	130	3. Throw all male babies born into river (including Egyptian)	*Exodus 1:22*
				Moses is born	*Exodus 2:1*
	2380	*1381*	142	Moses flees Egypt	*Exodus 2:14*
	2420	*1341*	182	Moses leaves for Midian	*Exodus 2:15*
	2430	*1303*	192	Moses marries Tzipporah	*Exodus 2:21*
	2444	*1317*	206	New pharaoh comes to power	*Exodus 2:23*
	2447	*1314*	209	Moses sees the burning bush	*Exodus 3:1*
				Pilot trip to Pharaoh and his refusal and additional burdens	*Exodus 5:1*
				Moses returns six months later to confront Pharaoh	*Exodus 7:10*
				Ten Plagues begin, one a month until the Exodus	*Exodus 7:19*
End of exile	**2448**	*1313*	210	**Exodus from Egypt**	*Exodus 2:37*

GENEALOGICAL OVERVIEW 4 / *The Twelve Tribes* 2191–3043/1569–717 BCE

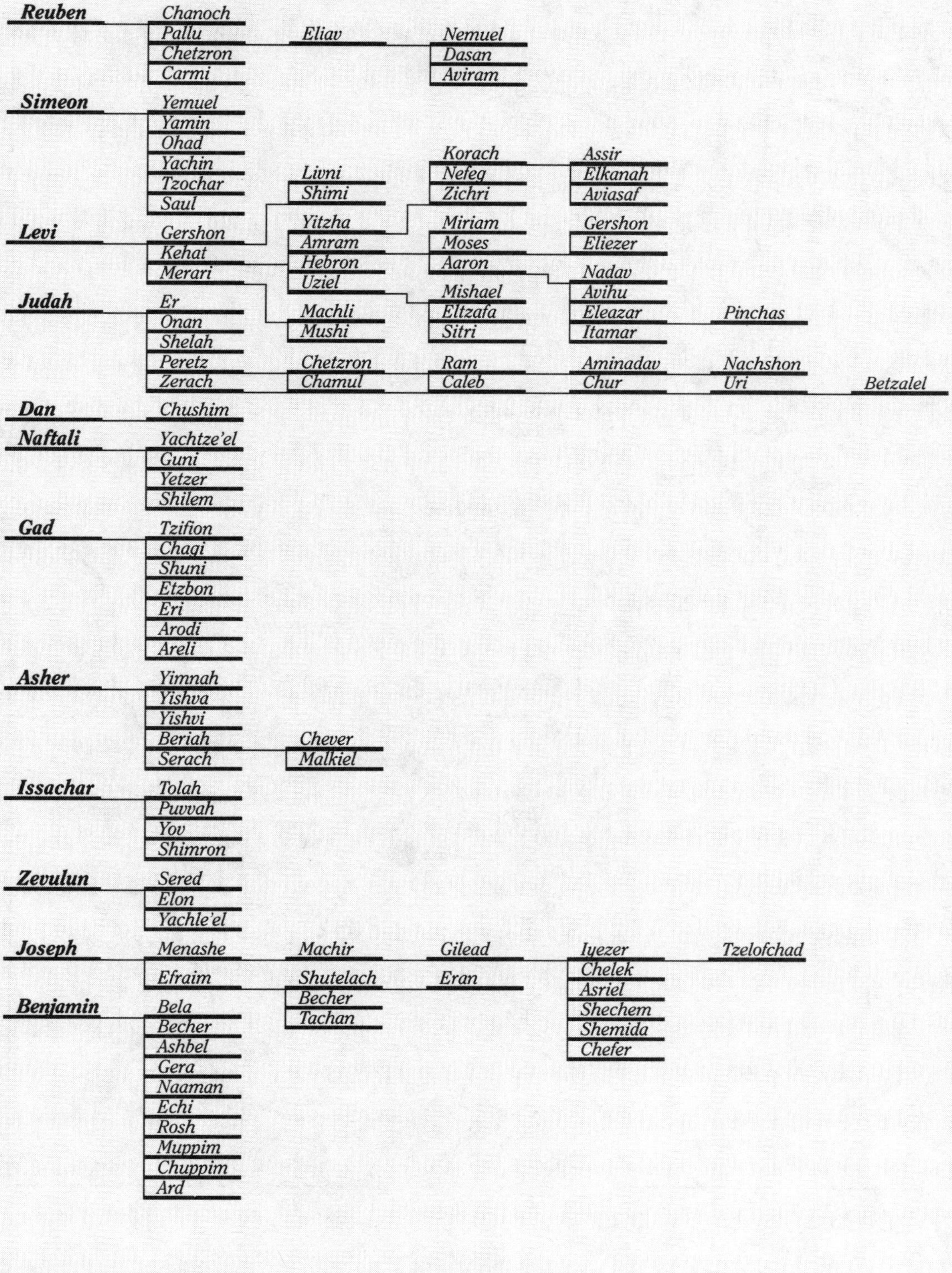

Reuben
- Chanoch
- Pallu → Eliav → Nemuel, Dasan, Aviram
- Chetzron
- Carmi

Simeon
- Yemuel
- Yamin
- Ohad
- Yachin
- Tzochar
- Saul

Levi
- Gershon → Livni, Shimi
- Kehat → Yitzha, Amram, Hebron, Uziel
- Merari → Machli, Mushi
  - Yitzha → Korach, Nefeg, Zichri
    - Korach → Assir, Elkanah, Aviasaf
  - Amram → Miriam, Moses, Aaron
    - Moses → Gershon, Eliezer
    - Aaron → Nadav, Avihu, Eleazar, Itamar
      - Eleazar → Pinchas
  - Uziel → Mishael, Eltzafa, Sitri

Judah
- Er
- Onan
- Shelah
- Peretz → Chetzron, Chamul
  - Chetzron → Ram, Caleb
    - Ram → Aminadav → Nachshon
    - Caleb → Chur → Uri → Betzalel
- Zerach

Dan
- Chushim

Naftali
- Yachtze'el
- Guni
- Yetzer
- Shilem

Gad
- Tzifion
- Chagi
- Shuni
- Etzbon
- Eri
- Arodi
- Areli

Asher
- Yimnah
- Yishva
- Yishvi
- Beriah → Chever, Malkiel
- Serach

Issachar
- Tolah
- Puvvah
- Yov
- Shimron

Zevulun
- Sered
- Elon
- Yachle'el

Joseph
- Menashe → Machir → Gilead → Iyezer, Chelek, Asriel, Shechem, Shemida, Chefer
  - Iyezer → Tzelofchad
- Efraim → Shutelach, Becher, Tachan
  - Shutelach → Eran

Benjamin
- Bela
- Becher
- Ashbel
- Gera
- Naaman
- Echi
- Rosh
- Muppim
- Chuppim
- Ard

MAP 3 / *Egypt to Mt. Sinai* 2448–2488/1313–1273 BCE (*One of several opinions*)

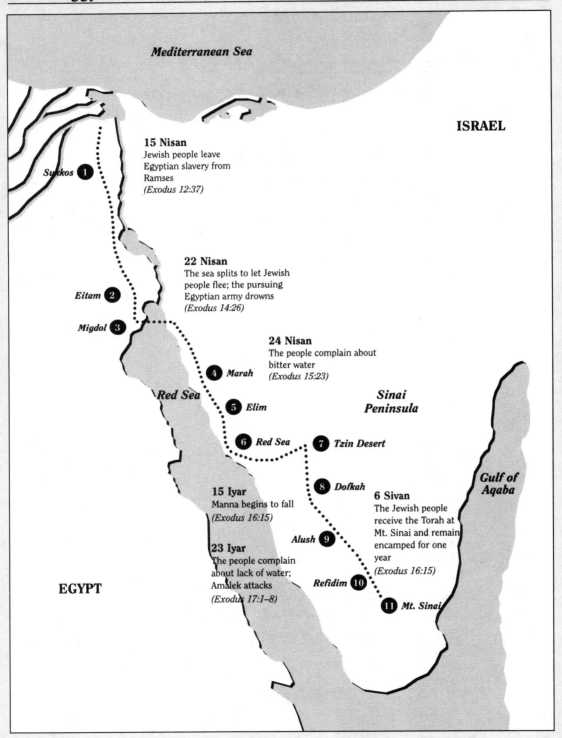

Mediterranean Sea

ISRAEL

Sukkos **1**

15 Nisan
Jewish people leave
Egyptian slavery from
Ramses
(*Exodus 12:37*)

Eitam **2**

Migdol **3**

22 Nisan
The sea splits to let Jewish
people flee; the pursuing
Egyptian army drowns
(*Exodus 14:26*)

24 Nisan
The people complain about
bitter water
(*Exodus 15:23*)

4 Marah

**Sinai
Peninsula**

Red Sea

5 Elim

6 Red Sea   **7** Tzin Desert

**Gulf of
Aqaba**

8 Dofkah

15 Iyar
Manna begins to fall
(*Exodus 16:15*)

6 Sivan
The Jewish people
receive the Torah at
Mt. Sinai and remain
encamped for one
year
(*Exodus 16:15*)

Alush **9**

23 Iyar
The people complain
about lack of water;
Amalek attacks
(*Exodus 17:1–8*)

EGYPT

Refidim **10**

11 Mt. Sinai

HISTORICAL OVERVIEW 5 / *Countdown to Sinai* 2448/*1313* BCE *(61 days)*

Date		Events along the way	Encampments
Nisan	15	**15 Nisan** *The Tenth Plague: Killing of the first-born began at midnight; the first Passover Seder is observed. The Jewish people leave Egypt in the morning.* (Exodus 12:29–36)	**Sukkot** *(Exodus 12:37)*
	16		
	17		
	18		
	19		**Eitam** *(Exodus 13:20)*
	20		
	21		
	22	**22 Nisan** *The Red sea splits, allowing the Jewish people to escape.* (Exodus 14:15)	**Migdol** *(Exodus 14:1)*
	23		
	24	**24 Nisan** *People arrive at Marah only to find bitter water.* (Exodus 15:23)	
	25		
	26		**Marah** *(Exodus 15:23)*
	27		**Elim** *(Exodus 16:27)*
	28		
	29		
	30		
Iyar	1		
	2		
	3		
	4		
	5		
	6		**Red Sea** *(Exodus 15:27)*
	7		
	8		
	9		
	10		
	11		
	12		
	13		
	14		
	15	**15 Iyar** *Manna begins to fall; some laws are given, including the laws of the Sabbath.* (Exodus 16:15)	**Sin Desert** *(Exodus 16:1)*
	16		**Dofkah** *(Numbers 33:12)*
	17		**Alush** *(Numbers 33:12)*
	18		
	20	**23 Iyar** *Complaints of lack of water cause Moses to bring water from a rock. Amalek attacks.* (Exodus 17:2–17)	
	21		
	22		
	23	**2 Sivan** *Moses ascends Mt. Sinai; God tells him to ask the people if they'll accept the covenant.* (Exodus 15:23)	**Refidim** *(Exodus 17:1)*
	24		
	25	**3 Sivan** *Moses descends and asks people who answer in the affirmative.* (Exodus 19:8)	
	26		
	27	**4 Sivan** *People accept the seven Noahide laws and laws taught at Marah; God tells Moses to sanctify the people.* (Exodus 19:3–10)	
	28		
	29		
Sivan	1		
	2	**5 Sivan** *Moses completes Genesis and Exodus on Mt. Sinai.* (Exodus 24:9) *Moses builds altars and twelve monuments.* (Exodus 24:7) *Moses, Aaron, Nadav, Avihu, and Elders ascend.* (Exodus 24:9)	**Sinai Desert** *(Exodus 19:1)*
	3		
	4		
	5		
	6	**6 Sivan** *The Ten Commandments are given on Mt. Sinai.*	
	7		
	8	**7 Sivan** *Moses ascends for 40 days to receive the first set of tablets.* (Exodus 24:12)	

Introduction to Leviticus/VaYikra

VAYIKRA

- *The Burnt-offerings*
- *The Meal-offerings*
- *The Peace-offerings*
- *The Mistake-offerings*
- *The Guilt-offerings*

TZAV

- *Additional offerings*
- *The priests' portion*
- *Installment of the priests*

SHEMINI

- *Inauguration of the Tabernacle • Death of Nadav and Avihu*
- *Warning against Priestly drinking • Laws of kosher animals and fish*

TAZRIA

- *Childbirth • Laws of the diseases of the skin*
- *Laws of the diseases on clothing*

METZORA

- *Purification from the diseases of the skin • Laws of the diseases on houses*
- *The laws of bodily discharges*

ACHAREI MOT

- *The Yom Kippur service*
- *Prohibition against eating blood • Forbidden sexual relationships*

The third book of the Five Books of Moses is "Leviticus" which in Greek means "the Levitical book." It deals with laws concerning Levites and priests. The Hebrew name of the book, derived from the first word, is *VaYikra*, "and he called."

Leviticus begins precisely where Exodus left off, with the completion of the Tabernacle, waiting to be officially put into commission. In preparation for the inauguration of the Tabernacle, the first two weekly readings discuss animal and food offerings, which become a major part of the daily service within the Tabernacle. They close with the initiation of the priests who will officiate over all services.

Leviticus has its own drama. With the third weekly reading which begins with the eighth day of the inauguration service of the Tabernacle (a festive day beyond imagination), Nadav and Avihu, the two eldest sons of the High Priest, Aaron, who are newly initiated priests, are dramatically killed as a result of Divine wrath (*10:1*). An unmitigated disaster and source of overwhelming disappointment, it serves as perhaps one of the most crucial lessons of the entire Torah: service of God, no matter how heartfelt and inspired, is only acceptable if performed *within the guidelines of the Torah*. The less obvious message learned from the episode of Nadav and Avihu, but also of extreme importance, is that one must still believe in God's love for the Jewish people, in spite of the harshness of Divine anger. God's commitment to the Jewish people and the need to carry on after a disaster, is a solemn lesson for generations of Jews who would suffer the hardships of bitter exiles.

A central theme of Leviticus is holiness, which is the essence of the mission statement of the Jewish people, first mentioned in Exodus (*19:5*). This statement is

KEDOSHIM

• Laws for a Holy nation
• Laws of the first fruits
• The consequences for
forbidden practices and
forbidden relationships

EMOR

• Laws of priests • Laws
of the High Priest • The
Holidays

BEHAR

• The Sabbatical year
• The selling and
redemption of land in
Israel • Laws of lending
money • Laws of slaves

BECHUKOTAI

• Reward and punishment
• Endowment evaluations

reiterated again in the weekly reading *Kedoshim* (*19:1*). Because Leviticus is about holiness, it is the most appropriate book in which to record the commandments dealing with *kashrut* (the eating of ritually certified food), ritual defilement and purification, the Day of Atonement service, forbidden relationships, priests, and Jewish holy days (a source of spiritual elevation explained in the *Guide to the Holidays*).

Another theme of Leviticus is community responsibility. Commandments such as *"Love your neighbor as yourself"* (*19:18*) and others dealing with behavior between people are prominent in this third book. Finally, Leviticus closes with the commandment to allow the land of Israel to lie fallow for one year every seventh year (*shemittah*). It also includes a detailed discussion of the rewards or punishments for either obeying or ignoring the commandments.

All of Leviticus can be related to the Jewish mission of striving to be holy, and in its process, elevating the spiritual level of mankind. Leviticus stresses the need for personal and national sacrifice. Though society today rejects the notion of animal sacrifices, the Torah emphasizes them as a means of bringing social consciousness to a higher level of appreciatiation for the value and sanctity of life, two values that have weakened over the millennia, often with horrible consequences.

Leviticus is the shortest book of the five and it contains only ten weekly readings. It covers the course of the year in which the Jewish people remained encamped at the base of Mt. Sinai, from the first day of *Sivan, 1313 BCE* until the 20th day of *Iyar, 1312 BCE* (approximately 13 months). Only with the final redemption and the construction of the third and final Jewish Temple will we adequately appreciate the depth and beauty of the Book of Leviticus.

CHART 3 / *The Offerings* *Leviticus 1:1–5:1*

	Type of animal or food allowed	Type of animal offered	Accompanying wine libation (fl. oz.)	Accompanying meal offering (fl. oz.)
Burnt-offering	bull, sheep or male goat, turtle-dove, common dove	Bull Yearling lamb	220 73	61.2 30.6
Guilt-offering	**Adjustable:** female sheep or goat, turtle-dove, meal **Misappropriation:** ram **Questionable:** ram **Dishonesty:** ram	Ram Yearling lamb	147 73	40.8 30.6
Meal-offering	**Meal-offering:** best grade wheat meal **Baked-offering:** wheat meal mixed with olive oil **Pan-offering:** wheat meal mixed with olive oil **Deep fried-offering:** wheat meal mixed with olive oil			
Mistake-offering	young bull (*High Priest*) young bull (*community*) male goat (*King*) female goat or sheep (*commoner*)	Bull Yearling lamb	220 73	61.2 30.6
Peace-offering	**Thanksgiving vow or pledge:** bull, sheep or goat	Bull Yearling lamb	220 73	61.2 30.6

GENEALOGICAL OVERVIEW 5 / *Generations of Levi* 2195–3043/ *1565–717 BCE*

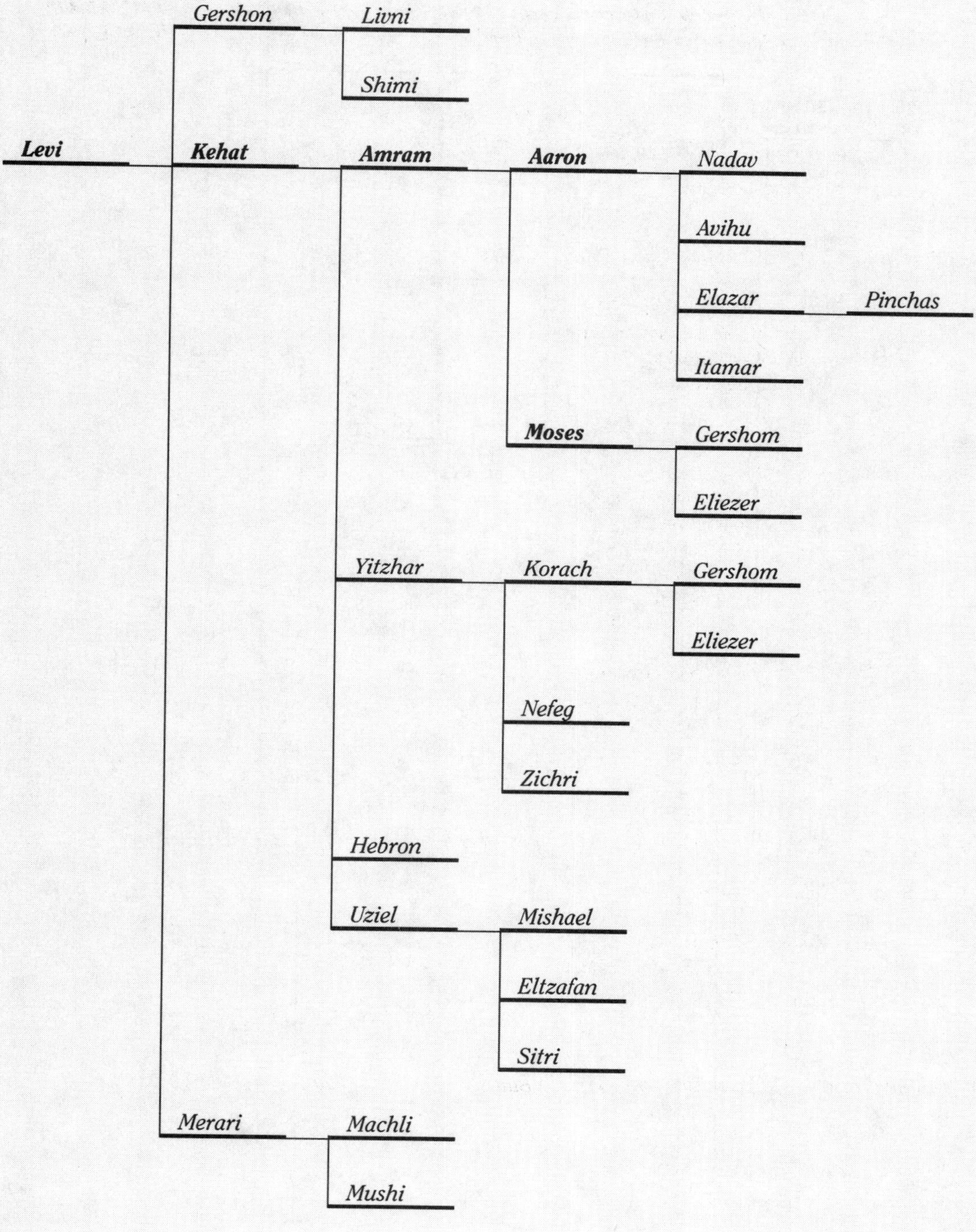

Levi
- **Kehat**
  - *Gershon*
    - *Livni*
    - *Shimi*
  - **Amram**
    - **Aaron**
      - *Nadav*
      - *Avihu*
      - *Elazar* — *Pinchas*
      - *Itamar*
    - **Moses**
      - *Gershom*
      - *Eliezer*
  - *Yitzhar*
    - *Korach*
      - *Gershom*
      - *Eliezer*
    - *Nefeg*
    - *Zichri*
  - *Hebron*
  - *Uziel*
    - *Mishael*
    - *Eltzafan*
    - *Sitri*
- *Merari*
  - *Machli*
  - *Mushi*

FIGURE 1 / **Plan of the Tabernacle** *Exodus 25:10–27:19*

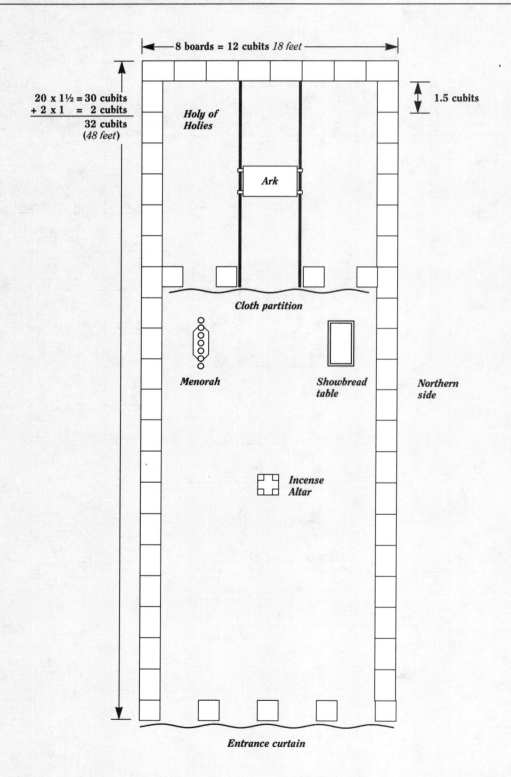

8 boards = 12 cubits *18 feet*

20 x 1½ = 30 cubits
+ 2 x 1 = 2 cubits
32 cubits
(48 feet)

1.5 cubits

Holy of Holies

Ark

Cloth partition

Menorah

Showbread table

Northern side

Incense Altar

Entrance curtain

FIGURE 2 / *The Tabernacle* *Exodus 25:10–27:19*

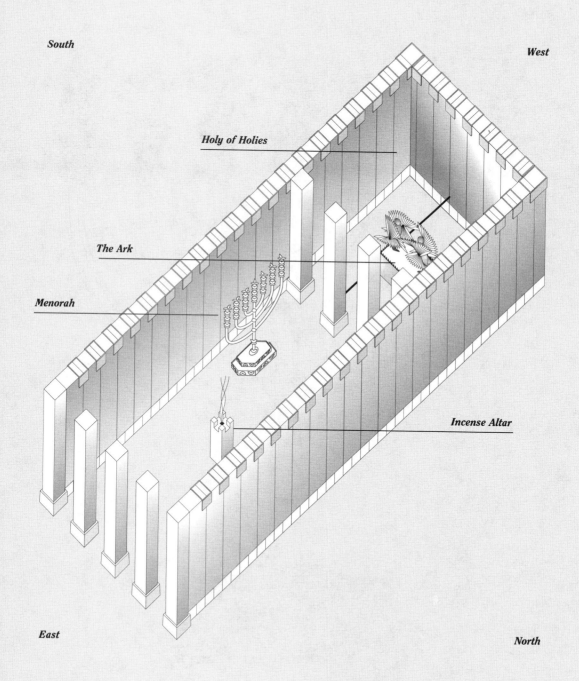

South

West

Holy of Holies

The Ark

Menorah

Incense Altar

East

North

FIGURE 3 / *The Menorah* Exodus 25:31

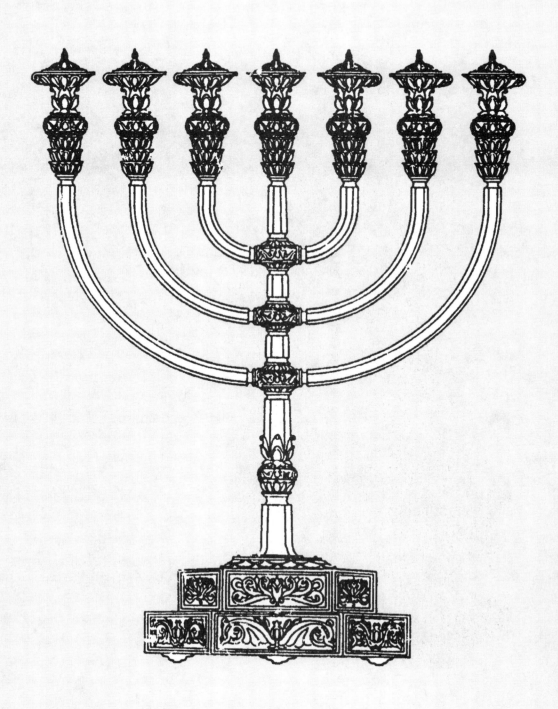

FIGURE 4 / *The High Priest's Clothing* Exodus 28:1

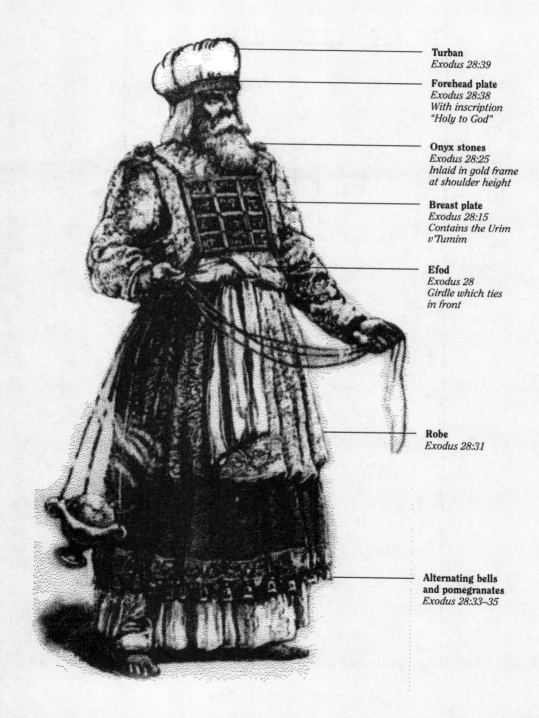

Turban
Exodus 28:39

Forehead plate
Exodus 28:38
With inscription
"Holy to God"

Onyx stones
Exodus 28:25
Inlaid in gold frame
at shoulder height

Breast plate
Exodus 28:15
Contains the Urim
v'Tumim

Efod
Exodus 28
Girdle which ties
in front

Robe
Exodus 28:31

Alternating bells
and pomegranates
Exodus 28:33–35

FIGURE 5 / *The Enclosure* Exodus 27:9

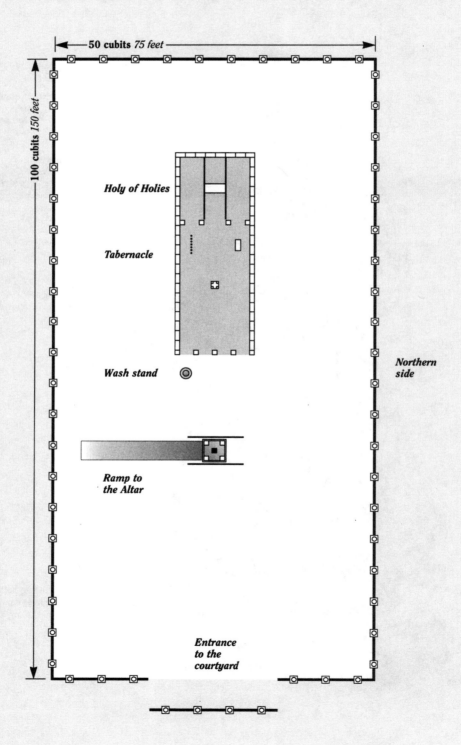

50 cubits *75 feet*

100 cubits *150 feet*

Holy of Holies

Tabernacle

Wash stand

Ramp to
the Altar

Northern
side

Entrance
to the
courtyard

Introduction to Numbers/BaMidbar

BAMIDBAR

• *The census* • *The camp arrangement* • *The census and the duties of Levites* • *Redemption of the first born*

NASO

• *The Gershon family's responsibilities* • *Merari's responsibilities* • *Camp purification* • *Suspected adulteress* •*The Nazirite* • *Leader's dedication offering*

BEHA'ALOT'CHA

• *Menorah* •*Inauguration of Levites* • *Passover* • *Departure from Sinai* • *Complaints and the Quails* • *Miriam's and Aaron's complaint* • *Miriam's punishment*

SHELACH

• *Moses sends the twelve spies* • *The decree of forty years* • *The laws of offerings* • *The Sabbath violator*

KORACH

• *The rebellion of Korach* •*The punishment for the rebellion* • *The almond-blossoming staff* • *Responsibilities of priests and Levites* • *Priests' and Levites' shares*

CHUKAT

• *The Red Heifer* • *The death of Miriam* • *Moses hits the rock* • *Near war with Edom* • *Aaron dies* • *The war with Canaan* • *Snakes* • *Confrontation with Sichon and Og*

T he fourth book of the Five Books of Moses is "Numbers," so named because it begins with a commandment from God to count the Jewish people. The Hebrew name of the book, derived from the first verse, is *BaMidbar*, "in the desert." The narrative that left off at the end of Exodus in the Sinai Desert is about to continue in Numbers.

A glance at *Historical Overview 6 (p.126)* shows that there is some overlap between the Books of Leviticus and Numbers. Throughout the Bible, the sequence of the narrative does not always coincide with the historical sequence of events.

For the most part, this book covers the travels of the Jewish nation starting with their departure from their camp at the foot of Mt. Sinai, to their arrival at the border of the Land of Canaan, a period of thirty-eight years.

The journey to Canaan (Israel) should have taken only one year. The Jewish people were brought to Mt. Sinai in the Sinai Desert to receive the Torah, and then they were supposed to have traveled straight to Canaan to conquer and settle it. In the fourth weekly reading (*Shelach*), however, ten of the twelve men sent to investigate the Land return to the people with a discouraging message, and thereby precipitate a Divine wrath, leading to a decree of thirty-eight additional years of wandering (*13:1*).

In many respects, Numbers is about preparing for life in the Land of Israel. Israel represents far more than a geographic homeland for a once homeless people. It is the only land capable of supporting a holy people. This union of the people with the land can trigger the fulfillment of the Divinely ordained mission (*see the summary of Exodus*). Therefore, whether it be the story of the spies (*13:1*), the account of the rebellion against Moses (*16:1*), or the story of Moses' error which prevented him from crossing the Jordan river into

BALAK

• Balak hires Bilam to curse Israel • Bilam's donkey speaks to him • Bilam's attempted curse becomes a blessing • Israel is lured by Moab

PINCHAS

• Pinchas' reward for zealousness • Orders to attack Midian • A new census • The division of Israel • The laws of inheritance • Daily and holiday sacrifices

MATOT

• Laws of vows • The war against Midian • Reuben and Gad request Transjordan

MASEI

• Journeys of Israel • The borders of Israel • New leaders • The Levitical cities • The cities of refuge • Inter-tribal marriage

Canaan (20:11), there is always some crucial message for every generation to learn regarding the proper attitude for living in the Land of Israel.

Numbers is very dramatic and it even contains some bizarre episodes. For example, Bilam, the non-Jewish prophet contracted to curse the Jewish people (22:2), is forced to converse with his donkey. One can imagine the looks on the faces of the emissaries sent by King Balak to escort the "great" Bilam from Midian to Moab! In the end, Bilam's curse is turned into a blessing, one whose words are said every morning upon entering a synagogue ("How good are your tents, O Jacob..." 24:5).

One of the climaxes of Numbers comes towards the end of the book and at the end of the forty years of wandering in the desert. Set to enter the Land, the Jewish people falter one last time, becoming involved with the worship of the idol, Ba'al Peor. "From amongst the congregation," Pinchas, the son of Elazar the priest, performs a zealous act that mitigates God's anger and ends the plague (25:7). As a reward, Pinchas is inducted into the priesthood, teaching us a very important lesson: no matter who you may be, if you are in a position to prevent immorality, it is your responsibility to do so.

As Numbers comes to a close, the leadership is passed onto the next generation, through Joshua, Moses' loyal disciple. Also, the Land of Israel is divided amongst the tribes. Finally, the Torah recounts the forty years of wandering with an overview of all the encampments from the time the people left Egypt, until the last stop at the border of Israel. All that remained to be done was to review the laws previously given, strengthen the people's commitment to Torah, and for Moses to bid the nation farewell, all of which are themes of the fifth and final book, Deuteronomy.

HISTORICAL OVERVIEW 6 / *Historical Sequence of Leviticus and Numbers* 2448–2488/*1313–1273* BCE

Year from creation/ *Common Era year*	Time periods	Bible books Time periods	The chronology of weekly portions
2448/*1313 BCE*	**40 years in the desert**		**Shelach**
2449/*1312 BCE*		**Exodus**	*Numbers 15:32–36*
2450/*1311 BCE*	**19 years in Kadesh**	**Leviticus**	**Chukat**
2451/*1310 BCE*		**Numbers**	*Numbers 19:11–22*
2452/*1309 BCE*			**Naso** *Numbers 7:1–7:89*
2453/*1308 BCE*			**BeHa'alot'cha** *Numbers 9:1–10:11*
2454/*1307 BCE*			
2455/*1306 BCE*			**BaMidbar** *Numbers 1:1*
2456/*1305 BCE*			**Naso**
2457/*1304 BCE*			*Numbers 4:21–7:11*
2458/*1303 BCE*			**BeHa'alot'cha** *Numbers 8:1–26*
2459/*1302 BCE*			**BeHa'alot'cha**
2460/*1301 BCE*			*Numbers 10:11–12:16*
2461/*1300 BCE*			**Shelach** *Numbers 13:1–14:45*
2462/*1299 BCE*			
2463/*1298 BCE*			
2464/*1297 BCE*			
2465/*1296 BCE*			
2466/*1295 BCE*			
2467/*1294 BCE*			
2468/*1293 BCE*			
2469/*1292 BCE*			
2470/*1291 BCE*			
2471/*1290 BCE*			**Korach**
2472/*1289 BCE*			*Numbers 16:1–17:15*
2473/*1288 BCE*			
2474/*1287 BCE*			
2475/*1286 BCE*			
2476/*1285 BCE*			
2477/*1284 BCE*			
2478/*1283 BCE*			
2479/*1282 BCE*			
2480/*1281 BCE*			
2481/*1280 BCE*			
2482/*1279 BCE*			
2483/*1278 BCE*			
2484/*1277 BCE*			
2485/*1276 BCE*			**Chukat**
2486/*1275 BCE*			*Numbers 20:1–21*
2487/*1274 BCE*			**Chukat** *Numbers 20:22–21:4*
2488/*1273 BCE*			**Masei** *Numbers 35:1–36:13*

Note: *There is a principle in Torah that not all events follow chronologically. This is especially so with weekly portions in the Book of Numbers, where many events take place in the time frames of the Book of Leviticus and one occurring as early as the Book of Exodus.*

Order of Weekly Portions

Leviticus
1. VaYikra
2. Tzav
3. Shemini
4. Tazria
5. Metzora
6. Acharei Mot
7. Kedoshim
8. Emor
9. BeHar
10. BeChukotai

Numbers
1. BaMidbar
2. Naso
3. BeHa'alot'cha
4. Shelach
5. Korach
6. Chukat
7. Balak
8. Pinchas
9. Matot
10. Masei

CHART 4 / *The Census* *Exodus 38:26, Numbers 1:2, Numbers 26:1*

	First count	First census	Second census
The tribes excluding Levi			
Reuben		46,500	43,730
Simeon		59,300	22,200
Gad		45,650	40,500
Judah		74,600	76,500
Issachar		54,400	64,300
Zevulun		57,400	60,500
Efraim		40,500	32,500
Menashe		32,200	52,700
Benjamin		35,400	45,600
Dan		62,700	64,400
Asher		41,500	53,400
Naftali		53,400	45,400
Total Israelites		**603,550**	**601,730**
The Levites			
Gershon		7,500	
Kehat		8,600	
Merari		6,200	
Total Levites		**22,300**	
National total	**603,550**	**625,850**	

Note: *The first count included all the tribes, and was totalled by adding together all the half-shekel pieces collected. The first and second census totalled the individual members of each tribe (again, by counting the half-shekel pieces contributed) and they both excluded the Levites, who were counted separately as commanded by God (Numbers 1:49; the first census of the Levites is in Numbers 3:21–34). Each count was only of males 20 years and older who were fit for military service.*

FIGURE 6 / *The Camp in the Desert* Numbers 2:1

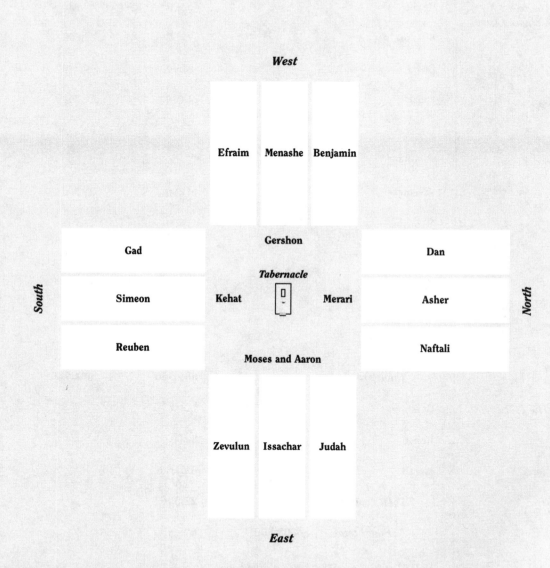

MAP 4 / *Biblical Borders of Israel* *Genesis 15:18; Genesis 35:10–15; Numbers 34:1*

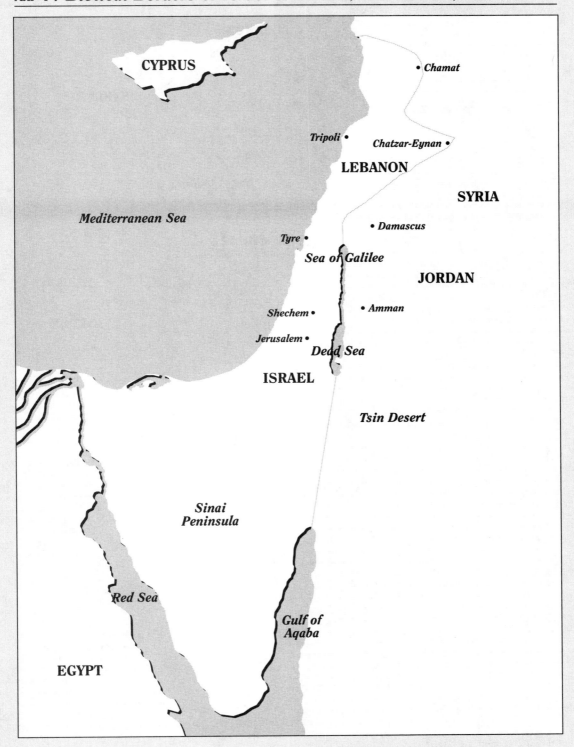

MAP 5 / *Division of the Land of Israel* 2495/1267 *BCE*

LEBANON

Dan

SYRIA

Mediterranean Sea

Asher

Naftali

• Haifa

Sea of Galilee

Zevulun

Issachar

Menashe

JORDAN

Menashe

• Tel Aviv

Efraim

Gad

Dan

Benjamin

Jerusalem •

Reuben

Judah

• *Hebron*

Dead Sea

Beersheva •

Simeon

MAP 6 / *Forty Years in the Desert* 2448–2488/1313–1273 BCE (*One of several opinions*)

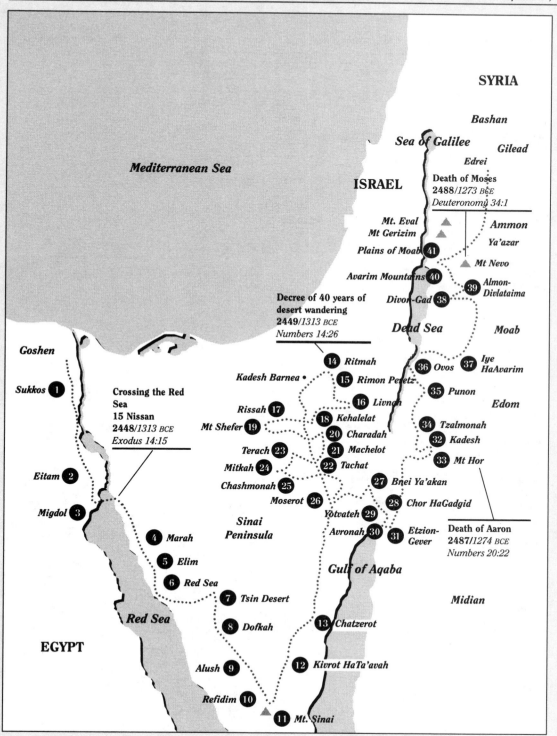

SYRIA

Bashan

Sea of Galilee

Gilead

Edrei

ISRAEL

**Death of Moses
2488/1273** *BCE*
Deuteronomy 34:1

Mediterranean Sea

*Mt. Eval
Mt Gerizim*

Ammon

Ya'azar

Plains of Moab **41**

Mt Nevo

Avarim Mountains **40**

39 Almon-
Divlataima

**Decree of 40 years of
desert wandering
2449/1313** *BCE*
Numbers 14:26

Divon-Gad **38**

Dead Sea

Moab

14 *Ritmah*

Kadesh Barnea •

36 *Ovos*   **37** *Iye
HaAvarim*

15 *Rimon Peretz*

35 *Punon*

Goshen

16 *Livnah*

Edom

Sukkos **1**

Rissah **17**

**Crossing the Red
Sea
15 Nissan
2448/1313** *BCE*
Exodus 14:15

Mt Shefer **19**

18 *Kehalelat*

34 *Tzalmonah*

20 *Charadah*

32 *Kadesh*

Terach **23**

21 *Machelot*

33 *Mt Hor*

Mitkah **24**

22 *Tachat*

Eitam **2**

Chashmonah **25**

27 *Bnei Ya'akan*

Moserot **26**

28 *Chor HaGadgid*

Migdol **3**

Yotvateh **29**

4 *Marah*

Avronah **30** **31** *Etzion-
Gever*

**Death of Aaron
2487/1274** *BCE*
Numbers 20:22

5 *Elim*

*Sinai
Peninsula*

Gulf of Aqaba

6 *Red Sea*

7 *Tsin Desert*

Midian

8 *Dofkah*

13 *Chatzerot*

Red Sea

EGYPT

Alush **9**

12 *Kivrot HaTa'avah*

Refidim **10**

11 *Mt. Sinai*

HISTORICAL OVERVIEW 7 / *Forty Years in the Desert* 2448–2488/1313–1273 BCE

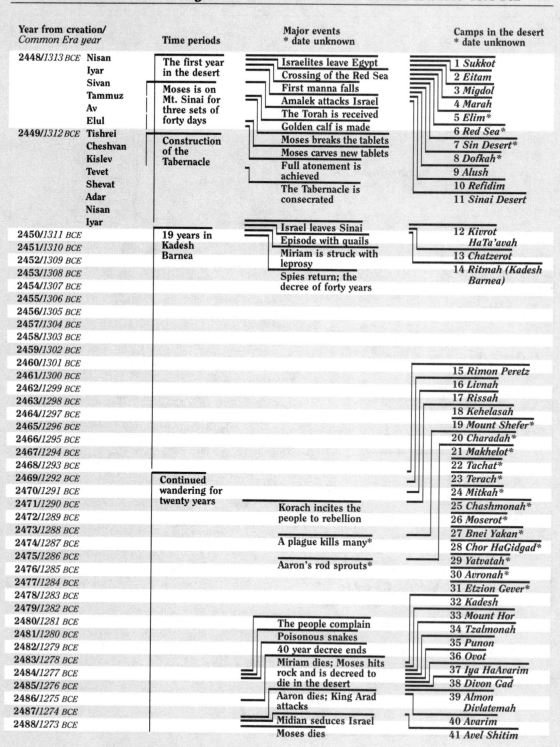

Year from creation/ *Common Era year*	Time periods	Major events * date unknown	Camps in the desert * date unknown
2448/*1313 BCE* Nisan Iyar Sivan Tammuz Av Elul	**The first year in the desert** **Moses is on Mt. Sinai for three sets of forty days**	Israelites leave Egypt Crossing of the Red Sea First manna falls Amalek attacks Israel The Torah is received Golden calf is made	1 *Sukkot* 2 *Eitam* 3 *Migdol* 4 *Marah* 5 *Elim**
2449/*1312 BCE* Tishrei Cheshvan Kislev Tevet Shevat Adar Nisan Iyar	**Construction of the Tabernacle**	Moses breaks the tablets Moses carves new tablets Full atonement is achieved The Tabernacle is consecrated	6 *Red Sea** 7 *Sin Desert** 8 *Dofkah** 9 *Alush* 10 *Refidim* 11 *Sinai Desert*
2450/*1311 BCE* **2451**/*1310 BCE* **2452**/*1309 BCE* **2453**/*1308 BCE* **2454**/*1307 BCE*	**19 years in Kadesh Barnea**	Israel leaves Sinai Episode with quails Miriam is struck with leprosy Spies return; the decree of forty years	12 *Kivrot HaTa'avah* 13 *Chatzerot* 14 *Ritmah (Kadesh Barnea)*
2455/*1306 BCE* **2456**/*1305 BCE* **2457**/*1304 BCE* **2458**/*1303 BCE* **2459**/*1302 BCE* **2460**/*1301 BCE*			
2461/*1300 BCE* **2462**/*1299 BCE* **2463**/*1298 BCE* **2464**/*1297 BCE* **2465**/*1296 BCE* **2466**/*1295 BCE* **2467**/*1294 BCE* **2468**/*1293 BCE*			15 *Rimon Peretz* 16 *Livnah* 17 *Rissah* 18 *Kehelasah* 19 *Mount Shefer** 20 *Charadah** 21 *Makhelot** 22 *Tachat**
2469/*1292 BCE* **2470**/*1291 BCE* **2471**/*1290 BCE* **2472**/*1289 BCE* **2473**/*1288 BCE* **2474**/*1287 BCE* **2475**/*1286 BCE* **2476**/*1285 BCE* **2477**/*1284 BCE* **2478**/*1283 BCE* **2479**/*1282 BCE*	**Continued wandering for twenty years**	Korach incites the people to rebellion A plague kills many* Aaron's rod sprouts*	23 *Terach** 24 *Mitkah** 25 *Chashmonah** 26 *Moserot** 27 *Bnei Yakan** 28 *Chor HaGidgad** 29 *Yatvatah** 30 *Avronah** 31 *Etzion Gever**
2480/*1281 BCE* **2481**/*1280 BCE* **2482**/*1279 BCE* **2483**/*1278 BCE* **2484**/*1277 BCE* **2485**/*1276 BCE* **2486**/*1275 BCE* **2487**/*1274 BCE* **2488**/*1273 BCE*		The people complain Poisonous snakes 40 year decree ends Miriam dies; Moses hits rock and is decreed to die in the desert Aaron dies; King Arad attacks Midian seduces Israel Moses dies	32 *Kadesh* 33 *Mount Hor* 34 *Tzalmonah* 35 *Punon* 36 *Ovot* 37 *Iya HaAvarim* 38 *Divon Gad* 39 *Almon Divlatemah* 40 *Avarim* 41 *Avel Shitim*

Introduction to Deuteronomy/Devarim

DEVARIM

• Recollection of events, encounters and victories

VAETCHANAN

• Moses' plea • Loyalty to God • Setting up the cities of refuge • The Ten Commandments • Hear O Israel (Shema) • Warnings • The Exodus

EKEV

• Reward for obedience • Warning against overconfidence • Warnings • Following God

RE'EH

• The choice • Non-sacrificial meat • Idolatrous prophet and city • Kosher and non-kosher animals • Tithes • Sabbatical year • Firstborn animals • Holidays

SHOFTIM

• Establishing judges and police • Penalty for idolatry • Supreme court • Kings • Levitical priests • Divination • Cities of refuge • Witnesses • Going to war • Unsolved murders

KI TETZE

• Female captives • Firstborn's inheritance right • The rebellious son • Rape • Exclusions from Jewish people • Divorce • Remarriage • Laws of employees • Widows and orphans • Gifts for the poor • Amalek

The name of the fifth and last book of the Five Books of Moses is "Deuteronomy," which in Greek literally means "the second law," because it repeats many of the commandments discussed in previous books and reviews the events of the past forty years of wandering in the Sinai desert. The Hebrew name, derived from the second word of the book is "Devarim," which means "things" or "words."

Deuteronomy is Moses' final discourse to the Jewish people before climbing Mt. Nevo (north of the Dead Sea), to depart from this world. He begins by criticizing the people for having strayed from the Torah and for having acted rebelliously and ends by blessing them (all within a period of weeks). In between, he poses a question to the nation which stands around him, enraptured by his every word but saddened by the thought of his imminent departure, "Now, Israel, what does God, your God, want from you, except to fear God..." (10:12).

Moses even goes one step further with an advance warning to the Jewish people of the dangers of overconfidence and of their eventual straying from the Torah, calling "heaven and earth to bear witness" to this fact (30:19). He reviews once again the blessings that result from living according to the Torah's laws and the negative consequences for abrogating our covenant with God (27:11). He also emphasizes the accessibility of the Torah (30:11).

Perhaps the strongest and clearest summation of not just Deuteronomy, but of

KI TAVO
• First fruits • End of
commandments
• Blessings and curses
• Moses' final words

NITZAVIM
• The covenant with God
• Returning to God
• Life's choice

VAYELECH
• New leadership • Final
preparations for entering
Israel

HA'AZINU
• Moses' song • Moses told
to ascend Mt. Nevo

**V'ZOT
HABERACHAH**
• Moses blesses the tribes
• Moses' death

the entire Torah, is *"I call upon heaven and earth to witness today that I have set before you life and death, blessing and curse. Choose life! So you and your descendants may live..."* (30:19). Life, in the context of this verse and Moses' entire dialogue, refers to more than mere physical survival; it alludes to a life which is spiritually inclined, one based upon the moral values of the Torah. This, the Torah instructs, is the true definition of Life.

One of the most touching scenes in Deuteronomy is the description of Moses' death. It attests to the unwavering loyalty of Moses to God and of God to Moses. As harsh as Moses' punishment not to enter the Land may have been, one still senses God's love for Moses, and Moses' commitment to follow Him anywhere God may lead him. Above all, the final paragraphs of Deuteronomy prove that the last four books were not only about the Jewish people growing into their role as a "light unto the nations," but also about the leader who brought them to this level of achievement.

Finally, Deuteronomy, through the life of Moses, teaches all mankind what it means to fulfill one's personal potential, as the Torah points out:

> *Moses was one hundred and twenty years old when he died. His eyes had not weakened, nor had his strength dissipated... (34:7).*

Having completed the mission he was destined to perform, Moses was taken from this world. *"There never again arose a prophet in Israel like Moses..."*

HISTORICAL OVERVIEW 8 / *The Life of Moses* 2368—2488/1393—1273 BCE

Year from creation *Common Era year*	Portion of the week	Landmark events	Moses' location	Moses' age	Others' ages
2360/*1401 BCE*	**Shemot** *Exodus 1:1–6:1*				**Yocheved** *(130 years old at Moses' birth)*
		Moses is born *Exodus 2:2* **2368**/*1393 BCE*	*Egypt*	birth	
2370/*1391 BCE*				10	
2380/*1381 BCE*		**Moses strikes Egyptian** *Exodus 2:12* **2380**/*1381 BCE*	*Cush (Ethiopia)*	20	**Amram** *137 years*
2390/*1371 BCE*				30	
2400/*1361 BCE*				40	
2410/*1351 BCE*				50	
2420/*1341 BCE*			*Midian*	60	
2430/*1331 BCE*				70	
2440/*1321 BCE*		**The burning bush** *Exodus 3:1* **2448**/*1314 BCE*		80	
2450/*1311 BCE*	**VaEra** *Exodus 6:2–9:35* **Bo** *Exodus 10:1–13:16*		*Egypt* *Desert*		
		Exodus *Exodus 12:51* **2448**/*1313 BCE*		90	
2460/*1301 BCE*	**BeShalach** *Exodus 13:17–17:16*	**The Torah** *Exodus 19:1* **2448**/*1313 BCE*		100	
2470/*1291 BCE*	**Numbers** *1:1–36:13*	**Moses hits the rock** *Numbers 20:1* **2487**/*1275 BCE* *As a result, neither Moses nor Aaron were to enter Israel.*		110	**Miriam** *126 years (7 years old at Moses' birth)*
2480/*1281 BCE*				120	**Aaron** *123 years (3 years old at Moses' birth)*
2490/*1271 BCE*	**Deuteronomy** *1:1–34:12*	**Moses' death** *Deuteronomy 34:5* **2488**/*1273 BCE*			**Joshua** *(82 years old at Moses' death)*

GENEALOGICAL OVERVIEW 6 / *David's Lineage* 1958–2216/*1803–1545* BCE

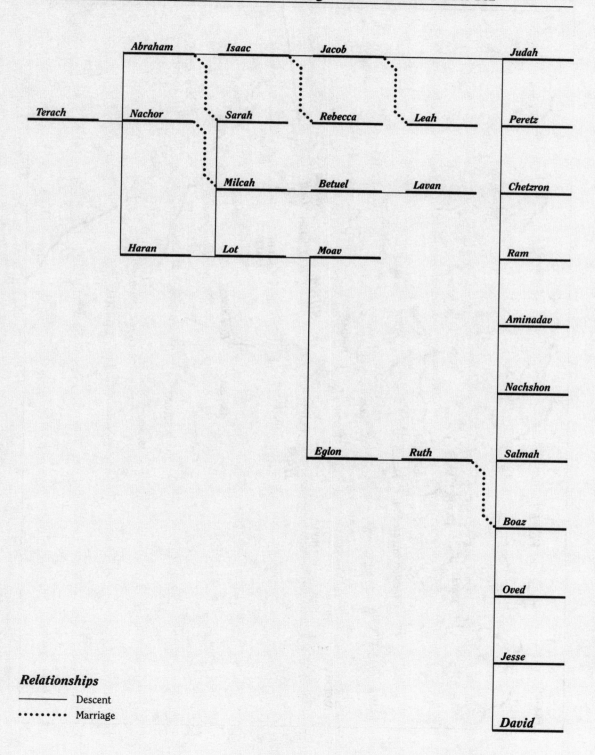

Relationships

—————— Descent

•••••••••• Marriage

MAP 7 / *The Seventy Nations* Post-flood 1657/2104 BCE; Genesis 10:1–32

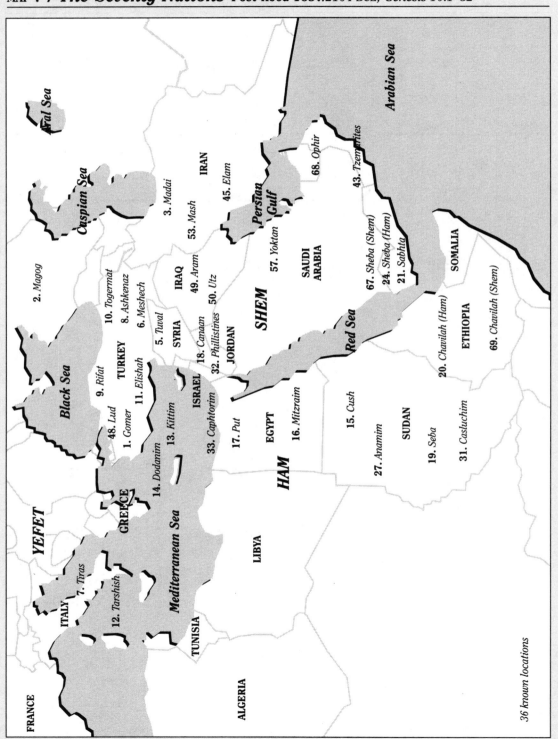

The Bible Basics Text

Book One: *Genesis/Bereshit*

Bereshit

Noah

Lech Lecha

Bereshit

....

🙿 *Six days of creation* 🙿 *The mistake
of eating from the Tree of Knowledge*
🙿 *Expulsion from the Garden* 🙿 *Cain
kills Abel* 🙿 *Decree of destruction*

The Tree of Knowledge

The First Day: Creation and Light

1 ¹ In the beginning [*bereshit*], God created the heaven
and the earth. ² The earth was formless and void, and
darkness was upon the surface of the deep; God's spirit hovered over the surface of the water.

³ God said, "Let there be light," and there was light.
⁴ God saw that the light was good, ***and God separated
between the light and the dark.*** 🜨 ⁵ God called the light,
"Day," and the dark, He called "Night."

There was evening and there was morning, one day.

The Second Day: Formation of the Sky

⁶ God said, "Let there be a sky within the water," and it
will divide between water and water. ⁷ God made the sky, ***and
it separated between the water which was below the sky
and the water which was above the sky;*** 🜨 and it was so. ⁸
God called the sky, "Heaven."

There was evening, and there was morning, a second
day.

The Third Day: Formation of Land and Vegetation

⁹ God said, "***Let the water gather under the sky into
one place, and let dry land appear.***" 🜨 And it was so.
¹⁰ God called the dry land, "Earth" and He called the gather-
ing of water, "Seas." God saw that it was good.

¹¹ God said, "Let the earth sprout vegetation—seed-
bearing plants and fruit trees that produce their own kinds of

🜨 1:4 **Orderly**
***"and God separated between
the light and the dark."*** (Good
and Evil?—Life and Death?)
Arranging things in a clear and
orderly manner in every aspect of
one's life is the way to begin any
undertaking and is the key to
success.

🜨 1:7 **Divisive**
***"and it separated between the
water which was below the sky
and the water which was above
the sky."*** This time He did not
say "It was good." Why? Because
this second division was an internal division of one entity. A clear
warning against internal strife—
divisiveness causes strife.

🜨 1:9 **Respectful**
***"Let the water gather under the
sky in one place and let dry
land appear."*** This is a third kind
of separation; a respectful separation of boundaries for two different purposes—teaches us not to
violate another person's domain.

🜨 📖 *symbols explained on page 35*

fruits with seeds shall be on the earth." And it was so.

¹² The earth brought forth vegetation, plants that bear seeds according to their species, and specific kinds of trees that produce fruits with seeds according to their species. God saw that it was good.

¹³ There was evening, and there was morning, a third day.

The Fourth Day: Formation of the Sun, Moon, and Stars

¹⁴ God said, "*Let there be lights in the sky of heaven to separate between the day and the night. They will be signs for the festivals, the days, and the years.* ¹⁵ They will be lights in the sky of heaven, to shine upon the earth." And it was so.

¹⁶ God made two great lights: a great light to dominate the day, and a small light to dominate the night; and the stars. ¹⁷ God put them in the sky of heaven to light up the earth, ¹⁸ to dominate during the day and during the night, and to separate between the light and the dark. God saw that it was good.

¹⁹ There was evening, and there was morning, a fourth day.

The Fifth Day: Formation of Creatures in the Water and Air

²⁰ God said, "Let the water be filled with swarms of living creatures, and let flying creatures fly above the earth on the surface of the sky of heaven."

²¹ God created the great sea creatures and all the creeping living creatures which the water produces according to their species, and all the flying winged creatures according to their species. God saw that it was good. ²² God blessed them saying, "Be fruitful and multiply, and fill the water in the seas, [while] the flying shall increase on the land."

²³ There was evening, and there was morning, a fifth day.

The Sixth Day: Formation of Land Animals and of Man

²⁴ God said, "Let the earth bring forth living creatures according to their species: domestic animals, creeping things, and wild animals of the land according to their species." And it was so; ²⁵ God made the wild animals according to their species, the domestic animals according to their species, and the creeping things according to their species. God saw that it was good.

²⁶ God said, "*Let us make Man* in our image, in our likeness. He will subdue the fish of the sea, the flying crea-

⚖ 1:14 Time-efficient
"Let there be lights in the heaven to separate between the day and the night. They will be signs for the festivals, the days and the years." God set up an infallible system for tracking time. He not only created day and night, but placed the stars in the heavens as well. Man has further developed systems of measurement in accordance with his needs. Man should organize his time, the greatest gift of all, to take advantage of all the opportunities afforded to him, and thus be able to achieve according to his true abilities.

⚖ 1:26 Humble
"Let us make Man..".. Who is the *us*? We are taught that God consulted with the angels before he made man. This teaches us that even God follows the modest and productive practice of seeking advice from others. Every person should believe in himself, but not be ashamed to consult with others.

tures in the sky, the domesticated animals throughout the earth, and all the creeping things that crawl on the ground." [27] *God created mankind in His image;* ⚖ He created him in the image of God, male and female.

[28] God blessed them, and said to them, *"Be fruitful and multiply.* 📖 8 Fill the earth, and conquer it. Subdue the fish of the sea and the flying creatures in the sky and all the creatures that move on the ground."

[29] God said, "I have given to you all the seed-producing plants upon the face of the entire earth, and all trees which have seed-producing fruits. They will be your food. 30 *All plant vegetation will be food for all the creatures of the earth,* ⚖ the flying creatures of the sky, and all living, moving creatures on the earth." And it was so. [31] God saw all that He had made, and it was very good.

[32] There was evening, and there was morning, the sixth day.

The Sabbath

2 [1] The heavens and the earth were completed, with all their components. [2] God completed His creative work that He had done, and abstained from such creative work on the seventh day. [3] God blessed the seventh day, and sanctified it, because on it He abstained from all His creative work.

The Garden of Eden

[4] This is what occurred after the creation of heaven and the earth, after the day on which God made earth and heaven.

[5] All plants of the field did not yet exist on the land, and all grass of the field had yet to sprout, because God had not yet caused it to rain on the earth [while] there was no man to work the land. [6] Then, mist rose from the earth and watered the entire surface of the land.

[7] *God formed Man from the dust of the earth. He blew into his nostrils the breath of life,* ⚖ and Man became a living creature. [8] God planted a garden in the east of Eden; there He placed Man whom He had formed.

[9] God caused to sprout from the land all trees which are pleasant to look at and good to eat. The Tree of Life and the Tree of the Knowledge of Good and Evil were in the middle of the garden.

[10] A river went out from Eden to water the Garden; from there it separated into four major rivers. [11] The name of the first is Pishon, and it encircles all the land of the

---

⚖ 1:27 **Creative**
"God created Mankind in His image..." This means with potentially the same attributes as God. We should know and appreciate that God is the creator of everything and that He gave us the potential ability to be similarly creative in our world.

📖 1:28 **Family oriented**
"Be fruitful and multiply."
God's first commandment to Adam and Eve was to have children. While this is the prime commandment for the continuation of man's existence, it is also essential to appreciate that having children gives purpose to our lives and brings us the ultimate happiness.

⚖ 1:30 **Sharing**
"All plant vegetation will be food for all the creatures of the earth..." God created abundant food for all living creatures, as well as mankind. There is more than enough for all. This teaches us the concept of sharing our blessings with others.

⚖ 2:7 **Spiritual**
"God formed Man from the dust of the earth. He blew into his nostrils the breath of life..."
Man was created as a combination of the material and the spiritual. Although we tend to concentrate on the physical, the dust of the earth, it was only when God gave him His breath, the spiritual, that man actually became a living creature and became capable of fulfilling his mission of living. Remember that your spirituality is a gift given to you by God and that unlike the material, no one can take it away from you. Live it and revel in it for a deeper appreciation of all which is around you.

Chavilah, where there is gold. ¹² The gold of that land is good; crystal and the shoham stone can also be found there.

¹³ The name of the second river is Gichon, which encircles all the land of Cush. ¹⁴ The name of the third river is the Tigris, which traverses eastern Assyria; the fourth river is the Euphrates.

¹⁵ God took the man and placed him in the Garden of Eden to work it, and to watch over it. ¹⁶ God commanded the man, saying, *"You may eat from every tree in the Garden,* ¹⁷ *except from the Tree of Knowledge of Good and Evil.* ⚖ *If you do, you will certainly die,* ⚖ from that day."

¹⁸ Then God said, *"It is not good that the Man is alone.* ⚖ I will make a mate to complement him."

¹⁹ God produced from the land all the animals of the field, and all the flying creatures in the sky. He brought them to the man to see what he would name them. Whatever the man called the animals, that was their names.

²⁰ The man gave names to all the domestic animals, the flying creatures in the sky, and all the animals of the field. Yet the Man did not find a mate like himself. ²¹ God caused a deep sleep to fall upon the man, and he slept. He then took one of his ribs, and after, closed the flesh in its place. ²² God fashioned the rib, which He took from the man, into a woman, and He brought her to the man.

²³ The Man said, "She is bone of my bones, and flesh of my flesh. She will be called 'Woman' for she was taken from man." ²⁴ *Therefore a man will leave his father and his mother and cling to his wife, and they will become one flesh.* ⚖

²⁵ Both the man and the woman were naked, but were not embarrassed.

3 ¹ The serpent was the most cunning of all the animals of the field which God had made. He said to the woman, "Didn't God say not to eat from any of the trees of the Garden?"

² The woman answered the serpent, "We may eat from [all] the fruits of the trees of the garden, ³ except for the fruits of the tree in the middle of the garden. God said, "Do not eat from it, or touch it, because if you do you will die."

⁴ The serpent told the woman, "You will not die! ⁵ God knows that once you eat from it, your eyes will be opened, and you will be like God, knowing good and evil."

⁶ *The woman saw that the tree was good for food, appealing to the eyes* ⚖ and an attractive means for gaining understanding. She took some of its fruit, and ate. She also

---

⚖ **2:16–17 Self-controlled**
"You may eat from every tree in the garden, except from the Tree of Knowledge of Good and Evil." In many aspects of life you may indulge and receive pleasure, but there are always some restrictions for your own well-being.

⚖ **2:17, 3:3 Misleading**
"If you do, you will certainly die..." God said to Adam not to eat from the Tree. Eve changed God's instruction by adding "and don't touch it." She touched it and didn't die. Then she ate its fruit, and instantly lost her immortality. Misleading statements can lead to personal disaster.

⚖ **2:18 Sociable**
"It is not good that the man is alone." One should be inclined to associate with or be in the company of others. A key aspect of our lives is our relationships with others. True fulfillment of life requires this characteristic.

⚖ **2:24 Filial**
"Therefore a man will leave his father and his mother and cling to his wife, and they will become one flesh." The prime responsibilities and loyalties of both husbands and wives shall be to each other.

⚖ **3:6 Lustful**
"The woman saw that the tree was good for food, appealing to the eyes..." Lust and being desirous of the forbidden must be controlled.

gave some to her husband, and he ate.

7 Thus the eyes of both of them were opened, and they know that they were naked. ***They sewed fig leaves together, and made loincloths for themselves.*** ⅗ **8** Then they heard the voice of God moving through the Garden like the day breeze, and ***the man and his wife hid from God*** ⅗ among the trees of the garden.

9 God called out to the man, "Where are you?"

10 He answered, "I heard Your voice in the Garden. I was afraid because I was naked, so I hid."

11 He said, "Who told you that you were naked? Did you eat from the tree from which I commanded you not to eat?"

12 The man said, ***"The woman you created to be with me gave to me from the tree, and I ate."*** ⅗

13 God said to the woman, "What have you done?" And the woman said, "The serpent deceived me, and I ate."

14 God said to the serpent, "Because you did this, you, of all the domesticated animals and the animals of the field, are cursed. You will move on your belly, and will eat dirt all the days of your life. **15** I will create animosity between you and the woman, and between your offspring and her offspring. He will stamp on your head, and you will bite his heel."

The Woman's Punishment

16 To the woman, He said, "I will greatly increase your pain in pregnancy, and childbirth will also be painful. Your desire will be for your husband, and he will dominate you."

Man's Punishment

17 To the man, He said, "Because you listened to your wife, and you ate from the tree from which I commanded you not to, the land will be cursed for you; with struggle you will eat from it all the days of your life. **18** Thorns and thistles will grow for you, and you will eat of the grass of the field. **19** ***By the sweat of your brow will you eat bread,*** ⅗ until you return to the earth [*adamah*] from where you were taken. You are dust, and to dust you will return."

20 The man called his wife "Eve" [*Chavah*] since she was the mother of all life [*chai*]. **21** God made leather garments for Adam and his wife, and clothed them.

Banishment from the Garden

22 God said, "Adam has become like one of us, knowing good and evil. Now he might stretch out his hand and also take from the Tree of Life and eat, and live forever."

23 So God sent him from the Garden of Eden to work the

⅗ **3:7 Modest**
"They sewed fig leaves together, and made loincloths for themselves." We learn of the importance of modesty very early in the text. It is important to assure modesty in our dress as well as in all aspects of our lives.

⅗ **3:8 Concealing**
"...the man and his wife hid from God..." When one attempts to commit misdeeds in secret, we all know the true facts are usually revealed at one time or another. It is like pretending one can hide from God.

⅗ **3:12 Blame-passer**
."..the woman you created to be with me gave to me from the tree and I ate." Adam not only passed the blame for his disobedience on to Eve, but on to God himself, who created Eve for the benefit of Adam (Man). Take responsibility for your own actions.

⅗ **3:19 Hardworking**
"By the sweat of your brow shall you eat bread..." Although it may sound like a curse, very often what seems like a curse can be a blessing. Man will always derive more pleasure from accomplishing things which required more effort on his part, than from the things which required little or no effort. We are all well aware of this phenomenon in our life every day. "According to the effort, comes the reward."

earth from which he was taken. ²⁴ He banished Adam, and He placed Cherubs and a rotating, flaming sword to the east of the Garden of Eden, to guard the way to the Tree of Life.

Cain and Abel

4 ¹ Adam knew his wife Eve. She became pregnant and gave birth [to a son and named him] Cain, saying, "I have acquired [*kaniti*] a man with God." ² In addition, she gave birth to his brother, Abel. Abel was a shepherd, and Cain worked the land.

³ After some time, Cain brought a food offering to God from the fruit of the land. ⁴ Abel also brought [an offering], but from the firstborn of his sheep and of their milk. God favored Abel and his offering, ⁵ but not Cain and his offering, and ***Cain became very angry and dejected.*** ⚖

⁶ God said to Cain, "Why are you angry, and why are you dejected? ⁷ If you did the right thing would I not accept it? But by not doing the right thing, mistake crouches at the doorstep. It desires you, but you can rule over it." ⁸ [One day], Cain engaged his brother Abel in conversation, and when they were in the field, Cain attacked his brother Abel and killed him.

⁹ God said to Cain, "Where is your brother Abel?" He answered, "I don't know. ***Am I my brother's keeper?"*** ⚖

¹⁰ Then [God] said, "What have you done? The voice of your brother's blood shouts out to Me from the ground. ¹¹ You are now cursed by the land that has opened its mouth, taking your brother's blood from your hand. ¹² You will work the land, but it will no longer give you of its bounty. You will be a wanderer in the land."

¹³ Cain said to God, "My sin is too great a burden to bear. ¹⁴ You have already banished me from upon the surface of the land, and from You I will have to hide; I will be a wanderer, and anyone who finds me will kill me."

¹⁵ God said to him, "What you say is true. Therefore, for anyone who kills Cain, a vengeance will be taken against him seven times more." God placed a sign upon Cain, disallowing anyone who finds him from striking him. ¹⁶ Cain left from before God, and settled in the land of Nod, to the east of Eden.

¹⁷ ***Cain knew his wife, and she became pregnant. She gave birth to Enoch. Cain built a city, which he called "Enoch," after his son.*** ⚖

¹⁸ Enoch fathered Irad, and Irad fathered Mechuyael. Mechuyael fathered Metushael, and Metushael fathered Lemech.

¹⁹ Lemech married two wives. The name of one was

⚖ **4:5 Jealous**
"Cain became very angry and dejected." Jealousy only breeds anger and misery. In this extreme case, it led to murder. Jealousy always leads to unhappiness.

⚖ **4:9 Caring**
"Am I my brother's keeper?" Yes, you are your brother's keeper. In fact, you should strive to be your brother's keeper. Caring for and working together with others helps you to reach your personal and collective goals.

⚖ **4:17 Optimistic**
"Cain knew his wife...She gave birth to Enoch...Cain built a city, which he called "Enoch," after his son." Even though he was cut off from the rest of the world, he did not despair. On the contrary, he had children, and on his own initiative, built a whole city. You too can look forward to the future with an optimistic outlook. You will be surprised how you can reverse trends.

Adah, and the name of the second was Tzillah.

²⁰ Adah gave birth to Yaval, who was the ancestor of those who live in tents and have cattle. ²¹ His brother's name was Yuval who was the ancestor of all those who play the lyre and the pipes. ²² Tzillah also fathered Tuval-cain, the maker of copper and iron implements. The sister of Tuval-cain was Naamah.

²³ Lemech said to his wives Adah and Tzillah, "Listen to me, wives of Lemech, listen to my words. I have killed a man by wounding [him], and a young man by bruising [him]. ²⁴ If Cain will be avenged seven times, then for Lemech it will be seventy-seven times!"

²⁵ *Adam knew his wife again, and she gave birth to a son.* She called him Seth [*Shet*], "because God has given [*shat*] me another child to replace Abel, whom Cain killed."

²⁶ A son was also born to Seth. He called him Enosh. *It was then that people began to pray using God's Name.*

The Generations of Adam

5 ¹ This is the book of the generations of Adam, from the day God created Man, whom He had made in the likeness of God. ² He created a male and female, and He blessed them. He called them Man [*adam*] on the day they were created.

³ Adam lived one hundred thirty years and he fathered a son in his likeness and his image. He called him Seth.

⁴ The days of Adam, after he fathered Seth, were eight hundred years. He [also] had [other] sons and daughters. ⁵ Adam lived for nine hundred thirty years, and then died.

Seth: Second Generation

⁶ Seth lived one hundred and five years and he fathered Enosh. ⁷ Seth lived eight hundred seven years after he fathered Enosh, and had [other] sons and daughters.

⁸ Seth lived for nine hundred twelve years, and then died.

Enosh: Third Generation

⁹ Enosh lived ninety years and he fathered Kenan. ¹⁰ Enosh lived eight hundred fifteen years after he fathered Kenan, and had [other] sons and daughters.

¹¹ Enosh lived nine hundred five years, and then died.

Kenan: Fourth Generation

¹² Kenan lived seventy years and he fathered Mahalalel. ¹³ Kenan lived eight hundred forty years after he fathered Mahalalel, and had [other] sons and daughters.

4:25 Determined
"Adam knew his wife again, and she gave birth to a son..." Even though Abel was dead, and Cain was in exile because of his actions, Adam was undaunted, and determined to have an expanding family. Only with a wife and children can the ultimate pleasures of life be experienced.

4:26 Appreciative
"It was then that people began to pray using God's Name." With the realization that his hopes and aspirations were being accomplished through the actions of God, not only Adam, but others realized the beneficence of God and began to pray in His name. All of us can experience the emotional satisfaction of having our prayers answered—but, first we must pray.

14 Kenan lived nine hundred ten years, and then died.

Mahalalel: Fifth Generation

15 Mahalalel lived sixty-five years and he fathered Yered. **16** Mahalalel lived eight hundred thirty years after he fathered Yered, and had [other] sons and daughters.

17 Mahalalel lived eight hundred ninety-five years, and then died.

Yered: Sixth Generation

18 Yered lived one hundred sixty-two years and he fathered Enoch. **19** Yered lived eight hundred years after he fathered Enoch, and had [other] sons and daughters.

20 Yered lived nine hundred sixty-two years, and then died.

Enoch: Seventh Generation

21 Enoch lived sixty-five years and he fathered Methuselah. **22** Enoch walked with God for three hundred years after he fathered Methuselah, and had [other] sons and daughters.

23 Enoch lived for three hundred sixty-five years. **24** Enoch walked with God, and was taken by God.

Methuselah: Eighth Generation

25 Methuselah lived one hundred eighty-seven years and he fathered Lemech. **26** Methuselah lived seven hundred eighty-two years after he fathered Lemech, and had [other] sons and daughters.

27 Methuselah lived nine hundred sixty-nine years, and then died.

Lemech: Ninth Generation

28 Lemech lived one hundred eighty-two years and he fathered a son. **29** *He called him Noah, saying, "This one will console us from our work and from the toil of our hands* ⚖ caused by the ground which God cursed."

30 Lemech lived five hundred ninety-five years after he fathered Noah, and had [other] sons and daughters. **31** Lemech lived seven hundred seventy-seven years, and then died.

Noah: Tenth Generation

32 Noah was five hundred years old when he fathered Shem, Ham, and Yefet.

⚖ 5:29 **Forward-looking** *"He called him Noah, saying, 'This one will console us from our work and from the toil of our hands'…"* Even though the ground had been cursed and man was burdened by his toiling over the land, Lamech had the ability to look forward to a better time for all mankind through Noah. The ability to look forward to "better times" is a most important trait which enables us to cope with "today's problems."

6 ¹ Eventually Man began to multiply abundantly, and daughters were born to them. ² The sons of the rulers [*Nefilim*–The Fallen Ones] saw that the daughters of men were beautiful, ***and they took whomever they chose as wives.*** ⚖

³ God said, "My Spirit will not struggle with man forever. He is but flesh, and his days will be only one hundred and twenty years."

⁴ The Fallen Ones were on the earth from those days and onwards. The sons of the rulers came to the daughters of men, and fathered from them. They were the greatest men who ever existed, men of renown.

Destruction is Decreed

⁵ God saw that the evil of Man increased, and that all the desires of his inner thoughts were always evil. ⁶ God regretted that He ever made Man in the land, and His heart was saddened.

⁷ God said, "I will destroy Man, whom I created, from upon the face of the earth; from Man to beast, to the creeping things, and the flying creatures in the sky; I regret that I made them."

⁸ However, Noah found favor in God's eyes.

⚖ **6:2 Lustful**
"...and they took whomever they chose as wives." As the population grew, men became lustful and "took" women when and where they chose. They did not restrain themselves. It was then that the life span of men was shortened. Even today, as mankind yields to various forms of lust, (alcohol, smoking, overeating, and the like) he shortens his life.

The Flood and the Covenant

Noah

....

- ❧ *The Flood* ❧ *The Covenant*
- ❧ *The curse of Canaan* ❧ *The tower of Babel*
- ❧ *Ten generations to Abram*

⚖ **6:9 Righteous**
"Noah was a perfect and righteous man in his generation."
In the period when the people were so corrupt that God condemned them all to death in the flood, Noah stood out as the most righteous of men. We must all rise above the temptations in our environments and live righteous lives.

⚖ **6:11 Violent**
."..the land was filled with violence." When violence is ignored at the beginning, it will grow and spread without limit. It can pervade an entire nation. It must be nipped in the bud in any individual or group.

⚖ **6:18 Dependable**
"I will keep My covenant with you." Keeping one's word is one of the most important of all character traits. A person who doesn't keep his/her word is doomed to be friendless and even shunned by all who become aware of this trait. Alternatively, the person who is dependable and reliable is respected by all, and others take special efforts to befriend this person.

⁹ These are the generations of Noah. ***Noah was a perfect and righteous man in his generation;*** ⚖ Noah walked with God. ¹⁰ Noah fathered three sons: Shem, Ham, and Yefet.

¹¹ The world was corrupt before God, and ***the land was filled with violence.*** ⚖ ¹² God saw that the world was corrupt, and that all flesh across the land had perverted its ways.

The Flood

¹³ God said to Noah, "The end of all flesh has come before Me, because the land is filled with corruption. I will annihilate them from the land.

¹⁴ "Make an ark out of gopher wood for yourself. Make rooms in the ark, and seal it on the inside and outside, using pitch. ¹⁵ This is how to construct it: the ark must be three hundred cubits long, fifty cubits wide, and thirty cubits high. ¹⁶ Make a window for the ark, and slant it from the top so that it is one cubit wide. Place the door of the ark on the side. Make a lower level, a second level, and a third level.

¹⁷ "I, Myself, am bringing a flood of water upon the earth to destroy all living flesh which is under the heavens; all that is on the earth will die. ¹⁸ ***I will keep My covenant with you.*** ⚖ You will come into the ark, you, your sons, your wife, and the wives of your sons.

¹⁹ "Of every living creature of flesh, bring two of each kind into the ark with you, male and female. ²⁰ From the species of flying creatures, the species of livestock, and from all species of creeping things on the earth, two of each will come to you to survive.

21 "For yourselves, gather all kinds of food to be eaten, food for you and for them."

22 *Noah did all that God had commanded him to do.* ⚖

7 **1** God said to Noah, "You and all your household will go into the ark, since I have seen that you are righteous before Me in this generation. **2** From each of the pure [kosher] livestock you must take seven pairs, male and female. From the livestock that is not pure [unkosher], [take] two — male and female. **3** Also, of the flying creatures of the sky, [take] seven pairs, male and female, to keep their seed alive on the face of all the earth.

4 "In another seven days, I will cause rain to fall down upon the earth for forty days and forty nights. I will obliterate the entire world that I made, from upon the face of the earth."

5 Noah did according to all that God had commanded him.

6 Noah was six hundred years old when the Flood came upon the earth. **7** Noah, his sons, his wife, and the wives of his sons, came into the ark with him, because of the waters of the Flood. **8** The pure livestock, the impure livestock, the flying creatures, and all that crept on the land, **9** came by pairs of male and female to Noah and to the ark, as God had foretold to Noah.

10 After seven days, the waters of the Flood came upon the earth. **11** In the six hundredth year of Noah's life, in the second month [*Cheshvan*], on the seventeenth day of the month, all the fountains of the depths burst open; the windows of the skies opened up. **12** It rained on the land for forty days and forty nights.

13 On that day, Noah came to the ark, with Shem, Ham, and Yefet [the sons of Noah], as well as Noah's wife and the wives of his sons, **14** every species of animal according to its kind, all species of livestock according to its kind, every species of creeping thing, every species of flying creature– every bird and winged creature. **15** *All the living creatures came to Noah in pairs,* **16** *male and female,* ⚖ as God had foretold to him.

God shut him in [the ark].

17 The Flood was upon the land for forty days, [and] the waters increased until they raised and carried the ark above the earth. **18** The waters became stronger, and increased even more on the earth, while the ark floated on the face of the water. **19** The waters surged on the earth, until they covered the highest mountains, **20** and were fifteen cubits higher than the mountains.

⚖ **6:22 Diligent**
"Noah did all that God had commanded him to do." Although it took many years to carry out the program, he was diligent in carrying out every minute detail. Thus, he was successful in providing for the continuation of Man on earth.

⚖ **7:15-16 Orderly**
"All the living creatures came to Noah in pairs, male and female,..." Once again we are taught this trait. Organization and orderliness are mentioned many times in the Bible in order to reinforce this essential character trait. In these two verses, the concept of the orderliness and continuity of the world is emphasized by specifically mentioning "male and female".

21 All flesh perished from upon the earth: flying creatures, livestock, animals, creeping things that creep on the land, and all of mankind. 22 Everything on dry land that breathed, died; 23 everything that existed on the face of the earth was eradicated, from man to animal, from creeping things to the birds in the sky. Only Noah and all that was with him in the ark survived.

24 The waters strengthened their flow on the earth for one hundred fifty days.

8 1 Then God remembered Noah, and all the animals and livestock that were with him in the ark. God caused a wind to pass over the earth, and the water subsided. 2 The fountains of the deep and the windows of the sky were shut, and the rain from the skies ended. 3 The waters continually receded from the land, and at the end of one hundred fifty days, the waters subsided.

4 On the seventeenth of the seventh month, the ark rested on the mountains of Ararat. 5 The waters continued to wane until the tenth month. On the first of the tenth month, the tops of the mountains could be seen.

6 At the end of forty days, Noah opened the window of the ark that he had made. 7 He sent out a raven, which went back and forth until the water dried on the land.

8 Then he sent the dove out to see if the water had receded from the earth's surface. 9 But the dove couldn't find a place to rest its feet, so it returned to him and the ark; the water was still on the surface of the earth. He put out his hand and took it into the ark.

10 He waited another seven days, and again he sent the dove from the ark. 11 Then, toward evening, the dove returned to him, carrying a plucked olive leaf in its mouth. Noah then knew that the waters had receded from the land. 12 He waited another seven days and again sent out the dove, *but this time she didn't come back.* ⚖

⚖ 8:6-12 **Testing .".. but this time she didn't come back."** Noah conducted the tests with the birds to assure the safety of his leaving the ark and to assure the safety of his cargo. It is always wise to test unknown situations before plunging ahead.

13 By the six hundred first year [of Noah's life], in the first month [*Tishrei*], on the first day of the month, the waters had dried up from upon the land, and Noah removed the hatch from the ark, looked out, and [saw that] the surface of the ground was drying. 14 By the twenty-seventh of the second month [*Cheshvan*], the land had dried up.

The New World Order

15 Then God told Noah, 16 "Leave the ark, you and your wife, your sons, and your son's wives. 17 Bring out all the animals that are with you, the birds, the livestock, and every creeping

thing that crawls on the land; bring them out with you so that they can breed and be fruitful and multiply on the land."

18 Noah went out, as did his sons, his wife, and his son's wives with him. **19** Every animal, every creeping thing, and every flying creature that crawls on the land, each according to their species, left the ark.

20 Noah built an altar to God and took [offerings] from all the pure [kosher] livestock and from all the pure [kosher] fowl, and offered burnt-offerings on the altar.

21 God smelled the pleasing odor, and God said, "I will never again curse the land because of mankind, *for the impulse of man's heart is evil from his youth.* ⚏ Nor will I ever again exterminate all living creatures as I have done. **22** For the rest of the earth's history, seed time and harvest, cold and heat, summer and winter, day and night, will not cease to occur [ever again]."

9 **1** God then blessed Noah and his sons, and He said to them, "Be fruitful and multiply and fill the earth. **2** The fear of you, and the dread of you will be upon every living creature on the land, every bird in the sky, all that creeps on the ground, and all the fish in the sea; everything is given over to you. **3** Every creeping creature that is alive may be food for you, just like the green vegetation that I have given you. **4** But meat of a living creature you may not eat while it is alive.

5 "Only for your own blood will I require an accounting. I will require it from every living creature, from the hand of man, [and from] the hand of one's own brother; I will require it of [every] human life. **6** *Whosoever sheds a man's blood, by man will his blood be shed,* ⚏ because *man was made in the image of God.* ⚏

7 "Be fruitful and multiply, and breed abundantly on the land."

The Rainbow

8 God said to Noah and to his sons with him, **9** "I will keep My covenant with you and with your descendants after you, **10** and with every living animal that is with you from the birds, the livestock, and from all animals of the earth—with all that came out of the ark. **11** I will establish my covenant with you and will never cut off all life again by the waters of the Flood; never again will there be a Flood to destroy the earth."

12 God said, "This is a sign of the covenant that I make between Me and you, and between all living animals that are with you, for all generations forever. **13** I have placed My rainbow in the clouds, and it will serve as a covenant, as a sign

⚏ **8:21 Evil Minded**
"for the impulse of man's heart is evil from his youth." The evil inclination is pointed out as a natural tendency from our youth, which makes it all the more difficult to conquer. It is an ongoing battle, but one which must be fought to achieve morality and success in life through our own unfettered free will.

⚏ **9:6 Destructive**
"Whosoever sheds a man's blood, by man will his blood be shed..." Murder stems from a destructive desire to obliterate another person from the world. When a person is destroyed, so is all his potential in this world. Gossip and tale bearing, according to Judaism, is a spiritual form of murder. When a person gossips about another, the one who gossips is destroying the other person's potential for accomplishments in this world, and the one who listens is just as guilty.

⚏ **9:6 Appreciative**
"...man was made in the image of God." All human beings have the Divine spark in them. When you realize that your spouse, your children, and your neighbors have that spark, you will appreciate them more and respect their ideas more. You will learn that something can be learned from everyone and you will have a heightened appreciation of those around you.

between Me and the earth. **14** When I cloud the earth, the rainbow will be seen in the clouds. **15** I will remember My covenant between Me and you, and between all living animals. Never again shall the waters become a flood to destroy all flesh. **16** The rainbow will be in the clouds, and I will see it to remember the eternal covenant between God and between all living animals — all flesh which is upon the earth."

17 God said to Noah, "This is the sign of the covenant which I have established between Me and between all flesh which is upon the earth."

Shem's Blessing, and Canaan's Curse

18 The sons of Noah who left the ark were Shem, Ham, and Yefet. Ham was the father of Canaan. **19** These three are the sons of Noah, from whom the whole earth was populated.

20 Noah began to be a man of the soil, and he planted a vineyard. **21** *He drank from the wine and became drunk, and lay uncovered in the tent.* ⚖ **22** Ham, the father of Canaan, saw the nakedness of his father and told it to his two brothers outside.

23 Shem and Yefet took a cloak and placed it on both their shoulders, *and walked backwards to cover their father, facing backwards in order to avoid seeing their father's nakedness.* ⚖

24 Noah awoke from his wine and realized what his youngest son had done to him. **25** He said, "Cursed be Canaan! A slave's slave shall he be to his brothers!" **26** And then he said, "Blessed is God, the Lord of Shem, may Canaan be a slave to him! **27** May God enlarge Yefet, yet may He dwell in the tents of Shem. May Canaan be a slave to them."

28 Noah lived after the flood for three hundred fifty years. **29** Noah lived nine hundred fifty years, and then died.

Descendants of Yefet and Ham

10 **1** These are the generations of Noah's sons. Shem, Ham, and Yefet, [to whom] children were born after the Flood.

2 The sons of Yefet were Gomer, Magog, Madai, Yavan, Tuval, Meshech, and Tiras.

3 The sons of Gomer were Ashkenaz, Rifat, and Togarmah.

4 The sons of Yavan were Elishah, Tarshish, Kittim, and Dodanim.

5 From these the island nations branched out into their lands, each according to his language, according to their families in their nations.

⚖ **9:21 Alcoholic**
"He drank from the wine and became drunk, and lay uncovered in the tent." Even though he was a righteous man, he became drunk. When one becomes drunk, one loses complete control of his thinking and actions. Almost anything can happen and quite often does — from driving accidents to violent personal arguments and perhaps even physical violence. Be very wary about this character trait.

⚖ **9:23 Respectful**
"...and walked backwards to cover their father, facing backwards in order to avoid seeing their father's nakedness." They did this in order to show proper respect to their father, despite his failings. This character trait is again expressed later when God includes "Honor your father and mother" in the Ten Commandments.

6 The sons of Ham were Cush, Mitzrayim, Put, and Canaan.

7 The sons of Cush were Seba, Chavilah, Sabtah, Ramah, and Sabteca. The sons of Ramah were Sheba and Dedan.

8 Cush fathered Nimrod, and he began to be powerful in the land. 9 He was a great hunter before God, [and] thus was born the expression, "Like Nimrod, a great hunter before God." 10 The beginning of his kingdom was Babylon, Erech, Akkad, and Calneh in the land of Shinar.

11 From that land came Ashur who built Nineveh, Rechovot-ir and Kalach, that is the great city.

13 Mitzrayim fathered Ludim, Anamim, Lehavim, Naftuchim, 14 Patrusim, and Casluchim, from whom the Philistines descended, and the Caftorim.

The Descendants of Ham
15 Canaan fathered Sidon, his firstborn, and Chet, 16 as well as the Jebusites, the Amorites, the Girgashites, 17 the Hivites, the Arkites, the Sinites, 18 the Arvadites, the Tzemarites, and the Chamatites. After that, the Canaanite families became scattered.

19 The Canaanite borders were from Sidon toward Gerar until Gaza, towards Sodom, Gomorah, Admah, and Tzevoyim [until Lasha].

20 These are the sons of Ham according to their families, and their languages, according to their lands and their nations.

The Descendants of Shem
21 Shem, the ancestor of the descendants of Ever, [and] the brother of Yefet the elder, also had children. 22 The sons of Shem were Elam, Ashur, Arpachshad, Lud, and Aram.

23 The sons of Aram were Utz, Chul, Getter, and Mash.

24 Arpachshad fathered Shelach, and Shelach fathered Eber.

25 Eber had two sons; the name of one was Peleg, because in his days the land was divided [*niflagah*]. The name of his brother was Yoktan.

26 Yoktan fathered Almodad, Shelef, Chatzarmavet, and Yerach, 27 Hadoram, Uzal, and Diklah, 28 Oval, Avimael, and Sheba, 29 Ophir, Chavilah, and Yovav—all these were the sons of Yoktan. 30 They lived [in the land] from Mesha to Sephar, the eastern mountain.

31 These are the descendants of Shem according to their families, their languages, by their lands and according to their nations.

32 These are the families of the sons of Noah according to their generations, according to their nations. From these the nations spread out upon the earth after the Flood.

The Tower of Babel

11 **1** At that time, all the earth spoke one language, and was united in speech.

2 As they journeyed from the east, they found a valley in the land of Shinar, and settled there. **3** Then, each man said to his neighbor, "Let's make bricks and burn them thoroughly." They had brick to use as stone, and they used asphalt as mortar.

4 Then they said, *"Let us build a city, with a tower whose top will reach into Heaven. We'll make ourselves famous* ☍ [to prevent ourselves] from being scattered over the face of the earth."

5 God descended to see the city and the tower that the people had made. **6** God said, "They are one nation with one language, and this is what they do! Now nothing will stop them from what they set out to do. **7** Come, let us go down and confound their language, so that one person will not be able to understand the language of the other."

8 Therefore, God scattered them from there over the face of the whole earth, and they stopped building the city, **9** which is called "Babel," because that is where God confounded [*balal*] the language of the whole earth. From there God scattered them over the face of the earth.

Shem: The Eleventh Generation

10 These are the generations of Shem. Shem was one hundred years old when he fathered Arpachshad, which was two years after the Flood.

11 Shem lived after he fathered Arpachshad five hundred years, and fathered [other] sons and daughters.

Arpachshad: The Twelfth Generation

12 Arpachshad lived for thirty-five years and fathered Shelach.

13 Arpachshad lived after he fathered Shelach for four hundred three years, and fathered [other] sons and daughters.

Shelach: The Thirteenth Generation

14 Shelach lived for thirty years and fathered Eber.

15 Shelach lived after he fathered Eber for four hundred three years, and fathered [other] sons and daughters.

☍ **11:4 Arrogant**
"Let us build a city, with a tower whose top will reach into Heaven. We'll make ourselves famous..." This is a negative character trait which eventually leads to one's downfall. While unity in language and speech is a most important element amongst people, these people became arrogant and used this blessing to reach into, and attempt to control, Heaven. The punishment for this ultimate arrogance is well known, yet the lesson of Babel in our everyday world is yet to be appreciated.

Eber: The Fourteenth Generation

16 Eber lived for thirty years and fathered Peleg.

17 Eber lived after he fathered Peleg for four hundred thirty years, and fathered [other] sons and daughters.

Peleg: The Fifteenth Generation

18 Peleg lived for thirty years and fathered Reu.

19 Peleg lived after he fathered Reu for two hundred nine years, and fathered [other] sons and daughters.

Reu: The Sixteenth Generation

20 Reu lived for thirty-two years and he fathered Serug.

21 Reu lived after he fathered Serug for two hundred seven years, and fathered [other]sons and daughters.

Serug: The Seventeenth Generation

22 Serug lived for thirty years and fathered Nachor.

23 Serug lived after he fathered Nachor for two hundred years, and fathered [other] sons and daughters.

Nachor: The Eighteenth Generation

24 Nachor lived for twenty-nine years and he fathered Terach.

25 Nachor lived after he fathered Terach for one hundred nineteen years, and fathered [other] sons and daughters.

Terach and Abram: The Nineteenth and Twentieth Generation

26 Terach lived for seventy years and fathered Abram, Nachor, and Charan.

27 These are the generations of Terach: Terach fathered Abram, Nachor, and Charan; Charan fathered Lot. **28** Charan died before Terach his father did, in his birthplace, Ur of the Chaldees.

29 Abram and Nachor married. The name of Abram's wife was Sarai, and the name of Nachor's wife was Milcah, the daughter of Charan who was also the father of Iscah. **30** Sarai was barren and had no children.

31 Terach took Abram his son, Charan's son, Lot, Sarai his daughter-in-law, the wife of his son Abram, and left Ur of the Chaldees for the land of Canaan. When they arrived in Charan, they settled there [instead].

32 Terach lived for two hundred five years, and Terach died in Charan.

Abram's departure from Ur

Lech Lecha

· ·

&. *Abram journeys to Canaan*

&. *Pharaoh takes Sarai* &. *Abram battles the Kings*

&. *Covenant With God* &. *Birth of Ishmael*

&. *Name Changes* &. *Circumcision*

⚖ 12:1 **Selective**
.".. Go for yourself, from your land, from your birthplace, and from your father's house..."
Be selective about your environment, your community, and your friends for your own benefit. Choose an atmosphere that will raise your positive values, not diminish them. Sometimes it is very difficult to make such a change in one's lifestyle, including giving up certain comforts and conveniences, but the road to self-improvement requires such efforts and the reward is worth the effort.

Abram's Journey to Canaan

12 ¹ God said to Abram, ***"Go for yourself [lech-lecha] from your land, from your birthplace, and from your father's house,*** ⚖ to the land which I will show you. ² I will make you into a great nation; I will bless you and I will make your name great. You will be a blessing, ³ [and] I will bless those who bless you; the one who curses you, I will curse. All the families of the earth will be blessed through you."

⁴ Abram left as God told him to, and Lot went with him. Abram was seventy-five years old when he left from Haran. ⁵ Abram took Sarai his wife, Lot, his brother's son, all the property that they had acquired, and the souls that they had converted in Haran, [and] went toward the land of Canaan. Upon arriving in Canaan, ⁶ Abram traveled to Shechem [and] to Plain of Moreh. The Canaanites were in the land at that time.

⁷ God appeared to Abram and said, "I will give this land to your descendants." He built an altar there to God who had appeared to him. ⁸ He moved from there toward the mountain to the east of Beth-El, and pitched his tent with Beth-El to the west, and the city of Ai to the east. He built an altar there to God, and called out in the name of God.

⁹ Abram continued on his way toward the South.

Famine, Sojourn in Egypt, and Return

¹⁰ A famine occurred in the land, and Abram went down to Egypt for a while because of the severity of the famine.

11 As he approached Egypt, he said to Sarai his wife, "I have known how beautiful a woman you are. 12 When the Egyptians see you they will say, 'She is his wife,' and will kill me and keep you alive. 13 Please tell them you are my sister so that they will treat me well on your behalf, and my life will be spared because of you."

14 When Abram came to Egypt, the Egyptians saw that the woman was very beautiful. 15 The Pharaoh's ministers saw her and praised her to Pharaoh. The woman was taken to Pharaoh's house. 16 He treated Abram well on her behalf, [and] Abram acquired sheep, cattle, donkeys, slaves, maid-servants, female donkeys, and camels.

17 But God inflicted Pharaoh and his household with severe plagues because of Sarai, Abram's wife. 8 Pharaoh summoned Abram and said, "What have you done to me? Why didn't you tell me that she was your wife? 19 Why did you say, 'She's my sister,' and let me take her for a wife for myself? Now, take your wife and go!"

20 Pharaoh gave men orders concerning him, and they sent him away, with his wife and all that he had.

13

1 Abram went up from Egypt toward the South with his wife, with all that he had, and with Lot. 2 Abram had become very rich with cattle, silver and gold.

3 He went on his journey from the South up to Beth-El, where his tent had originally been, between Beth-El and Ai, 4 to the altar that he had first made there. There Abram called out in the name of God.

5 Lot, who was traveling with Abram, also had sheep, cattle, and tents. 6 The land couldn't support them both while they lived together because they had so may posses-sions; they weren't able to remain together.

7 An argument broke our between the herdsmen of Abram's flocks and of Lot's flocks. At that time the Canaanites and the Perizites were living in the land.

8 Abram said to Lot, "***Please, let no argument occur between me and you,*** ⚖ between my herdsmen and your herdsmen. We are brothers. 9 Is not the whole land before you? Please separate from me. ***If you go to the left, I'll go to the right. If you go to the right, then I'll go to the left.***" ⚖

10 Lot looked and saw the whole plain of the Jordan, and how well it was watered. This was before God destroyed Sodom and Gomorah. It was like a garden of God, like the land of Egypt was as you come to Tzoar. 11 Lot chose the whole plain of the Jordan for himself, and journeyed east-ward, and the two separated from one another.

⚖ **13:8 Peace Pursuing**
"Please, let no argument occur between me and you..." Abram chose to part from Lot rather than fight with him over land for the cattle, but before he leaves he offers a gesture of peace. This illustrates the importance of striving for peace even if it means making a material sacri-fice. Peace between people leads to one of the most important aspects of living—peace of mind.

⚖ **13:9 Unselfish**
"If you go to the left, I'll go to the right. If you go to the right, then I'll go to the left." Abram concedes to Lot by giving him first choice of the grazing ground. Permitting another person to choose first is an act of giving and giving is an act of love. The Hebrew word for love is *AHAVAH*. The root of this word, *HAV,* means "to give." When you give to another person, their joy becomes your joy.

⚖️ **13:12-13 Careless** . "..*Lot camped by Sodom. The men of Sodom were evil...*" Sodom was known as a wicked city and yet Lot chose to live there. He should have known better and surely there would come a time when he would rue this careless or poor judgment decision. The same is true for all of us. Life's decisions must be made carefully, taking all considerations into account.

[12] Abram dwelled in the land of Canaan; Lot lived in the cities of the plain, ***and camped by Sodom,*** [13] ***The men of Sodom were evil,*** ⚖️ and transgressed greatly against God.

[14] God said to Abram, after Lot had separated from him, "Look to the north, to the south, to the east, and to the west. [15] All the land that you see, I will give to you and to your descendants forever. [16] I will make your descendants like the dust of the earth. Just as the dust of the earth cannot be counted, so too will it be impossible for your descendants to be counted. [17] Go and travel around the land, on its length and its width, for I will give it to you."

[18] Abram traveled [and] came and settled at the Oaks of Mamre, which are in Hebron. There he built an altar to God.

War Amongst the Canaanite Kings

14 [1] In the days of Amrafel king of Shinar, Arioch king of Elasar, Kedorla'omer king of E'lam, and Tidal king of Goyim, [2] made war with Bera king of Sodom, Birsha king of Gomorah, Shinab king of Admah, Shemeber king of Tzevoyim, and the king of Bela, now Tzo'ar.

[3] All of these had joined together in the valley of Siddim, which is the Salt Sea. [4] For twelve years, they had served Kedorla'omer, and in the thirteenth year, they rebelled. [5] In the fourteenth year, Kedorla'omer came with the kings that were with him, and they defeated the Refaim in Ashterot-Karnaim, the Zuzim in Ham, and the Eimim in Shaveh-Kiryataim; [6] [they defeated] the Horites in the hill-country of Mount Seir, up to Eil-Paran, which is by the desert. [7] They returned, came to Ein-Mishpat, presently Kadesh, and they defeated the entire field of the Amalekites, as well as the Amorites who lived in Chatzatzon-Tamar.

[8] The king of Sodom, the king of Gomorah, the king of Admah, the king of Tzevoyim, and the king of Bela [which is Tzo'ar], went out and joined to do battle with them in the valley of Siddim, [9] against Kedorla'omer, the king of Eilam, [against] Tidal, the king of Goyim, [against] Amrafel, the king of Shinar, and [against] Arioch, the king of Elasar. [There were] four kings against the five.

[10] The valley of Siddim was full of tar pits, and when the kings of Sodom and Gomorah fled, they fell into them; the remaining ones fled to the mountains. [11] [The victors] took all the possessions of Sodom and Gomorah and all their food and left. [12] They [also] took Lot [the son of Abram's brother] and his possessions [he had been living in Sodom]. [13] One person [who escaped] came and told Abram the Hebrew, who

was living at the plains of Mamre [the Amorite]. [Mamre was] the brother of Eshkol, and the brother of Aner; they were allies of Abram.

14 **When Abram heard that his relative was taken captive, he armed his trained servants** ⚖ who were born in his house, **three hundred eighteen of them, and they pursued [the conquerors] to Dan.** ⚖ **15** He divided [the men] against them at night, he and his servants, and they attacked them and pursued them to Chovah which is north of Damascus.

16 [After his victory] he returned all the possessions, Lot his relative, [Lot's] possessions, and all the women and the people.

17 The king of Sodom went out to meet him after his return from the battle with Kedorla'omer and the allied kings, to the Valley of Shaveh [which is the Valley of the King]. **18** **Malki-tzedek, king of Salem** [and a priest to God, the Most High], **brought out bread and wine.** ⚖ **19** He blessed him and said, "Blessed be Abram to God, the Most High, the Owner of heaven and earth. **20** Blessed be God, the Most High, who delivered those who wanted to kill you, into your hand."

Abram gave him one-tenth of everything.

21 The king of Sodom said to Abram, "Give me the people, and the possessions take for yourself."

22 Abram said to the king of Sodom, "I have vowed to God, the Most High, the Owner of heaven and earth! **23** **I will not take even a thread to a shoelace from anything of yours.** ⚖ You will not [be able to] say, 'I made Abram rich. **24** [I won't take anything] except for what the young men ate, and the share of the men who went with me, Aner, Eshkol, and Mamre. They can take their share."

The Pact Between the Halves

15 **1** After these events occurred, the word of God came to Abram in a vision, saying, "Don't be afraid Abram, I am your shield; your reward is very great."

2 Abram said, "My Lord, God, what will You give to me? I go childless, and the custodian of my household is Eliezer! **3** You have not given me children, and a member of my household instead is my heir!"

4 The word of God came to him saying, "This one will not be your heir. Rather one who will go out from your own bowels—he will be your heir."

5 He brought him outside and said, "Look toward heaven and count the stars, if you are able to count them!"

⚖ 14:14 **Family Devoted**
"When Abram heard that his relative was taken captive, he armed his trained servants..." Although Lot and Abram had their differences, when Abram heard of Lot's capture he did not hesitate to run to his resentful relative's aid. No one can replace your parents, siblings, or other relatives. Be appreciative of your family relationships.

⚖ 14:14 **Courageous**
."..he armed his trained servants, three hundred eighteen of them, and they pursued [the conquerors] to Dan." It took exceptional courage to pursue the massive, conquering armies of four kingdoms with only three hundred eighteen men. But he did it, and for no personal gain or advantage. Courage is measured in many ways, but courage for a righteous cause is the most vital and the most durable.

⚖ 14.17-18 **Hospitable**
"Malki-tzedek, king of Salem... brought out bread and wine." The king of Salem (modern day Jerusalem) had come out to meet him and brought him bread and wine. These forms of greetings—actually going out to meet a guest and bring him in and offering food and drink are signs of true hospitality.

⚖ 14:23 - 24 **Altruistic**
"I will not take even a thread to a shoelace from anything of yours...." He could have easily justified receiving a reward for his actions, but he had saved everyone out of brotherly love. He never expected to be rewarded by others for his actions. We too can elevate ourselves above the rest of society with altruistic actions.

He said to him, "So will be your descendants."

⁶ He believed in God, and he considered it as righteousness.

⁷ He said to him, "I am God who brought you out of Ur of the Chaldees, to give you this land as an inheritance."

⁸ And he said, "My Lord God, how can I know that I will inherit it?"

⁹ He said to him, "Take a three-year-old female calf, a three-year-old female goat, a three-year-old ram, a turtle dove, and a young pigeon."

¹⁰ He took all of these, and he split them in the middle, and placed each piece opposite the other half. However, the birds he didn't cut up.

¹¹ Birds of prey descended upon the carcasses, and Abram drove them away. ¹² As the sun was setting, a deep sleep came to Abram, and a deep and dark dread fell upon him.

¹³ [God] said to Abram, "Know that your descendants will be strangers in a land that is not theirs, and [the host nation] will enslave them, and afflict them for four hundred years.

¹⁴ "However, the nation they will serve I will judge, and afterwards they will leave with great possessions. ¹⁵ You will come to your fathers in peace, and be buried in a good old age. ¹⁶ However, only the fourth generation will return here, because the iniquity of the Amorites will not be complete until then."

¹⁷ When the sun had set, there was a thick darkness. A smoking furnace and a flaming torch had passed between the [cut up] pieces [of the carcasses]. ¹⁸ On that day, God made a covenant with Abram, saying, ***"To your descendants I have given this land, from the river of Egypt to the great river, the Euphrates;*** ⌗ ¹⁹ [the land of] the Kenites, the Kenizites, the Kadmonites, ²⁰ the Hittites, the Perizites, the Refaim, ²¹ the Amorites, the Canaanites, the Girgashites, and the Jebusites."

16

¹ Sarai, Abram's wife, was barren, and she had an Egyptian maidservant named Hagar.

² Sarai said to Abram, "God has kept me from giving birth. ***Please, come to my maidservant. Perhaps I will have a son from her."*** ⌗

Abram listened to Sarai.

³ At the end of the ten years that Abram had lived in Canaan, Sarai, Abram's wife, took Hagar the Egyptian, her maidservant, and gave her to her husband Abram as a wife. ⁴ He came to Hagar, and she became pregnant. When [Hagar]

⌗ **15:18 Planner**
."..To your descendants I have given this land, from the river of Egypt to the great river, the Euphrates..." Although Abraham and his family and followers did not need such a large portion at that time, his descendants were to have need for the planned borders. It is always prudent to plan for the future.

⌗ **16:2 Altruistic**
" Please come to my maidservant. Perhaps I will have a son from her." Because Sarah sacrificed her position for the greater goal of producing a family, God rewarded her and she later gave birth to Isaac, the progenitor of the Jewish people. Once again, the rewards are proportional to the effort.

saw that she was pregnant, she despised her mistress [Sarai].

5 Sarai said to Abram, "You are to blame! I gave my maidservant to you, and now that she sees she is pregnant, she despises me! May God judge between me and you."

6 Abram said to Sarai, "Here is your maidservant; do with her as you see fit."

Sarai dealt harshly with her, and she ran away from her. **7** An angel of God found her by a spring of water in the desert, at the oasis on the way to Shur.

8 He said, "Hagar, Sarai's maidservant, *from where have you come, and to where are you going?* ⚖️ "

She said, "I am running away from Sarai my mistress."

9 The angel of God said to her, "Return to your mistress, and submit yourself to her." **10** The angel of God said to her, "I will greatly increase your descendants, so great in number that no one will be able to count them."

11 And the angel of God said to her, "You are pregnant, and you will give birth to a son. You will call him Ishmael, because God has heard [*shama*] your affliction. **12** He will be a wild man. His hand will be against everyone, and the hand of everyone [will be] against him. Yet, he will dwell over all of his brothers."

13 She called God, who had spoken to her, "You are a God of Vision," because, she said, "Did I not have a vision, and yet retain my sight?"

14 Therefore the well was called "The Well of the Vision of the Angel" [*Be'er LaChai Ro'i*]. It is between Kadesh and Bered.

15 Hagar bore a son for Abram. Abram called his son to whom Hagar had given birth, Ishmael. **16** Abram was eighty-six years old when Hagar gave birth to Ishmael.

Circumcision

17 **1** When Abram was ninety-nine years old, God appeared to Abram and He said to him, "*I am God Almighty; walk before Me and be perfect.* ⚖️ **2** I will make My covenant between Me and you, and I will multiply you very, very greatly."

3 Abram fell on his face, and God spoke to him saying; **4** "As far as I am concerned, My covenant is with you, and you will become a father of many nations. **5** *You shall no longer be called 'Abram,' but rather 'Abraham,' because I have made you a father of many nations* ⚖️ [*av hamon goyim*]. **6** I will make you very fruitful, and I will make nations from you. Kings will come out from you.

7 "I will establish My covenant between Me and you, and with your descendants after you throughout the generations.

⚖️ 16:8 **Goal-oriented**
"...from where have you come, and to where are you going."
This is one of the most critical questions one can ask oneself. It is the key to achievement and satisfaction and peace of mind. In every area of our lives we must have goals and must orient ourselves to achieving them. This simple question, which we should ask ourselves every day, would be a great aid in accomplishing the many objectives in our lives.

⚖️ 17:1 **Persistent**
"I am God Almighty; walk before Me and be perfect."
A person should always strive for perfection. Most people would think this is a frustrating goal and would not even know where to start. While the ultimate goal may not be fully achievable in every aspect, God's instructions to Abraham on the method for achieving this goal were very clear. "...walk before Me and be perfect." Abraham did, and he was the most perfect man who ever lived. Try it... it works.

⚖️ 17:5 **Acknowledging**
"You shall no longer be called 'Abram,' but rather 'Abraham,' because I have made you a father of many nations."
His name no longer reflected his outlook or his actions. His name was therefore changed to Abraham because he was and would continue to be "the father of nations," which translates as Abraham.

[It is] an eternal covenant to you and your descendants, I will be God. **8** I will give to you and to your descendants after you the land in which you now live—the entire land of Canaan, as an eternal possession. I will be their God."

9 And God said to Abraham, "And as for you, you must keep My covenant, you and your descendants after you throughout the generations. **10** This is My covenant between Me and you, which you, and your descendants after you must keep: circumcise every male among you.

11 *"You shall circumcise the flesh of your foreskin, as a sign of the covenant between Me and you.* 📖 **12** At the age of eight days you shall circumcise every male child born to you throughout the generations, or [slaves] purchased from any stranger that does not descend from you. **13** You must circumcise any [male] born in your house, and the one who is bought with your money. My covenant will be in your flesh as an eternal covenant. **14** The soul of the uncircumcised male, whose flesh of his foreskin is not circumcised, will be cut off from his people for having broken My covenant."

Promise of a Son from Sarah

15 God [further] said to Abraham, "Regarding Sarai, your wife, you shall no longer call her 'Sarai' but 'Sarah.' **16** I will bless her, and I will also give to you a son from her. I will bless her, and she will be [a mother] of nations. Kings of peoples will come from her."

17 Abraham fell on his face, and laughed. He said to himself, "Will someone who is one hundred years old have a son? Will Sarah, who is ninety-years old give birth?" **18** Abraham said to God, "If only Ishmael would live before You!"

19 God said, "But still, Sarah your wife will bear you a son, and you will call him Isaac, and I will establish My covenant with him as an eternal covenant, and with his descendants after him. **20** As for Ishmael, I have listened to you. I have blessed him, [and] I will make him fruitful and I will multiply him very greatly. He will give birth to twelve princes, and I will make him a great nation. **21** But My covenant I will establish with Isaac, who Sarah will bear for you by this time next year."

22 He finished speaking with him, and God left Abraham.

23 Abraham took Ishmael his son, and all those born in his house, and all those acquired by money—every male of Abraham's household—*and he circumcised the flesh of their foreskins as commanded by God, on the same day God had spoken to him.* ⚖

📖 17:13
"You shall circumcise the flesh of your foreskin, as a sign of the covenant between Me and you." To circumcise all male children at the age of eight days.

⚖ 17:23 **Prompt**
"...and he circumcised the flesh of their foreskins...on the same day God had spoken to him." Abraham fulfilled God's command on the same day notwithstanding the awesome burden and responsibility of the command. Prompt response to our responsibilities and obligations gives others confidence in us and, just as vital, creates an inner satisfaction about ourselves.

24 Abraham was ninety-nine years old when he was circumcised. **25** Ishmael, his son was thirteen years old when he was circumcised. **26** On the very same day *Abraham circumcised himself, Ishmael his son,* **27** *and all the men of his household,* ⚖ born in his house, or acquired with money from a stranger.

⚖ 17:26-27 **Trustworthy**
"...Abraham circumcised himself, Ishmael his son, and all the men of his household..."
Though circumcision was painful to them and set them apart from the world, the people of Abraham's household did not hesitate to follow him and his instructions because they trusted him. It is a gratifying feeling when others show that they can trust you. However, first you must prove that you are reliable and trustworthy by always keeping your word.

Glossary of Hebrew Terms

adam · *man; Adam, the first man*

adamah · *earth*

ahavah · *love*

aliyah · *rising, pl.* **aliyot**

Amalek · *nation that attacked the people of Israel in the desert to prevent them from entering Canaan*

arba'ah minim · *four species; the four species that are used ritually on Sukkot. They are: lulav (palm), etrog (citron), hadassim (myrtle), and aravot (willow).*

Aseret Hadibrot · *the Ten Commandments*

atzeret · *festival (as in Shemini Atzeret)*

aviv · *spring*

BaMidbar · *In the desert (the fourth book of the Bible)*

ben · *son; the son of*

bayit · *house*

beit · *house of*

Beit HaKnesset · *house of assembly (synagogue)*

Beit HaMidrash · *house of study*

Bereshit · *In the beginning; the first book of the Bible*

bimah · *the podium from which the Torah is read*

beracha · *blessing, pl.* **berachot**

chai · *live*

chaim · *life*

chesed · *righteousness*

chametz · *leaven, which is prohibited on Passover*

Chumash · *five; the Five Books of Moses*

darom · *south*

Devarim · *words; things; the fifth book of the Bible*

d'rash · *learning through investigation*

efod · *the breastplate worn by the High Priest*

esh · *fire*

etrog · *citron (one of the four species used on Sukkot)*

gadol · *large; one in a high stature, f.* **gedolah**

gan · *garden*

gaon · *title of the head of the yeshivot of Babylonia between the 6th and 11th centuries* CE

goy · *nation, pl.* **goyim**

Haggadah · *narration; the Book of the Passover Seder service*

halachah · *law, pl.* **halachot**

har · *mountain*

havdalah · *separation; the Sabbath closing ceremony*

kabbalah · *receiving; Jewish mysticism*

Kaddish · *sanctification; the prayer for the dead*

kadosh · *holy*

kavod · *honor*

kedushah · *holiness*

ketubah · *marriage contract*

Kiddush · *Sabbath and festival sanctification ritual*

kiddushin · *betrothal*

kippur · *atonement*

kohen · *priest, pl.* **kohanim**

Kohen Gadol · *the High Priest*

Kotel HaMa'aravi · *the Western Wall, a remnant of the wall surrounding the Second Temple in Jerusalem*

lechem · *bread*

luach · *chart; calendar*

lulav · *a palm branch (one of the four species used on Sukkot)*

ma'arav · *west*

ma'aser · *tithe given to the priests*

Maccabean · *one of the band of warriors who liberated the Temple from the Hellenists*

maror · *bitter herbs, eaten with the Pascal lamb at the Passover Seder*

matzah · *the unleavened bread eaten on Passover*

metzora · *one with a certain skin disease*

megillah · *scroll; specifically, one of five Bible books: Ruth, Esther, Song of Songs, Lamentations, and Ecclesiastes.*

Megillat Esther · *the Book of Esther*

middah · *character trait, pl.* **middot**

midrash · *investigating; learning; philosophical interpretations of the Bible in the form of parables*

mikveh · *ritual bath*

mishnah · *teaching; the oral law committed to writing*

mitzvah · *commandment, pl.* **mitzvot**

mizrach · *east*

mo'ed · *specified time; holiday, pl.* **mo'adim**

Nazirite · *one who accepts upon himself vows of abstention*

Negev · *the desert that forms the southern part of Israel*

Nezikin · *damages (one of the books of the Talmud)*

oleh · *that which ascends; one who is called to the reading of the Torah; an emigre to Israel*

oleh regel · *one on a pilgrimage to Jerusalem during a festival*

pardes · *paradise; garden; acronym for p'shat, remez, d'rush, and sod*

parasha · *chapter or portion (of the Bible), pl.* **parashiyot**

parshat · *chapter of*

patuach · *open; a break in the Torah text that starts on a new line, f.* **petucha**, *pl.* **petuchot**

Pesach · *Passover*

p'shat · *simple explanation*

remez · *hint; learning through connotations*

rishon · *first*

Sanhendrin · *the governing body of 70 members*

sefer · *book*

sha'atnez · *a forbidden mixture of wool and linen*

Shabbat · *the Sabbath*

shama · *heard*

Shamai · *a great scholar of the Tannaic era*

shanah · *year*

Shavuot · *weeks; the Feast of Weeks*

shema · *hear*

Shemot · *names; Exodus, the second book of the Bible*

shemittah · *the seventh year that is a Sabbatical for the land*

shemoneh esrei · *eighteen; the eighteen blessings that comprise the Amidah, recited at each of the daily prayers*

sheni · *second*

sheratzim · *crawling creatures*

shofar · *ram's horn, heard on Rosh Hashanah*

Shulchan Aruch · *the Code of Jewish Law*

simchah · *happiness*

Simchat Torah · *Feast of Rejoicing with the Torah*

sod · *secret*

setumah · *closed; a break in the Torah text that does not begin a new line, pl.* setumot

sukkah · *the booth that is used for eating and sleeping on Sukkot*

Sukkot · *booths (The Feast of Tabernacles)*

tallit · *prayer shawl*

talmud · *learning; the compilation of the Mishnah, elaborations on the Mishnah, and the Midrash*

talui · *dependent*

taryag · *the acronym for the number 613, the number of command- ments in the Torah*

tefillin · *phylacteries, the black leather boxes containing scriptures worn by men during morning weekday prayer*

tel · *hill, sometimes the site of an archaeological mound*

Torah · *the Bible, pl.* Torot

torat · *the Torah of*

terumah · *donation to the Tabernacle or Temple*

tzafon · *north*

tzelem · *image; shadow*

tzitzit · *fringes that are attached to a four- cornered garment*

tzora'at · *a disease affecting the human skin or a disease on the walls of houses*

vadai · *certain*

VaYikra · *And He called (Leviticus, the third book of the Bible)*

yeshiva · *sitting; Jewish house of learning, pl,* yeshivot

yom · *day*

Jewish Months

Nisan

Iyar   *Spring*

Sivan

Tammuz

Av   *Summer*

Elul

Tishrei

Cheshvan   *Fall*

Kislev

Tevet

Shevat   *Winter*

Adar

Some Selected Transmitters of Torah and Kabbalah

Chafetz Chaim · *Rabbi Yitzchak Kagan, (1837– 1933) best known for his works, the Mishnah Berurah and the Chafetz Chaim, the laws of proper speech*

Hillel · *a great scholar of the early Tannaic era, leader of Pharisees (1st century BCE)*

Hirsch, Samson Raphael · *German rabbi of the 19th century. A Biblical commentator*

Karo, Yosef · *famous Rabbi of 15th–16th century Safed, author of the Shulchan Aruch, the Code of Jewish Law. Also of the Beit Yosef, and the Kesef Mishnah.*

Luzzatto, Moshe Chaim · *mystical scholar of the 18th century, author of "The Path of the Just"*

Maharal · *Rabbi Judah Lowe, a leading rabbi of Prague in the 16th century CE. Renowned as the creator of the Golem, a legendary automaton.*

Rambam · *Maimonides, a great philosopher, commentator, codifier of laws, and physician of the 10th century CE. Author of Mishneh Torah and A Guide for the Perplexed.*

Ramban · *Rabbi Moshe ben Nachman, a scholar and commentator of the 12th century CE*

Rashi · *Rabbi Shimon Yitzchaki, a great scholar, author, and commentator of the 12th century CE*

Vilna Gaon · *a great talmudist and leader of Jewry in eighteenth century Lithuania*

The Hebrew Alphabet

Letters

Name	Pronunciation	Letter	Script	Rashi	Meaning	Value
Alef	silent	א	k	ﬠ	ox	1
Bet	B	בּ	ﬡ	ﬡ	house	2
Vet	V	ב	כ	כ		
Gimel	G (hard)	ג	ﬡ	ﬡ	camel	3
Dalet	D	ד	?	7	door	4
Hey	H	ה	ﬣ	ﬣ	window	5
Vav	V	ו	/	ו	hook	6
Zayin	Z	ז	ﬢ	ﬢ	weapon	7
Chet	Ch	ח	ﬣ	ﬣ	fence	8
Tet	T	ט	ﬣ	ﬣ	snake	9
Yud	Y	י	,	י	hand	10
Kof	K	בּ	ﬡ	כ	palm of hand	20
Chof	Ch	כ	ﬡ	כ		
Lamed	L	ל	ﬥ	ﬥ	ox goad	30
Mem	M	מ	ﬡ	ﬡ	water	40
Nun	N	נ	ﬡ	ﬡ	fish	50
Samech	S	ס	O	ﬡ	tent prop	60
Ayin	silent	ע	ﬡ	ﬠ	eye	70
Pey	P	פּ	ﬡ	פ	mouth	80
Fey	F	פ	ﬡ	פ		
Tzadi	Ts	צ	3	ﬥ	fish hook	90
Kuf	K	ק	ﬡ	ﬣ	back of head	100
Resh	R	ר	ﬧ	ﬥ	head	200
Shin	Sh	שׁ,שׂ	e,é	ﬢ,ﬡ	tooth	300
Sin	S	שׂ	é	ﬢ		
Taf	T	ת,ת	ﬡ,ﬡ	ﬡ,ﬡ	sign	400

The Hebrew Alphabet

Word-ending letters

Name	Pronunciation	Letter	Script	Rashi	Meaning	Value
Kof sofit	*K*	ךּ	ךּ	ך	*palm of hand*	20
Chof sofit	*Ch*	ך	ך	ך		
Mem sofit	*M*	ם	ם	ם	*water*	40
Nun sofit	*N*	ן	ן	ן	*fish*	50
Fey sofit	*F*	ף	ף	ף	*mouth*	80
Tzadi sofit	*Ts*	ץ	ץ	ץ	*fish hook*	90

Long vowels

Name	Pronunciation	Sign
Tzeyrei	*ay as in stay*	ֵ
Cheereek	*ee as in feet*	ִי
Cholam	*o as in toe*	וֹ
Shoorook	*oo as in too*	וּ

Short vowels

Name	Pronunciation	Sign
Patach	*a as in what*	ַ
Chataf patach	*a as in what*	ֲ
Segol	*e as in met*	ֶ
Chataf segol	*e as in met*	ֱ
Cheereek	*i as in big*	ִ
Kamatz	*a as in father*	ָ
Chataf kamatz	*o as in son*	ֳ
Koobootz	*u as in put*	ֻ
Shva	*silent*	ְ

HISTORICAL OVERVIEW 9 / *The Unbroken Chain* 0–present/3761 BCE–present

Year from creation/ *Common era year*	Writings	Periods and writings	Transmitters of the law	Periods of transmission
2000/*1761 BCE*		**Period of the Forefathers** *1948–2255/1813–1506 BCE*		
2250/*1511 BCE*				
2500/*1261 BCE*	**Torah** *2448/1313BCE* The Torah was received in two parts from God: the Written Law and the Oral Law. Moses began a transmission process that has suffered little distortion, and continues on to this very day.	**Period of Prophecy** *2448–3448/1313–313 BCE* Prophecy existed prior to the giving of the Torah at Mt. Sinai, but it became widespread after that time. During the best of times, there were millions of prophets among the nation of Israel. Having direct access to God made it possible to resolve disputes and doubts concerning the proper observance of the commandments. The Torah transmission took place between the leader and the court of his generation, and the leader and the court of the next generation.	*Moses* *Joshua* *Pinchas and Elders* *Eli* *Samuel* *King David* *Achiah HaShiloni* *Elijah* *Elisha* *Yehoidah HaCohen* *Hoshea* *Amos* *Isaiah* *Michah* *Joel* *Nachum* *Chavakuk* *Zephaniah* *Jeremiah* *Baruch* *Ezra* *Shimon HaTzadik* *Antigonos Ish Socho* *Yose ben Yoezer/Yosef ben Yochanan* *Yehoshua ben Perachiah/Nittai Ha'Arbeli*	**Judges** *2488–2964/* *1273–797 BCE* **Kings** *2881–3338/* *880–423 BCE* **Transition** *3338–3550/* *423–211 BCE*
2750/*1011 BCE*				
3000/*761 BCE*				
3250/*511 BCE*				
3500/*261 BCE*				

Periods

Zugot 3550–3770/ 211 BCE–9 CE

Tanna'im 3750–3960/ 11 BCE–199 CE

Amora'im 3960–4235/ 199–474 CE

Savora'im 4235–4350/ 474–589 CE

Geonim 4349–4798/ 588–1037 CE

Early Rishonim 4725–5060/ 964–1299 CE

Rishonim 4725–5372/ 964–1611 CE

Early Acharonim 5230–5414/ 1469–1653 CE

Acharonim 5310/1549 CE

Sages

- Yehudah ben Tabbai/Shimon ben Shetach
- Shemaiah/Avtalyon
- Hillel/Shammai
- Rabbi Shimon ben Hillel HaZaken
- Rabbi Gamliel HaZaken
- Rabbi Shimon ben Gamliel
- Rabbi Gamliel of Yavneh
- Rabbi Shimon ben Gamliel II
- Rabbi Yehuda the Prince
- Rav/Shemuel/Rabbi Yochanan
- Rav Huna
- Rabbah/Rav Yosef
- Abaye/Rava
- Rav Ashi
- Mar Zutra
- Rav Achai Gaon
- Rav Yehudai
- Rav Amram
- Rav Hai Gaon
- Rabbenu Gershon Me'or HaGolah
- Rav Shemuel HaNagid
- Rav Shemuel Yitzchaki (Rashi)
- Rav Avraham ibn Ezra
- Rav Moshe ben Maimon (Rambam)
- Rabbenu Yona Gerondi
- Rabbenu Asher (Rosh)
- Morenu HaRav Yitzchak Levi (Maharil)
- Rav Yitzchak Abarbanel
- Rav Ovadiah Bartenura
- Rav Yaakov ibn Chaviv (Ein Yaakov)
- Rav Yosef Karo (Beit Yosef)
- Morenu Harav Yehudah Lowe (Maharal)
- Adonenu Rabenu Yitzchak Luria (Arizal)
- Rav Chaim Vital
- Rav Yaakov Emden
- Vilna Gaon
- Tzemach Tzedek
- Rogachover Gaon

Mishnah
3948/188 CE

The Mishnah was written by Rabbi Judah the Prince and his colleagues under six major headings:

1. Seeds (laws of agriculture)
2. Times (holidays)
3. Women (laws of marriage, divorce, etc.)
4. Damages (torts and acquisitions, etc.)
5. Holiness (laws of sacrifices, kosher laws)
6. Purity (laws of family purity, etc.)

Talmud (Babylonian)
4260/499 CE

The Talmud was written by Rav Ashi and his colleagues, preserving and providing the oral discussions necessary to understand the concise teachings of the Mishnah. It also provides stories and accounts to teach protocol and character development. This is the main body of learning in traditional study houses to this day.

Timeline markers

- 3750/11 BCE
- 4000/239 CE
- 4250/489 CE
- 4500/739 CE
- 4750/989 CE
- 5000/1239 CE
- 5250/1489 CE
- 5500/1739 CE
- 5750/1989 CE

IT

INTERNATIONAL
TRADITIONS
CORPORATION

FULLY ILLUSTRATED & USER-FRIENDLY

BIBLE BASICS

AN INTRODUCTION & REFERENCE GUIDE
TO THE FIVE BOOKS OF MOSES

Maps and charts

Historical timelines

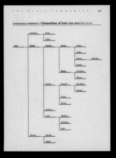

Bible text

Genealogical trees

"It is truly 'user friendly'—all readers will gain tremendously from it."
S. Zelig Pliskin, Author

"The graphics are great and really helps both the novice and the advanced student conceptualize."
Ephraim Z. Buchwald, National Jewish Outreach Program

"...a great pleasure to read... Regardless of his or her background, everyone will gain immensely from it."
Rabbi Noah Weinberg, Founder and President of Aish Hatorah World Center, Jerusalem, Israel

"The Torah is not an easy read—Bible Basics is a relief... illustrative and easy to read... an outstanding work."
Peter Johnson, Columnist, USA TODAY

"A comprehensive and enjoyable reference guide... the clear organization of the material allows for quick reference... A perfect addition to any library."
Rabbi Kenneth Brander, Boca Raton Synagogue, Dean of Judaic Fellows Program (Community Kolel)

"Bible Basics is a must for any library, whether you are a beginner or a scholar... essential to understanding the Five Books of Moses"
THE GAP—Magazine of the Noachides, Memphis, Tennessee

"The most concise, comprehensive and easy to use book for both beginning and advanced students available today."
Charles Samuel, Author

"A rare gift to new-comers to Judaism."
Rabbi David Aaron, Founder and President of Israelight Institute, Jerusalem, Israel

"An indispensable masterpiece to accompany the Torah... virtually a must for any student... You'll be ecstatic that you have a copy."
Rabbi Kalman Packouz, Internationally acclaimed Editor and Publisher of the *"Shabbat Shalom Fax"*